American Vaudeville as Ritual

ALBERT F. McLEAN, JR.

American Vaudeville as Ritual

UNIVERSITY OF KENTUCKY PRESS

For My Mother and Father

Preface

AS A PROLOGUE to *The Adventures of Huckle-berry Finn*, its author gave notice that readers attempting to find a "moral" in his narrative would be "prosecuted." Some who pick up this book antici-pating the nostalgic memorabilia of vaudeville may feel that for my attempt to find general meaning beneath the surface of entertainment, I deserve some mild prosecution. For this book takes vaudeville seriously, as a manifestation of psychic and social forces at work in American history. It deals not with memories or gossip but with symbols, not with "bills" and "acts" but with ritual. In short, this book attempts to make sense and some sort of order out of the tinsel and glitter known as vaudeville.

While not immune to the gay and picturesque elements of this entertainment form, I am convinced that there is a place for raising serious questions and examining current illusions. I am of a generation which has known vaudeville only through family tradition, hearsay, and its vestigial remains, and perhaps because of this I find it possible to seek intelligent perspectives from gazing upon what has now become the national past.

This book had its genesis in a small packet of letters in our family attic, letters written to my maternal grandfather by his friend and former employer, B. F. Keith. The letters themselves are autobiographical, full of recollections about Keith's early wanderings as a messboy, a door-to-door salesman, and a grifter with the circus, but they provide as well full accounts of American vaudeville in the eighties and nineties. These letters, since edited by me and published in *Theatre Survey*, fall into the familiar and predictable pattern of the American success story as Keith had found it in his own career. But the juxtaposition of this pattern with the rise of vaudeville as an institution prompted a further idea which lies at the heart of this book — that vaudeville as an entirety was a manifestation of the belief in progress, the pursuit of happiness, and the hope for material success basic to the American character. A decade and several trial papers after the initial discovery of the letters, the background materials which I had been laboriously collecting began to take shape. My excursions down the byways of humor, theology, dramaturgy, and folklore all pointed to what seems to me to be the underlying truth about American vaudeville.

It is not enough to say with the popularizers that vaudeville expresses the "American spirit." Nor is it sufficient to agree with R. G. Collingwood and other sophisticated observers that modern mass entertainment is merely a "grounding of emotional energy," a psychic safety valve for the mass man in his moments of quiet desperation. If the vaudeville performance as a unique set of expressive sights and sounds had value beyond the claims of its partisan supporters or critics, this value lay in that difficult area of modern scholarly investigation that is known as "mythic thought," an area in which idea and emotion become fused and complementary and in which generalities about the "spirit" of a people are subjected to critical examination. Myth itself consists of interrelated constellations of images and symbols that both singly and collectively express the unconscious assumptions upon which men base their functional attitudes and beliefs. Vaudeville, as became clear in the course of my investigations, stood in relation to the American dream of human progress and personal achievement as primitive ritual stood in relation to primitive myth. Its place in American life was neither that of a crude monument to national vitality and gaiety, nor was it simply a kind of relaxation. Instead it served as a means of assimilation and crystallization of very important and historically significant value judgments upon life in an expanding industrial democracy. Vaudeville, in short, was one way by which the American people, passing through a neoprimitive stage, sought perspectives upon their common experience.

Ritual, in this context, extends beyond its dictionary meaning as a recurring and systematic series of acts with formal (symbolic) meaning, to the point where Ernst Cassirer, in *The Philosophy of Symbolic Forms*, has found it—as a developmental stage in the process of myth creation in which it both accompanies and produces myth in its verbal forms. Thus it is that vaudeville could absorb into itself, into its humor, songs, and playlets, the verbal myths of the society at large or of distinctive segments of the society, but since its primary medium was that of dramatic *action*, it tended to move further away from conceptual thought than myth. Not *idea*, not even a formal *style* was essential to the expressiveness of vaudeville as ritual, but rather those more directly sensory experiences which are imparted by rhythmic patterns of gesture, color, and sound. Not all of vaudeville, of course, qualified as ritual gesture, for some of it was topical and ephemeral, a series of acts without particular or communicable symbolic meaning. Thus, the emphasis of this book upon ritual elements should not create the misconception that every vaudeville performance fulfilled a rigidly prescribed function and met an established standard. The very rapidity of its creation and of social change during its short life span precluded the development of a highly formalized or elaborate ritual. But ritual action and ritual meaning were implicit, nevertheless, in each gathering of an audience to watch the performers move through their various acts, and while the audience itself, like the primitive tribes participating in their indigenous rituals, was unaware of the myth-making process in which they were participating, it is now the role of the historian to extract thematic material from its ritual content and to interpret it as best he can.

As this thesis is developed, my debt to the philosophers, literary scholars, and historians who have brought to light the significance which symbol and myth have for civilized as well as for primitive cultures will become clear. It has required only a reasonable extension of their thought, provoked by the special problems of my investigation, to define popular stage entertainment as ritual—as one form of the symbolic activity appropriate to myth-making. The value and meaning of myth as a symbolic emergence from the realms of feeling and of will have already been well educed for the formal arts, particularly literature, and my innovation lies solely in applying many of the same principles to the popular arts. The accumulating evidence to support the insight of Cassirer and others, that the myth-making faculty in man is constant and compulsive, is becoming more impressive each year, and while there is an understandable reticence on the part of scholars to seek out the myths of contemporary society in the same dispassionate manner in which they have studied the ethnic mythologies of ancient cultures, yet the truth lies merely around the corner. There is no single dominant ethnic tradition in America, and thus the old folk traditions have withered away. But there is, in this heterogeneous society, still a folk element which too seeks to evolve its usable myths; only instead of linking these myths with the religious aspirations of the community, the new urban folk has drawn its symbols from the secular magic of its era—the very scientism which set out to dispell forever the prestige of myth. Vaudeville stands in the center of this secular myth-making and has been engaged in a process of real significance for modern society, a process which has gone largely unperceived because of inadequate perspectives and inattention to the nature and history of mass entertainment.

Necessarily this investigation leads off into two directions, one historical and the other critical. I have been forced by the nature of the material to engage in some rather wide, if elemental, sociological and anthropological considerations. Whereas in the formal arts the borrowing or creation of mythic types is solely an individual matter and may be understood primarily as a psychological process, the adaptation or creation of folk myth is a process with its roots in the basic structure of the society at large. In addition, when the myth is purely secular in its content, it will lack the clear articulation and graceful presentation of literary works. The audience, then, as well as the performer and his art, are under investigation here. This amorphous and shifting group I have called, for convenience, the New Folk and have sought to establish its values and its ideas as these related, within the historical context, to the pressures of other interest groups, particularly those of liberal Protestantism of the late nineteenth century. Without attempting a survey of American culture during the years from 1885 to 1930—and restricting my discussion to rough sketches of relevant background—I have attempted with some firmness to place the vaudeville ritual in both its mythic and historical context, to bring together the ritual with the forces which generated it.

At each stage of this study I have received inspiration and encouragement from many people, and I can only single out a few. From Howard Mumford Jones came the impetus to take vaudeville seriously; from Wisner P. Kinne, Alan S. Downer, David E. Philips, and the late William Van Lennep came a matured conception of theatrical history and the modern drama. From within the circle of those who knew vaudeville well, the Larsen family has been immensely helpful, as were both John Royal and William E. Collins. For diligent service upon the typewriter I would commend my wife, Jean, Mrs. Ann Parker, and Mrs. Angie Denny. To Miss Helen Willard and the other workers in the catacombs of the Harvard Theatre Collection, my deep appreciation for their generous aid in locating materials.

For financial assistance in research and writing, I wish to acknowledge and express my gratitude to the Roy E. Larsen Fund, the Penrose Fund of the

American Philosophical Society, the Tufts University Research Fund, and the Committee on Research of the Transylvania College Faculty.

Permission to use "The German Senator" by Aaron Hoffman was secured from William S. Bartman, trustee of the estate of Aaron Hoffman and agent for Mrs. Minnia Z. Hoffman.

Permission was received from Metro-Goldwyn-Mayer, Inc., to use the material from the book *Weber and Fields* by Felix Isman, copyright 1924 by The Curtis Publishing Company, renewed 1951 and 1952 by The Curtis Publishing Company, and copyright 1924 by Boni & Liveright, Inc., renewed 1952 by Helen G. Bishop.

Permission to use the material from *Weber and Fields* by Felix Isman, was also received from Mrs. Helen G. Bishop. For this permission in both instances I am deeply grateful.

Photographs are through the courtesy of the Harvard Theatre Collection.

ALBERT F. McLEAN, JR.

Contents

Illustrations

ONE

The Symbolism
of Vaudeville

AMERICAN VAUDEVILLE by 1915 had reached its full maturity. From its infancy, thirty years before, it had grown with such amazing rapidity that even in 1900 it had dominated popular amusements in the more thickly populated areas of the United States. During the first fifteen years of the twentieth century, however, vaudeville had not only increased the number and size of its theatres in such metropolitan centers as New York, Buffalo, St. Louis, Dallas, Chicago, and San Francisco, but had spread its circuits throughout the land to the point where vaudeville was accessible to all but the more removed rural areas. While the tempo and tone of this entertainment was being set by such mammoth circuits as those of Keith, Proctor, Considine, and Pantages, vaudeville also flourished in smalltime operations, in the so-called "family circuits" and in less respectable establishments which went under the ambiguous name of "variety-vaudeville." In newspapers, in magazines, in common speech, the mention of vaudeville served to designate something quite distinct and different in American life—distinct from other entertainments in its time, and different from anything which had preceded it. For vaudeville was, for at least four decades, not only a significant social institution but also a mythic enactment—through ritual—of the underlying aspirations of the American people.[1]

Viewed from the mythic perspective, vaudeville becomes not merely an "amusement" or means of killing leisure time—a preoccupation quite apart from the main business of American society. Nor was it just a fantasy in motley improvised by a clique of ambitious showmen and performers who foisted upon the public their artificial and eclectic medley of songs, monologues, dances, feats of skill, and exhibitions of the extraordinary. To the contrary, once the blinders of custom, sentiment, and nostalgia are removed, a pattern of social significance begins to emerge. Beneath the dazzle and the frenzy of the performances, a symbolism is revealed which not only increases our comprehension of the vaudeville era but also illumines the entire development of mass entertainment within modern culture. For vaudeville was neither a digression born of boredom, nor was it a conspiracy on the part of a few. Its roots lay deep in the experience of the millions who had swarmed into American cities in the latter decades of the nineteenth century and who sought images, gestures, and symbols which would objectify their experience and bring to their lives a simple and comprehensive meaning.[2]

It is the thesis of this book that vaudeville, as a ritual of a New Folk, was one means by which Americans came to terms with a crisis in culture. Though more formal modes of discourse—literature, the arts, scholarship—have recorded the sense which educated persons have developed of their national identity, a substrata of American thought has lain buried in almost primitive—or neoprimitive—modes of expression. Where discursive reasoning and the rarefied symbolisms of artistic disciplines have made only intermittent contact with the raw substance of the American city, the mass man encountered the city at firsthand and from his experience created his symbolism and his ritual. For neither the folk art of the settled societies from which he had come, nor the culturally impoverished surroundings in which he found himself upon arriving in the city could meet his immediate psychic needs. That urbanization came as a distinct trauma within the American experience and that it shook the foundations of the established social order has been the conclusion of a generation of American historians.[3] What has remained unclear, however, was just how the collective masses, both European immigrants and rural Americans, met this challenge to their traditions, standards, and even to their sanity. Vaudeville was one means—a primary one—by which the disruptive experience of migration and acclimatization was objectified and accepted. In its symbolism lies the psychic profile of the American mass man in the moment of his greatest trial.

Other modes of expression were open to this folk— as publishers, politicians, merchandisers, and evangelists quickly recognized—but the ritual mode as it

3

crystallized in American vaudeville was especially important. Committed to no particular tradition, capable of infinite variations and permutations, alien to all of the formalized modes by which educated persons communicate, the ritual of entertainment could absorb public sentiment and respond to it immediately. Ritual, as it has manifested itself throughout time, has been dynamic and effervescent, always evading the attempts of language to confine it. And within the heterogeneous society of the American city, composed of many peoples from many cultures, it was precisely this active, elusive form of expression which could be most effective. Vaudeville was catholic in its tastes, hospitable to the most ambiguous and contradictory symbolisms, open to old myths but also busy building new ones. Whereas the popular myths which served it were pointed and restrictive—symbolized through stereotyped characters and stories—vaudeville itself remained mobile and elusive as a form, capable of shifting in coloration and emphasis from one performance to the next.[4]

Through ritual the process of myth-making could be sustained; the symbols could be tested, and the gestures varied until the right combinations evolved. It was the essence of show business during the vaudeville era that popular taste had to be sought out and catered to, that offense be given to no one and satisfaction to the greatest number. As ritual, vaudeville could delve beneath conscious prejudices and deal directly with the encounter of the moment, always seeking the subject matter of maximum pertinence to its audience. Its myth-making contained some elements of backstage contrivance, and some organized pressures were brought to bear upon the industry to make the ritual conform to the moral and esthetic standards of the educated leadership of

4

American society, but basically the myths took their lives and meaning from the intimate contact between performer and his audience at the moment of presentation. Out of this process of dramatic trial and error arose the patterns of symbolic meaning which were the myths of a new industrial democracy.[5]

The crowded and machine-ridden world which credulous emigrants first met in New York, Trenton, Providence, Chicago, Cincinnati, or San Francisco was empty of the kind of myths familiar to them in rural America or the Old World. These people fell back, when they could, upon the stock of earthy or ethnic wisdom from their former lives. But the rapid development of American industrial civilization made it practically impossible to retain intact the older cultural traditions. Even the most reluctant or the most rigid of the new arrivals were at least aware of a new urban mythology crystallizing before their eyes, attended by all of the miracles and magical wonder of which all myths are made. Folklore, stringent religious and family disciplines, provincial or ethnic loyalties—all gave way over the span of three generations to the experience of Americanization—to the acceptance of vivid, collective myths which explained, at least in part, the new economic and social order.

Comprehensive in scope, the new mythology touched upon all pertinent areas of city life. The very substance of the physical world as defined by science took on mythic dimensions in the age of Edison and the Wright brothers. The very acts of invention and discovery were regarded by the common man as a kind of magic—and, thus, paradoxically the very groups who scorned myth as superstition and fantasy—scientists, physicians, and technicians—became the new priestly order. Money retained its prosaic function as an instrument for bar-ter but it also became transmuted into a *mana* capable of satisfying such psychic necessities as comfort, pleasure, and power.[6] Sex, which in primitive thought often shared with the earth mystical powers of regeneration, but which within the Puritan consciousness had become linked with a shameful bestiality, was refurbished into "glamour," a power accessible to even the most uneducated man or woman. Through "glamour," as vaudeville-goers and newspaper readers well knew, one could acquire popularity, wealth, fame, and happiness. Even the machines—dynamos, trolley cars, and Gramophones —had invaded everyday life, creating wonderful new possibilities for pleasure. In the mythical view which saw all human society as moving toward a collective, euphoric future, the machines were indispensable talismans.

To the expression of this mythic view, the ritual of vaudeville addressed itself. Though it was fundamentally naive and often misleading, it successfully derived from the experience of urbanization a symbolism of character, color, costume, and setting. As ritual, vaudeville arose in an era of crisis to offer the American people a definitive rhythm, a series of gestures which put man back into the center of his world, a sense of the human community, and an effective emotional release. In this respect, for all its similarity with European entertainments, vaudeville was a uniquely American achievement and fulfilled uniquely American needs. More formal rituals were inadequate to this task, and even popular entertainment was not responsive enough to the dynamic changes in American life. None of the leading entertainment forms—the stock company, the minstrel show, or the circus—were, by themselves capable of symbolizing the concerns of city folk, as a subsequent chapter will explain. While the major components of the vaudeville show—the song-and-dance, verbal and burlesque humor, stage magic, animal acts, acrobatics, and playlets—were all of utmost importance in the context of vaudeville, as isolated rituals their meaning was fragmented. It was the nature of the city itself that novelty, variety, and a quick succession of images upon the stage should express its complexity and constant motion. And it was in the nature of the human mind that symbolism combined former experience—images and patterns of images from rural and provincial life—together with the new and exciting symbols of urban life. Like most rituals, vaudeville combined without explanation or apology the means by which an audience could be lured, enthralled, and emotionally satisfied.

What is most transparently clear about American vaudeville is that it worshiped success. The star system, the lavish architecture of its theaters—appropriately called "palaces"—the pride with which it disclosed the financial manipulations of its circuits and syndicates—all pointed to a set of common assumptions about the desirability of making money, amassing it, and living richly off of the proceeds. Charles and Mary Beard, catching a glimpse of this opulence in their sweep through the late nineteenth century, concluded that such public amusements as vaudeville were exploitations of the newly-formed mass market by a few calculating businessmen.[7] That the masses wished, even demanded to be exploited in this manner, that is, to share in the myth of enterprise and aggrandisement, however, would be closer to the truth. The peculiar direction taken by the American Dream—what has come to be known as the "Myth of Success"—was not the exclusive domain of a few. The wealth and supposed happiness of the showmen and the favored performers have a far deeper significance than the Beards discovered, and the elements of economic conflict pale before the rich symbolic function served by these popular heroes. Not only the ritual itself smelled sweetly of success, but the entire structure of the industry testified to the importance of this particular myth.

As it has reached our time, the Myth of Success prevalent in late nineteenth century America is best known and most easily grasped through the glorified folktales in which Horatio Alger celebrated the rise from poverty to riches of the self-made businessman. Commentators have pointed out that the hero of Alger's dime novels derives not only from the pious, industrious entrepreneur of the Protestant ethic, but also from the rugged, self-reliant Western hero, who, from Natty Bumppo to Buffalo Bill, signified the American ideal of adventuresome self-fulfillment accessible to all men of courage and stamina. Unlike the pious Calvinist or the Western hero, however, the protagonist of the Alger tales encountered a world largely shaped by secular custom and institutions, a world in which physical prowess counted little, and a world in which simple honesty and goodwill were less effective than ambition and drive. Alger deliberately kept his story-line simple and blurred his moral with heavy strokes of coincidence and chance. But the public, and sensitive writers as well, knew that the myth he projected was the important fact of modern life, and that his cheap fiction was worth taking seriously. As Kenneth Lynn's study of the success myth in the American novel demonstrates, more powerful minds than Alger's could find rich materials for a vital and contemporaneous art in the myth itself and in the attempts of men to implement it in their lives.[8]

While Alger's novels concentrated upon the individualistic and moralistic aspects of the myth of business success — and thus provided an obeisance to

8

the Protestant ethic—he did not ignore the other aspects of equal importance for the urban mass man. The mythic ambiance in which the hero moved was that of the great city in all its diverse and contradictory phases—the life of the slums, the amusements of the rich, the lonely streetcorner and the crowded stock exchange, the dirt and waste of the tenements, and the conspicuous luxury of the mansions. It was a world of dust and glitter conveying no consistent pattern except clear levels of desirability which are measured by the basic unit of money. In the city of these novels, vigor and virtue had lost their intrinsic value and had become merely means by which the individual could move himself up the social and economic ladder. Money becomes, in this simplified, magical world of the Alger story, an all-effecting, all-moving *mana* of life. The sight, touch, and possession of money becomes the primary source of the hero's imaginative reality and the basis of his appeal to the reader. No longer did his individualism matter for itself, nor his piety, nor his ability to make his own way against external obstacles, for money has given him something greater than his own mere self and something more powerful than the threatening environment. Through money he has been transformed into the champion of the city, its possessor and at the same time, through the subtle logic of mythic thought, its personification. Success itself had lost its last vestiges of supernatural sanction and had become, for the generations reaching maturity in the closing decades of the nineteenth century, totally involved with the material forces of which the new industrial civilization was composed.

It is this mythic ambiance which the vaudeville ritual could depict and celebrate, rather than the pious morality supposedly involved in the rise-to-riches. The legend taken literally was an impossible

9

tale about an impossible business man, which appealed more directly to adolescents than to those who had tasted the disillusionments of the world. But in the vaudeville ritual the focus could shift away from the moral lesson of a simplified Protestantism toward the secular and magical elements of the myth. Pluck-and-luck might not in reality be a sure formula through which the individual could assert himself in city life, for there were other ways to make money, and others to make it besides industrialists and financial titans. The Myth of Success affected the common man, even though it might be quite removed from his experience, precisely because it was what had led him to the city in the first place and because it contained all of those imaginative elements upon which his mind could take hold. The vaudeville ritual worked with those very elements and translated the myth into terms readily appreciated by all of those unacquainted with literature or formal art. Glamour, glibness, and know-how were all avenues to success according to the vaudeville ritual, while its symbols were clothes, noise, and self-confidence. The fantasy on the stage was a glorified and idealized version of the life toward which all aspired, and an escape from the dirt, loneliness, and deprivation of present reality. Just as a few dimes would purchase some brilliant, satisfying hours at a vaudeville show, so would money transform the stuff of immediate existence into something called happiness.[9]

What vaudeville could do for the myth, which the stories could not, in spite of their persistence in journalism and juvenile literature, was to provide the compelling esthetic experience far more powerful than abstract ideas or discursive thought. For the roots of ritual lie deep in kinesthetic and unconscious processes which can be influenced directly with none of the doubts and conflicts involved in intellectual or rational activity. That surge of magical power evoked by brassy rhythms, the staccato wise-cracks, the poised charm of the "star," or the mastery over reality demonstrated by a juggler or animal trainer, were all more immediately assimilated by the mass audience than were the legends of Horatio Alger and his imitators. In this ritual, cause-and-effect relationships were completely bypassed, the question of ultimate ends was never raised, and the problem of higher values could be submerged in waves of pathos and humor. Not the happy ending but the happy moment, not fulfillment at the end of some career rainbow but a sensory, psychically satisfying here-and-now were the results of a vaudeville show. Its concern was not the making of money but the enjoyment of it. It offered, in symbolic terms, the sweet fruits of success neither as a reward nor as a promise, but as an accessible right for all those participating in the new life of the cities.[10]

Vaudeville, then, provided that esthetic encounter that immigrant and rural segments of the population longed to make with the urban civilization that was absorbing them. Not just the business or professional man, but a wide spectrum of technicians, clerks, artisans, managers, and housewives sought to share in the symbolic enactment of success. They were to make up, as a subsequent chapter will explain, a new and urbanized folk, different from the folk of less industrialized and more ethnically homogeneous areas, yet nonetheless just as susceptible to simple and primitive appeals to their unconscious fears and desires. That they should evolve a folk art expressive of these unarticulated feelings should surprise no one, although it is certainly anomalous

11

that this folk art should derive much of its substance from the unesthetic, flatly objective world of science and technology.

There are students of society and culture who, in the traditions of the Enlightenment, would deny symbolic value to popular pastimes, seeing in them only neurosis or, at best, immaturity. Educated observers like R. G. Collingwood and Johan Huizinga have seen in the symbols and rituals of the modern, industrial folk, only a means of "grounding" the hysteria evoked by the machine age, or a rampant and deplorable reversion of society toward "puerilism."[11] Even the folklorist, who manages to discover connotative values in the rituals, songs, and sayings of peoples in the pastoral backwaters of the modern world, is uncomfortable with the eclectic and commercialized products of the popular imagination which flourish all about him. While there seems to be little consensus among folklorists exactly what folklore *is*, there is considerable agreement that mass entertainment certainly does not belong in the list of approved materials for their research and study.[12] Yet the great foundation of all culture — whether described as the folk or the masses — goes on about its symbolizing ways indifferent to the distinctions and the objections raised by researchers and scholars. Certainly vaudeville solicited no learned apologists in its own day and, indeed, drew part of its strength from its very inaccessibility. Under the scrutiny of analysis and formal criticism its bloom would have soon withered, and its viable magic might well have been lost.

There were two articulate champions of vaudeville, however, who ventured some serious criticism of its form and content and thus broke some of the trails which this present book will follow. But neither of these critics respected the distinction which must be maintained between formal art—which is individual, knowledgeable, and concerned with self-understanding—and folk art—which is collective, mythic and oriented toward the immediate welfare of the group. The first of these critics, Caroline Caffin, whose book *Vaudeville* appeared in 1914, found this amusement rightly enough, "catholic and hospitable," in that it drew its acts and its audiences from all sectors. Justly seeing vaudeville as suspicious of everything "Highbrow," she also noted that in accord with popular taste it prostrated itself before successes in the formal arts. Although she did not press her observation to its conclusion, Miss Caffin saw vaudeville as inculcating a sense of community in the audience—at its best creating "an electrifying experience" in which the performer evoked from the audience "an answering vibration."[13] It is only when Miss Caffin describes the close effectual communion between performer and audience as "Something of that mysterious quality which we call Art" that her conclusions are open to objection.

Nor was the attempt of Gilbert Seldes, writing in the twenties, to place vaudeville among "the lively arts" much more successful in defining the function of popular entertainment. He rebuked, for example, his fellow critics for leaving vaudeville in the hands of the least cultivated audiences and declared that "We had asked nothing of vaudeville because we haven't suspected what it had to give." It was, he declared, in the nature of the American people that no single artist could be great enough "to do the whole thing," but "together the minor artists of America have created an American art." At times Seldes wrote in the vein of the editors of *Harper's*, who nourished for a short while the notion that somehow "uplift" could be applied to vaudeville, but elsewhere, like Caroline Caffin, he admired those elements of sparkle, impertinence, and liveliness in the best vaudeville shows. Like Miss Caffin also, he respected the proficiency of the skilled performer who, leaving nothing to chance, capitalized upon every second of his brief appearance in order to bring alive his contribution to the show.[14]

Such apologists as Caffin and Seldes have been rare; most writers on vaudeville have been content to extoll the "good old days" without reflecting upon their meaning. Understandably, educated persons and those of cultivated sensibilities have sought the higher values rather than the lower and with Collingwood have maintained a firm distinction between what he calls "art proper" and "art as amusement." Even intelligent critics like Caffin and Seldes, conditioned by the critical traditions of the humanities, which stress appreciation and exegesis, fail to discern the social myths which provide the basis for all folk art. Their application of the standards of drama criticism to vaudeville could do service neither to the amusement nor to the art of self-knowledge with which it was being compared. Neither Caffin's praise of the "electrifying experience," nor Seldes' approval of its liveliness could recommend vaudeville as a serious enterprise for informed persons, and the failure of these two critics to note the mythic elements in this mass entertainment only confirmed the suspicion of the sophisticated that "art as amusement" was fundamentally meaningless.

Vaudeville was not a disciplined or formal art and cannot be interpreted as such. It was born of social and economic pressures upon the masses and was nurtured by persistent anxieties. Their making of symbols sprang from a common need and from a primal compulsion, but the ritual evolved more from historical circumstance than it did from soul-searching or from imaginative effort. Through its symbolizing, vaudeville sought to allay those common tensions among city-dwellers brought about by their crowded lives, by their worries over employment and scarcity, by the growing depersonalization of their occupations, and by the erosion of their simple moral values.[15] But the symbolizing process went even further in pointing out continuously the positive goals of city life and giving life to the dream that someday all of these affronts to sanity and dignity would be dissolved. The Myth of Success was both an escape from the moment and a tangible promise for the future. Its glittering promises of pleasure and fulfillment, its easy answers for immediate problems, its roots in middle class values, and its cheerful materialism—all served to make it the primary myth celebrated by the New Folk. It met a hunger created by circumstance, a hunger which other social institutions could only begin to satisfy. Crude and vulgar as the ritual manifestation of the Myth of Success may have seemed to some observers, it was a powerful molder of the American way of life and was a foundation upon which other entertainment empires were to rise. The vaudeville palaces were not aberrations on the American scene, nor did they speak merely to the bold, the crass, the neurotic, or the alienated. Within the walls of these palaces gathered the hardworking and respectable members of society as well, caught up in the tinsel and gibberish, largely unaware that their world was being reshaped and revalued before their very eyes.

15

TWO

Evolution of a Ritual

AMERICAN VAUDEVILLE was shaped in the performances of the major circuits, and as such it was neither born whole nor imported from foreign shores. Its roots were only partially European, and its most evident sources were the itinerant amusements of the nineteenth century—the minstrel show, the circus, the troupes of traveling players who accommodated themselves to tents, show boats, opera houses, or town halls, whatever the particular stopping place provided. Vaudeville was itinerant amusement become stable and institutionalized in metropolitan centers. The players still traveled, but the circuits were no longer free and open. Beginning in the nineties, comprehensive networks of booking

16

offices and established theaters took on the important tasks of promotion, ticket vending, production, and plant maintenance. The impulsive and peripatetic player became a specialized agent within an industry. He played to larger audiences than tents could hold, and both his prestige and his income edged higher decade by decade. In this more complex scheme of organization the new managerial class assumed an important role. It served, on the one hand, an economic function, booking and producing the entertainments, while on the other it served also as an intermediary between the New Folk and the ritual, deciding which jokes, songs, and acts would "go over" and which would not. It played, therefore, a significant part in the adaptation of vaudeville to the American people at a crucial point in their development, and it is as an adaptation that vaudeville must be considered. What was new or novel about vaudeville was precisely what was new about urban society with its introduction of a vast new immigrant element into the American social order.

Vaudeville's history as a business venture and institution is easily traced and fairly obvious in its implications. Prior to 1860 there had been no massive amusement enterprises involving hundreds of persons, chains of theaters, and capital investments of millions of dollars. The public demand for entertainment was satisfied by traveling menageries, circuses, minstrel shows, independent repertory theaters, road shows, and show boats. Various kinds of musical entertainment, including musical comedy, appealed to scattered audiences of quality, while the less cultivated enjoyed the musical and humorous festivities of taverns, saloons, and brothels. On the fringes of these relatively stable operations would appear more ephemeral amusements such as "museums," panoramas, exhibitions of hypnotism and phrenology, medicine shows, and pseudo lectures. Only during the Gilded Age were the large scale troupes of the circuses and minstrel shows to discover a mass audience willing to support extravagant outlays of money, and only with the development of cheap railroad transportation were these troupes able to move from city to city, from one mass audience to the next, with a minimum of damage and wasted time. With P. T. Barnum's expansion of the circus into a variegated spectacle, with the absorption into the larger minstrel shows of a short variety show called an "olio," and with the wholesale assembly into traveling companies of whatever performing humans and animals a shrewd manager might lay his hands upon, arose the possibility of a conglomerate amusement which would appeal to a broadly diversified mass audience. The grandfather of a modern musical comedy, *The Black Crook*, was in fact such an assembly of acts, unified by only the most transparent excuse of a plot. Such well known productions as *Uncle Tom's Cabin* and *The Old Homestead* had a habit when en route of broadening or contracting their performances as specialty acts became available or were in demand. More and more the single acts and the small specialized companies were swallowed up by more skillfully managed, eclectic entertainments.

Nomenclature during these decades following the Civil War was loose and often misleading. The term "vaudeville" came into scattered use at this time to describe, in a general way, a variety entertainment. A showman of the period who later committed his long experience to print, M. B. Leavitt, claimed to have been the first to use the word *vaudeville* in this fashion, citing as evidence his traveling company of 1880 called "Leavitt's Gigantic Vaudeville

Stars."[1] However, one H. J. Sargent had organized in Louisville, Kentucky, some nine years previously "Sargent's Great Vaudeville Company,"[2] and other disputants to this claim of priority may still emerge. In each of these cases it is difficult to see that the term "vaudeville" meant much, for it seems to have been merely selected for its vagueness, its faint but harmless exoticism, and perhaps its connotation of gentility. During the nineteenth century, the traditional *vaudeville* of the French theater, a pastoral story line with musical interludes, had been revived for polite audiences,[3] and the name thus provided the cloak of respectability which Leavitt, Sargent, and perhaps others had desired. But nowhere in his memoirs does Leavitt, at least, show an awareness that a definite dramatic form existed; nor in the material on Keith, Proctor, or the other early managers of institutionalized vaudeville are there any indications that the precise nature of traditional vaudeville was recognized by them.

Leavitt accounted for the meaning of *vaudeville* by explaining that it was a corruption of "vaux de ville," or thus literally, "worth [sic] of the city," or "worthy of the city's patronage."[4] Scholars suggest a more plausible derivation—although perhaps one not so relevant—from the *chansons du Val de Vire*, those songs of the Vire River valley in Normandy which had been spread by the minstrel Olivier Basselin in the fifteenth century and were gradually incorporated into short pantomimes and plays.[5] In any case, the French name and the form seem to have little relation to nineteenth century practice outside of France, having been accepted by then as a general designation covering any sort of light amusement. The Vaudeville Theatre in London, in fact, sponsored legitimate drama during the height of its popularity in the seventies, and neither panto-

19

mimes, pastorals, nor variety shows are on record as having been performed there.[6]

B. F. Keith was only one of dozens of entrepreneurs who recognized the coming shape of the amusement business, but to Keith belongs most of the credit for institutionalizing "vaudeville" and making it preeminent among all of the competing entertainment forms at the close of the nineteenth century. Keith had led a varied career before finding success in downtown Boston. He had been a messboy on a tramp steamer, a sidewalk salesman and a grifter with the circuses of the 1870s. Before arriving in Boston, he had worked in Bunnell's Museum in New York, toured with Barnum's circus, and had even attempted a traveling museum show of his own. In 1883, with the financial backing of William Austin, he opened a small museum—afterwards known as Austin and Stone's Museum—on Washington Street, Boston, and thus brought about what he later fondly remembered as "the beginning of my permanent career in theatricals." His sole attraction at that time was "Baby Alice: the Midget Wonder," who was displayed on a stage six-by-six in a room fifteen feet wide at the front and only thirty-five feet long.[7]

Within four years he parlayed this small affair into the Bijou Theatre, a $100,000 "fire-proof" work of art which had dazzled the man on the street since its erection in 1882. It had claimed to be the first theater in America with electric lighting, and its heavy chandelier in ormolu, "made for the Khedive of Egypt," was centered in a forty-foot Moorish dome. The proscenium arch swept sixty feet upward in the shape of a huge horseshoe; the safety doors were supposedly capable of emptying the theater of a thousand people in three minutes.[8] In the Bijou in Boston in 1887, B. F. Keith had found the cornerstone for his mass-produced variety shows which would, within the following decade, occupy similar theaters in more than thirty cities in the heavily populated areas of the northeastern United States.

In similar fashion, F. F. Proctor, starting in New York City, developed a sizable empire which entered into fierce competition with Keith's. In the East also were S. Z. Poli, Klaw and Erlanger, and Marcus Loew. Moving westward Percy G. Williams was eventually to combine with the extensive Orpheum Circuit largely created by Martin Beck and pose a constant threat to eastern interests. In 1890 there had been no millionaires in show business, but according to a knowledgeable insider, Robert Grau, there were by 1910 more than a dozen, among them Keith, Poli, Loew, Williams, and Beck. If anything this estimate is conservative, for by 1910 the booking business itself was a multi-million dollar financial venture and the highly paid stars—Tanguay, Houdini, Lauder — might each have easily accumulated a million dollars.[9]

By 1900 vaudeville had outdistanced by many lengths its closest rivals—the circus, minstrel shows, musical comedy—and was ready to bask in two decades of glory and wealth. Its own "stars" had emerged, and while some were to drift off into independent ventures on the strength of the name made in vaudeville, for the most part they stayed by their well-known acts with few essential changes and left all else to the businessmen in charge. In the shadow of the stars, the lesser performers raised a few discontented voices in protest against the inequitable distribution of the box office profits, but the alliance of stars and managers was never seriously disturbed.

At one time or another vaudeville brought just about every form of entertainment known to man under its umbrella, but its main components were those drawn from the early variety shows—skits, songs, dances, and comic monologues—together with some of the minstrel show's humor and the staples of circus programs—acrobats and animals. In the early days performers moved easily in and out of vaudeville, readily adapting their particular acts to the shorter times which the vaudeville program would allow.

To this standard fare, from time to time, the more enterprising managers would add a brief glimpse of a name star from the legitimate stage or opera. Keith created a sensation when Sarah Bernhardt appeared on the stage of his Providence theater in 1893 in short scenes from *La Tosca* and *Cleopatra*, and the New York *Clipper* reported that: "The elite of the city has not been seen in such large numbers at any theatrical entertainment in this city before for many years."[10] Other managers were quick to take this example to heart. Proctor, for example, subsequently featured the opera tenor, Italo Campanini, in his Twenty-third Street Theatre (New York) for five days.[11] Over the years the roster of brilliant talent that appeared in vaudeville reads like a history of the American theater, as a Maud Adams or Ethel Barrymore was only too pleased to reap the large rewards accruing from short appearances at the major vaudeville theaters. Into the vaudeville format were also interjected as the demand warranted the early kinetoscopes, the public appearances of celebrities, and an occasional amateur night. High salaries and long-term contracts lured talented performers from European cabarets and British music halls, but also many American performers exported their talents and some, like Harry Houdini and Eddie Cantor, first found public acceptance abroad before returning in triumph to the United States.

22

Vaudeville provided a mirror which reflected the changes of American public taste through the period. Immigrant groups grew to resent being caricatured by vaudeville comics and so the first decade of the twentieth century was a period of gradual softening of ethnic humor. Middle class humanitarian and professional groups rose to decry the treatment of stage animals or the distortions of scientific knowledge as they manifested themselves in animal acts and stage hypnotism. The gradual relaxation of strict conventional attitudes toward sex can be followed in the career of vaudeville from 1900 through the roaring twenties. The form-fitting bathing suit was, after all, introduced by Annette Kellerman on the vaudeville stage, while Eva Tanguay's brazen and electric performance typified the new aggressiveness of the American female. The shifts in musical taste, from melancholy "coon songs" and Irish romantic ballads of the nineties into the catchy Tin Pan Alley tunes and lively jazz rhythms of the early twentieth century, are revealed in the life of vaudeville. Changes in American humor, the growing literacy of Americans, the nationalization of immigrant groups, a developing sophistication in regard to city ways, and a revised estimate of American family life were all expressed upon the vaudeville stage, as subsequent chapters of this book will demonstrate.

Yet there were other vehicles for the exploitation of stars and expression of popular attitudes, and even by 1915 they had begun to compete with vaudeville. Even before the movies were well underway and certainly a decade before radio brought entertainment into the home and shop, musical comedy as developed by George M. Cohan, had begun to drain off the better performers and more responsive audiences from vaudeville. The motion pictures themselves did not offer a severe threat in the early days because they could be included within the vaudeville performance itself. But in the twenties more and more of the smaller or local theaters, squeezed by the rising costs of "live" entertainment, resorted to large amounts of film presentation. Furthermore, both movies and radio had the effect of sapping vaudeville of its novelty, for the jokes and songs which had previously taken a year or more to spread throughout the country now took only weeks. Although the vaudeville managers saw the problem quite clearly, there was not much that could be done by the middle twenties. Larger, more spectacular theaters were built, fresh young stars were made, and the circuits engaged in an endless waltz of mergers and combines. But the lavish new palaces could do little for the faltering neighborhood vaudeville theaters, and eventually became merely the last strongholds in the long retreat. The fledgling stars waited long enough to have their name in lights on the marquee of the New York Palace, and then took their talents into media which in many ways could do more for them. By the time the Radio Corporation of America and Pathé News were ready to combine interests with the last of the great circuits—Keith's and the Orpheum—the fate of vaudeville was clear, and by 1930 the giant of the entertainment industry had been cut down to the point where it could no longer exist under its own terms.

The institutional development of vaudeville, in all of its economic and cultural phases, must ultimately be traced to the basic need of the American people to comprehend the new wave of industrialism and urbanization in symbolic terms. The preeminence of vaudeville in the entertainment field, the rapidity with which it overtook the itinerant amusements and easily surpassed them, the sentimental glorification of vaudeville not only in its own day but even now —all suggest that there was more behind its rise than the mechanics of distribution and supply. Earlier amusements, by the late nineteenth century, had already developed distinctive formats and were closely associated with the American past; hence they were incapable of accommodating to the radical changes taking place in American society, and the appeals of their myths and symbols no longer had force. No previous entertainment form had a symbolic vehicle which could clearly enunciate the Myth of Success for an urban audience. None could adequately celebrate the moneyed, mass-produced, collective social order which was the American Dream in the late nineteenth century.

Leading instances were the circus and the minstrel show. At least two decades before vaudeville emerged, they had been preparing American audiences for the succession of unrelated songs, sketches, dances, acts of physical prowess, and comic monologues, which was the distinctive characteristic of the vaudeville show. For many years previous to 1885 the minstrel shows had devoted the second major part of their presentation to a series of specialty acts variously called the "olio," "varieties," or "comicalities." By 1845, as Carl Wittke informs us, the olio began a transformation that moved it further and further away from its relation to the plantation life of the Old South.[12] The sixties and seventies even saw the inclusion of quite alien material into the minstrel olio—Irish ballad singers and Jewish comedians, for example.[13] Variety of course was the olio in its pure state, and the form had been a part of nineteenth century entertainment long before the appearance of vaudeville. Even the circus had contained the basic idea of a compart-

25

mentalized presentation, and the addition of acrobats, clowns, and menageries in the nineteenth century had furthered this tendency.

For neither of these itinerant entertainments, however, was the variety format essential, nor was it the means by which they were identified. What they held in common as parts of nineteenth century culture was a mythic conception of rural America. In this conception, as it has been described by Henry Nash Smith and other scholars, the independent yeoman farmer, drawing upon his own resources of virtue and will, and relying upon the benevolence of nature, stands as a hero in the drama of American Manifest Destiny. The theme of national literature during the middle decades of the nineteenth century was the ability of this self-sufficient, idealized stock to cultivate the Garden of the West and to provide the basis upon which a nation of free, industrious people might be built. Both the minstrel show and the circus applied this myth to the real problems of their era.

The minstrel show had emphatically relegated the figure of the Negro—a black intruder in a white world—to a role of comic inferiority. While making occasional concessions to his basic humanity, it nevertheless, as Negroes were soon to recognize, made of him a performing fool—an impotent and exotic creature in a land settled and governed by white stock. From the time of its inception in the 1840s, the black-faced minstrel show reenforced the prevailing social morality regarding the Negro and symbolized the tensions which occurred within its view. Behind his black face the actor could acquire the whimsical detachment from the real world which the clown needs to perform his psychic magic, yet at the same time, society was reminded of the Negro's childishness, his lack of ambition, and his mental inferiority. When Dan Rice and his troupe of fellow Yankees first developed the minstrel show, they did it without any real understanding of plantation life, but that made little difference to audiences which were as ignorant in this regard as were the actors. The minstrel show was not a directed attempt to conserve the plantation, nor in any way a comment upon the political aspects of the slavery question. But in its portrayal of the Negro it was implicitly a buttress of that entire state of mind which resisted the extension of slavery into the territories and tried to preserve at all costs the toil-won independence of a homestead social order.

The circus likewise spoke for the virtues of pioneer America, particularly in its agrarian phases. Physical strength and courage, intuitive knowledge of animals, and a complete mastery over them—this was the formula which made the circus an important part of nineteenth-century culture. That P. T. Barnum—like Rice, a Yankee—could shift the emphasis to include freaks and elephants was not a denial of this myth but an extension of it. The natural world was the yeoman's oyster, and having domesticated it, he was entitled to regard its wonders as a spectacle to entertain himself and to educate his family. Barnum promoted both his museum of the fifties, a more highly urbanized offshoot of the circus, and the great itinerant road shows with the same contempt for reality and the same braggart assurances of the moral and scientific validity of his exhibitions. For the circus myth may have begun in an epic mood of derring-do, but under Barnum's unsubtle touch, it came to acknowledge the wonders of exploration and science.[14] If the farmer at home had tamed nature with his ax and plow, so had the missionaries of progress captured and studied the rarer manifestations of nature in foreign lands.

Barnum had merely followed the American migrant to the cities and offered him a somewhat more sophisticated version of the American pastoral myth.

Vaudeville could assume the spectacle and pretentious nonsense, but the myth of an agrarian America nourished in the Garden of the West was irrelevant to America of the eighteen-nineties. Although the circus still maintained its strength into the twentieth century, it revealed none of vaudeville's capacities for growth, and characteristic of most amusements in their declining stages, it became thought of as a diversion for children. Nor did the clown, who was mainly an imported figure adapted from the *commedia dell'arte*, fare much better than his American counterpart, the black-faced darky of the minstrel show. His pantomime ran counter to the dominant verbalism of the new entertainment and his brand of whimsy seemed old-fashioned for the machine age.

The Tambo and Bones of the minstrel show appeared briefly on the vaudeville stage, but by 1900 they had become a definite encumbrance. Following emancipation and the nominal guarantee of constitutional rights, the image of the servile, child-like Negro not only lost its poignancy, but for cosmopolitan audiences, became actually absurd. Even when the minstrel show adapted itself to portray the pathetic Negro and the outcast of Reconstruction, it had not gone far enough, and it could hardly accept the Negro of the American city—pert, cocky, and dapper. He strutted the vaudeville stage, not in black face, but as the real Negro entertainer like Bon Bon Buddie Williams.[15]

The minstrel show had sought to hold its ground by more spectacular productions, but it could not return to the quaint dialect and the folk dancing of the mythic plantation. Neither could it move in the direction that variety and musical comedy shows were traveling—that of sex appeal. After the fantastic success of *The Black Crook* in 1866 and its successors, the major theater owners began to give the best bookings to musical troupes so that the larger minstrel shows like Haverly's Mastodon Minstrels or Christy's were frozen out of the best engagements.[16] Unlike musical comedies, the minstrel shows could not offer a mixed cast of males and females, represent romance on the stage, or exploit the humor of human sexuality. Simply to have added "sex appeal" to the minstrel show would have been to invite disaster. To the middle classes of the nineteenth century the purity of the white race was divinely decreed. Agonized at the possibility that the Negro could express himself sexually, they avoided reminders of this fact both on the stage and elsewhere. There were notable exceptions, of course, such as Dion Boucicault's careful treatment of the problem in *The Octoroon* (1859), but not until after the turn of the century do we find Negroes singing the music of Cole, Johnson and Johnson—"Tell Me, Dusky Maiden" and "Under the Bamboo Tree"—before Broadway audiences.[17] While the minstrel shows, one would gather, often included material that was suggestive and occasionally obscene, they could never exploit feminine beauty or the ritual of courtship. Female parts in the short sketches were played by male impersonators, usually for burlesque rather than sentimental effects.[18] The sexuality of this race was something that middle class America tried to forget.

To some degree, "variety" itself was also bound to the mythic conceptions of nineteenth-century society, and while it accommodated itself to the early stages of urban development, it could not maintain the pace set by vaudeville. By 1915 variety had fairly well

29

lost its distinctive identity and had become either the modern burlesque show, on the one hand, or an imitation of vaudeville. In its origins at about the time of the Civil War—M. B. Leavitt remembered soldiers attending a program of vocalists, minstrel acts, and a troupe of models in "Living Pictures" at the Adelphi Theater and Winter Garden—variety was an outgrowth of the saloon culture that had developed in the wake of the American frontier.[19] Overtly masculine in its salaciousness—bawdy, vigorous, intimate, and uncouth—it preceded a settled homestead society and yet lingered on as a reminder of the days when neither religion nor effeminate gentility encumbered the manly adventurer. Variety was distinguished from the minstrel show and the circus by its lack of a family audience, and its magic lay in a spirit of camaraderie and good fellowship quite at odds with a settled community life.

By the 1870's, however, variety acts were being performed under less bawdy conditions. The biographer of Weber and Fields tells us of the Bowery Theatre where these famous dialect comedians performed in juvenile comedies of their own devising. For ten cents at the Bowery the patron enjoyed a comedy, a drama, a pantomime, and three or four specialty acts. The spirit of even these nonalcoholic showplaces was vigorous. Isman describes the gallery of the period as "the pulse" of the popular stage. "It hissed and jeered the villain, shouted encouragement to the put-upon hero, guffawed and stamped at the clowning of the low comedian when it approved and stopped the show when it didn't."[20] This sense of familiarity with the audience was one of the characteristics which distinguished variety from vaudeville. Weber and Fields with their slapstick, knock-about act evoked this type of response. In the nineties they were playing in their own theater to a respectable audience yet maintained this feeling of intimacy, as David Warfield, who played with them for some years (as did Lillian Russell), testified: "A performance there went off in a chorus of laughter from the audience that was terrific and spontaneous. Sometimes it spread to the actors themselves till they had hard work to go on with their lines. And the theater was small enough to make the whole affair intimate."[21] Elsewhere on the Bowery the ethnic theaters played to Italians and Jews amid the screams, tears, and applause of a different kind of audience participation.[22]

The figure primarily responsible for leading variety out of the red light district was Tony Pastor. His story has been told often, and it is only necessary to notice here that he sold no liquor in his theater and required a level of decency in his performances which would encourage "ladies" to attend. Pastor's became a favorite entertainment spot in New York during the eighties and nineties, but it was always variety, distinguished by the masculine figure of Tony Pastor participating in his shows, not the impersonal ritual of vaudeville. Pastor had been a circus ringmaster at some time in his career, and he would present himself in tails and top hat to introduce his artists. As the *Dramatic Mirror* described it, he would rouse "a chorus of laughs loud enough to wake up a sleeping policeman outside."[23] The variety spirit of intimacy was prevalent at Pastor's and, perhaps because of this, it was patronized by many idle members of the theatrical profession.

Christy's Minstrels, Barnum, and Pastor all represented attempts to capture the mass audience, and all acknowledged that the secret lay in providing a family entertainment acceptable to the middle class that would appeal also to a general audience. The Negro, man and animals, or masculine horseplay

31

might each contribute something to this entertainment, but by itself not one of them was a sufficient lure for the mass audience. While the circus especially, with its hard-headed maxim of "Get the Coin" and its proclamations of moral purity and educational values, provided a good training ground for Keith, Proctor, and other pioneers of mass entertainment and was thus largely responsible for the synthetic formulation of vaudeville, yet it was to be no match for the new organizational techniques or for the mythic celebration of success in the new world of the machine.

One further component of the vaudeville synthesis, which has only been mentioned in passing, was the popular stage of the nineteenth century. From the stage vaudeville adopted the star system, undergoing refinement in the nineties by David Belasco—to say nothing of borrowing the stars themselves. From the "legitimate" theater vaudeville acquired also some knowledge of management, stage direction, and other niceties which the sawdust circuits had ignored. The other important transfers from the theatrical world were dramatic and musical pieces. Keith depended heavily upon light opera at first and formed his own company, which was not discarded until 1894. Although Proctor had announced in 1893 that he was changing to "continuous vaudeville," Professor Odell noted that his bill at that time included "the world-weary *The Mascot*, with Maggie and Frank Gonzales. . .and 'forty chorus voices,' all constituting the Marie Gurney English Opera Company."[24] Vaudeville bills of this early period contained melodramas, farces, and even rural dramas along the lines that Denman Thompson had made famous.

Of special note, however, because it reveals the growing sensitivity of the theater to city life, was

32

the increase in farces of the Charles W. Hoyt type. Hoyt specialized in depicting familiar city characters and exposing common fads and foibles. Typical were his *A Milk-White Flag* (on the militia), *A Hole in the Ground* (on station agents), and *A Brass Monkey* (on the plumbing trade). Hoyt followed in the path of Edward Harrigan, the realistic dramatist, who had won the acclaim of William Dean Howells, but he offered a simpler bill of fare with a greater emphasis upon plot and action.[25] This type of play, easily produced in a one-act, became the basis for the entire genre of one-acts which will be examined in Chapter 8.

From this brief survey of vaudeville's relation to other types of popular entertainment we can make several generalizations. Vaudeville was obviously highly derivative and eclectic. It grew from no one central tradition of either the theater or itinerant entertainment, but rather combined the elements from a number of established forms to appeal to a new and different sensibility. In some ways, it is true, the public taste did cling to its rural and frontier myths, and parts of the circus, minstrel and variety traditions persevered. But urban conditions had brought about the desire for new attitudes, new rhythms and new sensations. Whereas the earlier forms had concentrated on specific aspects of American life (the Negro, bawdiness, men and animals, the exotic) of special appeal to certain groups or classes, vaudeville widened the scope of the popular arts. If it had any one flaw, it was in trying to do too much, to express all things to all people. In fact, vaudeville was the first institution to face this particular dilemma of modern mass entertainment.

Mass entertainment as such was not, and is not now, distinctively American, any more than itinerant amusements had been. All nations which have undergone industrialization have had some sort of equivalents to vaudeville or the variety show. England particularly developed a widely diversified popular theater in the mid-nineteenth century and subsequently evolved the music hall, not unlike the vaudeville palace in its organization and performance. The similarities between vaudeville and the music hall are interesting and reveal the degree to which the United States was still predominantly Anglo-Saxon in its perspectives, but even more significant is the essential difference between the two. Whereas vaudeville was universally keyed to a peculiar response to urban life—designated here as the national Myth of Success—the music halls were much more diversified in their tone and informing vision. Differences of locale and social station played a much greater part in determining the content and pitch of the music hall show, and while there may have been minor differences of this sort in vaudeville, for the most part efficiency demanded that the acts be interchangeable parts which could move uptown, downtown, or across the country without excessive changes in costume, script, or stage business.

Vaudeville theaters were almost inevitably located in the heart of the city, the business or shopping center where communal life was its most active and where all elements of society were most likely to mingle, whereas the music halls tended to be located in the residential areas of their immediate audiences. This crucial difference led one observer of 1900 to classify the music halls of London into four distinct groups, on the basis not only of their location but also of the class level of each area.[26] Thus, at the top was the aristocratic music hall, best represented by the Alhambra and the other theaters near Leicester Square; at the bottom was the music hall of

34

the London slums, a cheap and shoddy entertainment for the most part but occasionally presenting singers or dancers of surprising talent. Somewhere between were the West End theaters, feeble imitations of the Alhambra, and the bourgeois music halls of the modest sections of the city and particularly of the suburbs. The content of these various theaters was well oriented to the tastes of their respective groups — nearly half the program at the Alhambra being filled by a *ballet divertissement,* the bourgeois theater offering a heavy dose of sentiment and melodrama, and the theaters of the working class specializing in Irish comics, imitators, and farces. For the aristocracy the theater was an appropriate setting for social intercourse: the audience was costumed in formal evening clothes, and for many years — much to the horror of moralists and B. F. Keith himself when he visited England in 1896 [27] — the ladies of little virtue strolled along the promenades to the sides and rear of the orchestra. For the proletariat the theater was a place for boisterous enthusiasm and vigorous expressions of approval or disapproval toward the performers. To a much greater extent than in the United States the music halls combined the sale of beverages with the stage entertainment and thus encouraged a more personal, or at least, sociable atmosphere.

Of course, these class distinctions must not be too rigidly interpreted, for many managers of American variety theaters quickly saw the prestige of "vaudeville" around 1900 and dubbed their entertainments as "variety-vaudeville," or even "vaudeville." Thus the real thing had to defend its integrity and leave no doubt as to its particular aims by calling itself "refined vaudeville," "polite vaudeville," or "family vaudeville." Even differences of pronunciation became important, ranging from the high-toned *vō´ dĕ vil*, derived from British usage, to the language of the streets as H. L. Mencken had found it —*vawdvil*.[28] But always the intent of the managers was to keep to a middle ground which would raise the ritual high enough to attract the middle classes, yet remain within the limits of acceptance recognized by the uneducated, working class. After a single season in New York, the Vaudeville Club, which catered to the closed circle of fashionable society, ceased its attempt to bring in the best artists from the local theaters for after-hours entertainment.[29] Nowhere else in this country did there seem to be sufficient impetus to start an aristocratic theater, and before long such creatures of the *beau monde* as Mrs. Jack Gardner would, with gracious condescension, attend the show at Keith's.[30]

In its ritual articulation of the American Myth of Success, vaudeville kept its doors open to the democratic mass. If the British music halls also glorified material values, they did so from the vantage of either the haves or have nots. But the American myth beckoned not merely those who had arrived but those on the way. What was for some a celebration of what had been done, was for others a dream or a promise. British and European scholars have looked at popular amusements and have found them to be reversions to puerile behavior or merely safety valves for the release of psychic energy. And as much has been said of American amusement. But vaudeville in its days of pristine vigor and symbolic sensitivity brought into form an energizing vision of the new civilization and its implications for the common man. If its immediate predecessors among itinerant entertainments could not inform it of a central, guiding purpose, neither

36

could its cousins abroad. The ritual evolved, certainly, making critical contact at many points with what had been done before and what was transpiring contemporaneously, but its central concern as an expressive ritual grew out of social and psychological necessity rather than from an inherited or acquired set of styles and symbols.

THREE

The New Folk and Their Heroes

THE VAUDEVILLE AUDIENCE, amorphous as it was, would appear to defy characterization, but even without precise quantitative definition, it takes on at least the outlines of an identity. We know, for example, that the theaters were generally located near metropolitan shopping areas, and thus the audience must have included both city-dwellers and shoppers from the suburbs. We know that the device of the "continuous performance" was a singular success, and thus that vaudeville appealed to groups with leisure time even during the normal working day. We know that a typical vaudeville show contained a good deal of fluent verbal humor, but that also there was a large proportion of the performance which required no firm control over the American language. We know that the humorous portrayal of ethnic types fell into disfavor after the turn of the century, and we know the shows were flavored with sex appeal—largely of a rather robust and plenteous variety. We know, and this from statistical information, that large numbers of children habitually attended the vaudeville shows—at least as early as 1910 and perhaps before. We know a great deal about the American city of the vaudeville era—its population, its economic and social structure—and can thus infer much about the audiences. But most of all, we know the persons with whom the members of the audience delighted in identifying themselves, and the insights provided in this fashion tell us much more essentially about the audience than do purely objective data.

The cities were, of course, manufacturing and distribution centers, and it was in this capacity, more than as centers of political or cultural life, that they expanded in the late nineteenth century. Laborers and factory workers, bookkeepers and clerks, entrepreneurs and professional persons entered the cities to man the growing industrial machine. They came from everywhere: from the small town of the American provinces, off farms handed down by pioneer progenitors, southward from Canada and north from Latin America, eastward from the Orient and westward from the Old World. If earlier immigrants had turned their eyes toward the rich farm lands of the territories, those of the eighties and after looked to the cities for their fulfillment, just as the second and third generations of native Americans were doing. A new way of life, different from that of European farm or city, even different from that of the American homestead or village, was in the making, and these masses were both curious and perplexed by its shape and meaning. Not all of these migrants and immigrants went to vaudeville performances, for many were either overworked, destitute, or so caught up in the trauma of transition that no external fantasy could redeem them. But the young and vigorous, those with newly acquired hours of leisure, those concerned and gratified by the new directions along which social life was traveling, sought out the vaudeville theater and listened to what it had to say about the bustling, energizing, affluent life of the cities.[1]

The mass audience was fundamentally altered during the decades after 1890 by the waves of immigration which brought ever-increasing numbers of the peasants and artisans of eastern and southern Europe into American ports. Whereas the earlier immigrants had been primarily from the British Isles, Germany, Scandanavia, Switzerland, and Holland, the fifteen million persons who arrived in the United States in the second of the great waves of immigration were largely from Austria-Hungary, Italy, Russia, Poland, Greece, Rumania, and Turkey.[2] The American city became a mélange of custom and a confusion of tongues. Folk habits, religious practices, family structures—all contributed to the differences and confusions. The Latin preference for exuberant public architecture, brighter colors, and larger families—the cynical humor of European ghettos—the peasant's phlegmatic indifference to personal property—the lower-class intellectual's endless verbalization—these were but a few of the attitudes that shook the primarily Anglo-Saxon and Germanic standards of taste and value. The streets, the buildings, the signs, and all of those peripheral social institutions of which vaudeville was one became brighter, more dynamic and boisterous.

But one must not suppose that the greater part of

a vaudeville audience, except perhaps from some of New York's East Side theaters, was made up of immigrants directly off the boat. The leisure time, the price of a ticket, and the frame of mind required to appreciate a vaudeville show were not available to the impoverished, unknowing newcomer. For him the immigrant theaters and cheap variety shows could offer more than the gilded palaces and highly paid performers of the circuits. Vaudeville was not prepared to initiate the Italian or the Slav directly into the American way of life, because it made so few points of contact with the ethnic culture of any one group. But for the mass as a whole, once the surface peculiarities had begun to blend into one another and once common denominators of taste and social habits had begun to crystallize, that is to say, once the process of Americanization had begun to take place, the palaces offered a redemptive vision of city life. The young men and women aspiring to the white-collar jobs in the expanding economy, the athletes, political bosses or contractors who had early established a basis of power among their fellow immigrants, the worldly wise and vain or sentimental—all were lured by the connotations of the vaudeville ritual—and were undismayed by its esthetic inadequacies.

Although even a sprinkling of professional people attended the better theaters, the symbolism of vaudeville was most appealing to the rising class of white-collar workers. Only one or two generations away from the pioneer homestead or from peasant life in southern Europe, these people aspired to the status and possessions of the mercantile middle class. This class expanded, between 1870 and 1910, to almost eight times its previous size until it included over five million persons.[3] It was to form the basis of the mass consumer market, and entertainment, publishing, and advertising were to aim their complex symbol-making apparatus at it. To this group, with its steadily increasing affluence, its appetite for consumer goods, its ambitions for its children, and its awed envy of the wealthy and the socially prominent, the ritual of abundance and vitality, of smartness and know-how, could offer the most.[4] Even further, this new white-collar class was groping for an identity, seeking to make known to the patricians above and to the laborers beneath—as well at to itself—its common interests and motivation. Vaudeville provided all that this class could ask for of a symbolic ritual: sentimentalized contact with its origins in the old folk, a community of feeling, and a sense of importance.[5] It gave them topics of conversation, sexual stimulation, memories, standards of taste, and a tangible presence located so centrally in the city that no one might overlook it. Vaudeville novelty, humor, movement, and sophistication were precisely calculated to bring meaning to lives destined for white collars and dark suits.

The taste-makers of this group were not necessarily the wage earners, however. The vaudeville ritual ran on through the working week and the working hours, catering in a large part to women and children. What the vaudeville managers thought of as "family entertainment" became the entertainment of those members of society which the industrial economy had released from domestic toil. Thus the vaudeville ritual included much material of appeal to women and children and exploited those aspects of the Myth of Success most appropriate to them. The emphasis upon clothes, jewelry, and cosmetics was obviously directed toward women, and the large number of female performers—especially among the stars—was a tribute to an emancipated feminism. For the children, of course, there were the feats of physical skill, stage magic, animal acts, and broad comedy. The ritual celebration of success was not directed merely at the white-collar worker as a justification of the demands placed upon him by the American enterprise, but it reached into his family as well and spelled out, with unmistakable clarity, what the new industrialism was to mean for their lives.

This new folk no longer respected the sharply drawn divisions among ethnic groups or the older caste or family values. They rejected former traditions and wished to be a part of the celebration of a brave new world. Collectively, they were a new audience for dramatists, a new readership for publishers, and a new listening group for musicians. Their tastes differed radically from those of the dominant Genteel Tradition, whose emphasis had been upon the classics and the art of the Romantic period, whose tastes tended toward the vaguely idealized and the "universal," and whose reservations about innovation in social or cultural institutions could become phobic at times. Lacking any clearly defined standards, the New Folk were faddish and volatile. They sought sensation and the impressions of the moment. They supported yellow journalism, political crusades, the naturalistic theater, and dozens of other novel turns in public taste. Arbiters of this taste were to be found, but even they lacked standards other than lipservice tributes to "realism," and all too often the taste-makers were also the money-makers—purveyors of novelty for the sake of personal gain. Yet the controlling factor was not individual taste or judgment but rather the mass imagination, the collective response of those most directly engaged in the new wave of social growth.

What quantitative information that can be obtained about the vaudeville audience serves to confirm its being denominated as a New Folk. The size of the vaudeville theaters, their large number, the scales of admission prices, the attendance, the proliferation of theaters from one decade to the next, and the enormous profits realized by the managers—all point to the firm base which vaudeville had among the expanding segments of the population.

Keith's Boston Theatre provides a useful yardstick for guaging the number of persons in a good-sized city who attended vaudeville performances in a given time. The theaters, naturally, were not expected to run at capacity, and managers had a way of exaggerating the capacities of their houses, but the best information points to a capacity of 2,000 for this particular theater. The major circuits generally considered around 60 percent of capacity as a profitable average for a season.[6] If we assume conservatively that Keith's, running about thirty performances per week, drew about 65 percent of its capacity, we find that each week nearly 40,000 persons (14 percent of the population of Boston in 1900) attended the theater. When we translate this into gross income, assuming the "average ticket" in the $1—$0.25 scale to have cost about 50 cents, a *conservative* estimate of the gross income would be about $20,000 per week. Granting the roughness of our figures, we still gain some idea how Keith could employ nearly a hundred persons in his theater and still pay from $500 to $2,000 weekly for the leading performers of the day. It is probable that Keith's Boston, which so dominated the city's amusement life that no other "big time" theaters were able to gain a foothold there, succeeded in "packing them in" during the regular theatrical season and kept fairly close to the 60 percent figure even in the summer months.

The capacities of other vaudeville palaces fell beneath the figure of 2,000. Although the Philadelphia Bijou, reconstructed in 1889 from a commercial build-

44

ing at the cost of $75,000, originally claimed to hold 2,700 persons, later figures indicated that 1,600 was a safer estimate. The Providence theater, Keith's Opera House, was the largest in that city and accommodated about 1,800 persons. Keith's first acquisition in New York, the Union Square Theatre, had a capacity of a mere 1,200 people. In the nineties Keith's New Theatre was surpassed only by Proctor's Pleasure Palace, the auditorium of which could take 2,200 persons. In general the theaters of the Keith and Proctor circuits tended to have capacities of 1,200-1,600—fully sufficient if one ran the "continuous performance."[7]

In the broader picture, however, the capacities of individual theaters lose significance. The circuits and combines multiplied incomes six, twelve, or thirty times. Keith's merger with Proctor in 1906 had put six theaters under their joint control at a capitalization of $8,000,000; and when Proctor fought his way out of the combine, Keith was reported to have bought the theaters of Percy G. Williams for nearly $6,000,000, giving him control of a string of thirty theaters.[8] In 1914, the year of Keith's death, the theaters bearing his name included two in Boston, six in New York City, six in Brooklyn, two in Jersey City, two in Philadelphia, two in Cleveland, and one each in Atlantic City, Columbus, Lowell, Indianapolis, Cincinnati, Louisville, Portland (Maine), Providence, and Pawtucket.[9] Shortly before F. F. Proctor died, he had sold out his holdings in vaudeville theaters to the Radio-Keith-Orpheum (RKO) interests for an estimated sixteen to eighteen million dollars.[10]

Yet the growth of these two major circuits represented only a portion of the entire picture, for the smaller circuits of three or four theaters, as well as independent theaters, had been proliferating in the decades following 1890. If we take as a rough measurement the relative number of vaudeville theaters listed in the *Official Theatre Guides* of 1896 and 1910, we find that in fourteen years New York City had grown from seven "Variety Theaters" to thirty-one "Variety Theaters." Included in this 1910 list were seven theaters belonging to the Keith-Proctor partnership, three owned by Percy G. Williams, two owned by William Morris, and three owned by E. D. Miner. Not all of the remaining sixteen theaters were dedicated to authentic vaudeville, but still the growth is impressive. Turning to Chicago for 1896, we find only a half-dozen theaters giving some sort of variety or burlesque performance, but in the 1910 listing there are twenty-two theaters under the heading of "Vaudeville." Philadelphia shows a somewhat different pattern, having had twelve variety or vaudeville houses in 1896, but then expanding its number of cheaper theaters during the fourteen years to a total of thirty in 1910. Only Boston, the site of Keith's New Theatre, remained relatively stable during this period, the few cheap vaudeville theaters which sprang up having quickly turned to burlesque or closed their doors, leaving Keith's two theaters the field.[11]

Some idea of the place that vaudeville and its companion amusements held in city life in 1911 can be gleaned from a survey sponsored by the Russell Sage Foundation. After considerable field work, the compilers of this survey estimated 700,000 persons attended some forty "low-price" theaters each week in New York City, a figure which represented about 16 percent of the total metropolitan population at that time. Weekly receipts from this audience were estimated to be about $315,000—an average of 45 cents per admission. This figure takes on additional weight when compared to the $190,000 weekly in-

EVA TANGUAY

MAY IRWIN

come of "high-priced theaters," and with the even smaller income of the motion picture shows.[12] Of course, the differences between the institutionalized vaudeville of the circuits and the imitations and mutations among the lower-priced theaters are not pinpointed by this survey, but the accompanying table of New York theaters in 1911 gives a clear enough idea of how well vaudeville was entrenched in New York in the early twentieth century.

TABLE 1 — New York Theaters[13]

Name of Theater	Price Range	Capacity
Alhambra	.25-1.00	1,566
American Music Hall	.25-1.00	2,150
Bronx	.25- .75	1,784
Colonial	.25-1.00	1,500
Columbia	.25-1.00	1,488
Dewey	.10- .25	1,600
Eden Musee	.50	400
Fourteenth St.	.25-1.50	1,500
Gotham	.05- .10	1,650
Hammerstein's Victoria	.25-1.00	1,350
Harlem Opera House	.05- .10	1,600
Keith and Proctor's (Union Square)	.10- .20	1,200
Keith and Proctor's (58th St.)	.10- .20	2,000
Keith and Proctor's (23rd St.)	.10- .20	1,551
Keith and Proctor's (5th Ave.)	.25-1.00	1,160
Keith and Proctor's (125th St.)	.10- .20	1,800
Lincoln Square	.10- .25	1,459
London	.25-1.00	1,800
Manhattan	.10- .25	1,100
Miner's Bowery	.15-1.00	1,000
Miner's Eighth Ave.	.15-1.00	1,000
Murray Hill	.15-1.00	1,400
Olympic	.25-1.25	1,350
Plaza Music Hall	.25-1.00	1,200
Star	.05- .10	2,000
Third Ave.	.10- .25	1,700
Yorkville	.15- .25	1,400

This mass audience, composed of many elements of the urban population but chiefly of the rising army of white-collar workers, gave rise to a new kind of folk culture, urban rather than rural in its orientation, expressive of a central faith in personal success and social progress, and tremendously effective in reshaping the entire basis of American society. This urban folk culture existed side by side with the remnants of folklore from the American frontier — the doughty settler, the fabular cowboy, the tall tale, the ballads, and masculine rough-and-tumble — and also with the folk customs and rites transplanted to America by the peasants of a dozen different ethnic and national groups. Mass culture at this transitional stage in American history cannot be written off as invidious commercialism, designed to supplant the common man's inherent gifts of expression. This folk culture, different as it may be from the folk cultures of less highly evolved societies, is nevertheless the closest to genuine expression which the mass man has yet enjoyed and must be considered seriously in this light.

There are, it must be acknowledged, theoretical difficulties in viewing mass entertainment as modern folklore, and the argument in favor of doing so must rest upon four premises. First, that folklore is essentially a form of symbolic discourse which connotes more for its proper audience than it does to objective observers. Second, as a consequence of the first premise, that any form of symbolic expression which is not readily defined as art, science, religious literature, or philosophical thought may possibly qualify as folklore, so long as it derives from a community of values and feelings. Third, that thus defined folklore need not be naive, child-like, or uncommercialized, but need only represent actual and significant values of the folk. Fourth, that a heterogeneous industrial society may seek community through folk-lore as well as a homogeneous, primitive one. While several of these premises run against the grain of professional scholarship in the area of folklore, they are an attempt to take into account both historical realities and our present understanding of symbol and myth. Such manifestations of psychic and sym-bolizing activity that one finds in mass entertain-ment can hardly be expected to rest in a critical limbo forever, and once the exclusiveness of tradi-tional folklore is broken down, a fresh and energiz-ing light is cast upon the entire field.

Constance Rourke wrestled with this theoretical problem, and her observations upon the folklore of the plantation Negro as it became absorbed into the minstrel show contain several implications for our view of modern mass entertainment. In *American Humor* she had perceived the direct relation between the minstrel show and Negro folklore, claiming that "From Negro humor early minstrelsy drew as from a primal source keeping the tradition for direct and ample portraiture."[14] And in those posthumous pa-pers, collected by Van Wyck Brooks under the title of *The Roots of American Culture,* she had described the similarities between the leading characteristics of the slave camp meeting and the minstrels' walk-around, their group singing, their use of the tam-borine and banjo, and their distinctive rhythms.[15] Yet Miss Rourke must have known also that the first commercial success of the blackface minstrels, which was created by Dan Rice and other itinerant Yankees, owed little to any personal roots the performers or producers had in plantation life. The removal of the black face and his walk-around from a homogeneous and localized culture did not necessarily entail a loss of meaning, although certainly the meaning became amplified beyond whatever original intentions had given rise to it. Perhaps, as a perceptive historian of the South has suggested, the minstrel show rose to meet a national, rather than a local need, and became a "defense mechanism" through which both North and South could regard Negro slavery without feelings of guilt.[16] What had been parochial became, as the symbolic need occurred, a piece of national folklore.

The circus, as we have already seen, quickly lost its identity as an equestrian performance, yet it too adapted itself to meet the symbolic requirements of a mass audience in the Gilded Age. Under Barnum and Forepaugh the circus became the symbolic prophecy of an age of opulence and splendor such as the imaginations of rural and provincial Americans could hardly conceive. Fantastic beauty, a fairy-like setting, and a sense of heightened sexual excitement —all pervade the account of the Missouri lad who crept under the tent flap and added one more to his string of "adventures":

It was a real bully circus. It was the splendidest sight that ever was when they all come riding in, two and two, and gentleman and lady, side by side, the men just in their drawers and undershirts, and no shoes nor stirrups, and resting their hands on their thighs easy and comfortable—there must 'a' been twenty of them— and every lady with a lovely complexion, and perfectly beautiful, and looking just like a gang of real sure- enough queens, and dressed in clothes that cost millions of dollars, and just littered with diamonds. It was a powerful fine sight; I never see anything so lovely. And then one by one they got up and stood, and went a-weaving around the ring so gentle and wavy and graceful, the men looking ever so tall and airy and straight, with their heads bobbing and skimming along, away up there under the tent-roof, and every lady's rose-leafy dress flapping soft and silky around her hips, and she looking like the most loveliest parasol.[17]

For Huck Finn, as for thousands of his contemporaries, a regional folklore was giving way before the enticing symbols of the materialism of the industrial age, which were national in their scope and fast becoming the basis for national folklore.

It is this very materialism which is the center of modern folklore, that modern criticism, of course, finds difficulty in accepting. Yet this materialism is, as Huck Finn's account demonstrates, full of wonder and awe. The mystery and magic of primitive animism, totemism, and incantations still exist in the mystery and magic of the machine and its products for the New Folk. The anomaly which Mark Twain explored in *A Connecticut Yankee in King Arthur's Court*—that empirical knowledge and applied science could be far more miraculous than any priestly subterfuges—became the basis for an entirely new kind of superstitious awe of the power of natural science. The modern folk, no less than their progenitors, had gone about their symbolizing way, utilizing the very methods and matter of science and spinning their fantasies around the very empirical, irreducible reality to which science had given authoritative approval. If, as R. G. Collingwood has observed, modern man is terrified of magic,[18] it is only that superstitious magic denounced by science that disturbs him. To those other kinds of magic tacitly approved by science—mass suggestion, "miraculous" medicine, and the wonders of technology—modern man consents without serious qualification.

But most important is the value of folklore in creating a community, and in this respect the symbolic activity of mass entertainment is difficult to ignore. Although rituals of the vaudeville kind could not integrate performers and audiences into a primitive tribe or arouse the public to confront specific communal crises, still the magical fellowship basic to folk rituals pervaded the vaudeville show and shaped the attitudes of the folk. Fireside ritual and stage ritual may present striking differences, but both serve to implant feelings of solidarity, enthusiasm, and purposefulness. The dynamism engendered by the vaudeville show differed, as does primitive folk art, from formal and humanistic modes of expression in the collective spirit which it encouraged and in its lack of self-consciousness. The New Folk, like the old folk, sought tangible symbols through which their spiritual and physical environments could be brought under control. That their collective problem was no longer the conquest of Nature but mastery of the Machine only serves to testify to the unbounded resources of the human consciousness.

Nowhere does the character of the New Folk reveal itself better than through its identification with the performers of the ritual. The dynamics of this identification were not simple, and it is easy to be misled into equating the stage images and groups within the audience. The performers were not merely what members of the public were in fact, but were also what they thought they were and what they thought they would like to be. The vaudeville performance had to present a varied and interesting cast of characters, representative of major components of city life: the verbal and nonverbal; the creatures of craft and skill and those of personality and wit; the exotic temperament and the prosaic mien; the scapegoat and the authority figure; the glamour girl and the homebody; the enterprising and the wary; those confident in the midst of personal success and those still ambitiously striving for it. In its larger capacity, however, vaudeville brought public opinion to a focus upon meaningful images and crystallized keys to success.

Out of thousands of performers the public would select an enterprising dandy like George Cohan, a pair of quarrelsome exotics like Weber and Fields, an oddly matched optimist and pessimist in blackface like McIntyre and Heath, a patrician beauty like Ethel Barrymore or a flamboyant beauty like Eva Tanguay. The channels to stardom were many, and sometimes mysterious, but once the type had been singled out, its relation to the rest of the bill was always clear, for it took featured billing and occupied the climactic position in the sequence of acts. Had vaudeville been a narrative folk art, these would have been the heroes and heroines of the drama; as it was they were isolated epitomes of what success was like in American society. Success was different and apart. It attracted money and admirers. It took what one was and made something distinctive out of this that would last as long as the audiences clapped and the theater's met one's demands. Of course, the stars found out, and some of the public might suspect before too long, that success in these terms was also a lonely thing, which froze one's personality and left one with nowhere to go. Yet so long as vaudeville flourished, the stars came forth to occupy the pedestals of public approval and to affirm the plausibility of the success myth.

The star system in vaudeville came about almost unintentionally as a result of a power struggle starting in 1893 between two rival managers, Keith and Proctor, in New York. J. Austin Fynes, an aggressive and imaginative showman, was Keith's manager of the Union Square Theatre. When he observed that Proctor was including opera favorites like Campanini in the vaudeville program, Fynes began offering generous salaries to encourage figures from the legitimate stage to make short appearances at his theater. As the competition waxed, performers of all kinds made double and triple the salaries in vaudeville that they were making elsewhere. The first well known performer at the Union Square was Alice J. Shaw who received $250 a week. She was followed by Ida Muller at $250 and then Verone Jarbeau at $400.[19]

For a one-act curtain raiser, Fynes had Robert Grau secure Charles Dickson and his wife, Lillian Burkhart, to appear in *The Salt Cellar* at $300 weekly. The salaries crept up, Grau reports, until by 1896 the limit was $600 per week. To one Charles Hawtry went the distinction of being the first actor from the legitimate stage to go over $1,000 a week (his figure was $1,250). In spite of managerial efforts to agree upon a maximum, renegades like Percy Williams found it expedient to "pay first and count afterwards." He paid Albert Chevalier $1,750, Henry Miller $1,500, and Vesta Tilly $1,750. Harry Lauder was probably the best remunerated: William Morris is supposed to have maintained him at $3,500 for each week in addition to some $1,500 for releases from European engagements.[20]

The stars had risen from petty cash to the big time. Lillian Russell had worked at Pastor's for $35 in the eighties but was to reach $3,000 a week in the first decade of this century. May Irwin had leapt from $150 to $2,000. The blackface comics, McIntyre and Heath, had earned about $400 weekly from Keith in the nineties but by 1911 they were making $2,500. Eva Tanguay received $3,500 a week at the height of her career around 1910. Will S. Cressy had moved down from Vermont to break into vaudeville about the turn of the century. He not only performed in popular one-acts with his wife, but he also wrote them in abundance. His weekly salary plus his royalties made him a millionaire in ten years.[21]

Even the lanterns of the managers seemed dimmer with these bright lights behind them.

One might expect that this exorbitant labor cost would have cut seriously into profits, but such does not seem to have been the case. As larger theaters were built to accommodate the throngs that came, the prices were edged up slightly from the old 10c — 30c levels, and the revenues held up. But the issue became one of relative power and prestige. The trend clearly anticipated the disintegration of the manager-centered circuit and could easily have led to a situation comparable to that today in motion pictures and television, where the prosperous actors and actresses of the forties have become the producers of the sixties.

Two of the greatest acts in early vaudeville were to leave the circuits to establish themselves independently. Their careers not only shed light on this weakness in the structure of vaudeville, but also show us one pattern of success. The first was that of Joe Weber and Lew Fields — Weber and Fields on the marquee — who had entered show business at the age of nine in the shoddy museums of the poorer sections of New York City. Forced out of the tight family life of the immigrant Jews more by the size of their families than by personal inclination, these two waifs became inseparable companions on and off the stage. Not until they reached a pinnacle of achievement was there the slightest rupture in that attachment for one another which had contributed hugely to their success. During the seventies theirs was largely a dialect act, mimicking the absurd speech of Irish, Germans, and their own people, but in 1883, when they first booked at the small museum in Boston operated by Keith and Bachelder, they had become firmly established in the rough and tumble burlesque for which they became famous. Weber was only 5 feet 4 inches in height and, with his stage padding in place, appeared to be nearly as wide as he was tall. The wiry Fields would push, strangle, and pummel this small blob of humanity, while they both would jabber a fantastic, nearly incomprehensible jargon which owed something to the German, something to the Yiddish, and something to the English language. Their exit became a byword for nearly a quarter of a century: Weber would shriek as he was hustled offstage, "Don't poosh me, Myer." As early as 1887 they were able to finance their own burlesque show, which traveled through the major eastern cities, and by 1894 they had crashed Broadway, appearing at Oscar Hammerstein's Olympia Theatre at $500 per week. In 1905, at the height of their career, they were able to ask $4,000 a week for short appearances at the New Keith Theatre in Boston.[22]

Another vaudeville turn which threw off the inhibiting reins of the managers was the song-and-dance skit of George M. Cohan. More properly, we should say that of the Four Cohans, for not until George entered musical comedy did he go off on his own. The Four Cohans, like Weber and Fields, were among the early performers at Keith's Washington Street museum, and previously they had toured the nation, performing in small halls, opera houses, county fairs, and the better variety shows. George and his sister Josephine, who made good with a "single" in vaudeville later on, entered their parents' act at some unspecified early age. George quickly established himself as their writer and was publishing his songs at the age of fifteen. His dramatic sense showed itself in such vaudeville skits as *A Game of Golf*, an ephemeral piece of nonsense which was revived annually along the circuits by less inventive comics. The Cohans broke into New York and the "big time" during the nineties, first appearing at Keith's Union Square Theatre. About 1899, however, they broke with Keith as the result of an argument over their billing—a constant source of friction between managers and performers. Legend maintains that the hotheaded young George had told Keith, "No member of the Cohan family will ever play for you again as long as we live."[23] From this point George drifted out of vaudeville and, shortly after, founded the partnership with Sam H. Harris which was to produce *The Governor's Son, Broadway Jones,* and *Get-Rich-Quick Wallingford.* Free from the restrictions of vaudeville and the domination of the managers, George M. Cohan, quick-tempered, quick-witted, young man on the make, was able to give full play to his talent and his sure sense of public taste.

Vaudeville did indeed develop and display a number of great American entertainers. Will Rogers, Texas Guinan, and Eddie Cantor—stars of the World War I period and later—were to make their most permanent marks after leaving the vaudeville format. Rogers' humor was too expansive in its rambling digressions, and his personality as uninhibited social critic from the prairies was too absorbing to the public to suit the compressed limits of the vaudeville "spot."[24] As long as Texas Guinan, another reminder of the frontier, stayed with Tin Pan Alley ballads and Gibson Girl poses, vaudeville provided her a sufficient medium. But her original talent was for a brawling sarcasm and a dramatic belligerence that made her the darling of the New York speakeasy set. At the height of prohibition her hoarse welcome to the patrons of her clubs—"Hello, sucker"—entered into the American language, while her parades into court and her well publicized ridicule of revenue agents, who never did send her to jail, made her too over-powering as a personality for vaudeville to restrain.[25] Eddie Cantor, who had taken his apprenticeship in smalltime vaudeville and cabarets previous to World War I, worked up his distinctive image as the bigtime lady fancier, signified by the popping eyes, during a tour of the London music halls, and when he was ready for high-paying vaudeville engagements in the United States, he was also being sought after by the producers of Broadway revues.[26] By 1920 the "stars" of vaudeville were "stars" in their own right, the "personalities" of show business who were readily adaptable to all of the various media that Broadway and technology could offer. That Rogers, Guinan, and Cantor all became featured performers in motion pictures — and they are merely representative — points out the function of vaudeville in creating a mobile, nationally-known corps of performers, a series of images in which Americans could identify something of themselves.

If the ritual was largely characterized by the stars, who explicitly enacted the myth of success, it was also fashioned by managers, making good in their own right, and supported by thousands of workaday show folk. For the managers, of course, the traditional lines of the Horatio Alger story were readily available, and the memorial volume on F. F. Proctor, and B. F. Keith's autobiographical letters both stick close to the stereotype. Proctor had been a performer, one of the Leventine Brothers, an acrobatic act, and Keith had risen from small museum enterprises, but both boasted of Yankee backgrounds and of how their native shrewdness was responsible for their success. Yet neither the managers themselves, like Proctor and Keith, nor the general public tended to think of these men as exploiters who were gulling the public with shoddy and irrelevant wares. Though they became self-conscious and deliberate as success stole upon them, in many ways they too retained the innocence of their age.

The public image, however, could be an ambiguous one. If Keith's name on the marquee of several dozen theaters and his widely quoted statements upon the "morality" of vaudeville served to present a positive image in the public mind, the accounts of the legal and financial struggles among the hierarchy, the references to Keith's estate or his yacht, and the hostile criticisms which appeared in *Variety,* all tended to encourage the kind of resentment of big money which lay at the root of both Populism and Progressivism in politics. Thus, in 1912, it became an ironic necessity to transform Keith, at the height of his success, into a plain, ordinary human being.

An unsigned feature article in the New York *Herald Sunday Magazine* eulogized Keith as much for his human warmth as for his success: "It is safe to say," states this piece of propaganda planted by Keith's associates, "that hundreds of performers love and honor the name of Keith, because it is synonymous with a square deal." The writer acknowledged that performers were "acts" rather than "persons" to Keith, and thus there was no element of "petty local managerial tyranny" in bookings, cancellations, and so forth. But still Keith was a human being in spite of what some might think: "Many of the performers have a mental picture of the big man slashing salaries, buying theatres, making up programmes and cancelling acts. How few of them picture the kindly old man as he really is, down in Florida, quietly enjoying his work amid flowers, foliage, and sunshine."[27] Years previously Mr. Frank J. Bonnelle, in a poem honoring Keith on the occasion of his fiftieth birthday, had tried to soften the harsh profile of success with joy and kindness. A few stanzas indicate sufficiently how strained the effort could become:

From the old Granite State came a brave-hearted boy
    Whom his playmates were wont to call "Ben,"
With a smile on his face and a soul full of joy
    To compete for a place among men.

Although baffled at first, and pursued by ill-luck,
    There was naught could his courage depress.
With ideas unique, perseverance and pluck,
    He at last won the greatest success.

The world owes him much—he has furnished it rest,
    Recreation, instruction and fun,
In a fairy-like palace, and always the best,
    In a way that no other has done.

The pride of achievement has not puffed him up,
    He is generous, thoughtful and kind;
And although he now sips from an o'erflowing cup,
    To misfortune he never is blind.

Now shines with full vigor Prosperity's sun
    On the man we are proud to call friend;
May Good Fortune's performance continuous run
    Through a season with far-distant end.[28]

Keith, like Proctor and others, carefully selected and cultivated his managers largely from the large city newspapers. The newspapers were, after all, like vaudeville in being collective repositories for the varied streams of taste and attitude which converged in the city. While the earlier managers had risen largely by virtue of their talents as businessmen— that is as distributors of goods and services—the second generation were trained interpreters of public opinion, men who understood the deeper vagaries of the mass mind.

For vaudeville to extend its life span, it had to retain a sensitivity to all of the peregrinations of popular myth, and it was through the work of this talented and perceptive group of newspaper-trained managers that the ritual was kept up to date. In their hands, for example, the "publicity stunt"—the skillful manipulation of news media—became a significant aspect of show business. In the early years of their influence—between 1905 and 1910—Eva Tanguay sold newspapers on a street corner accompanied by a trained elephant, Houdini jumped into the Charles River fully chained, a group of Harvard psychologists interviewed a precocious chimpanzee, and a strong man swam around the Statue of Liberty in the dead of winter. Such devices not only filled theater seats, but they also satisfied the public yearning for novelty and excitement.[29]

The ascendancy of vaudeville as a mass media however, brought with it economic problems which temporarily threatened the tight grip of the managerial clique. A system for the total control of booking operations had been agreed upon by independent managers in 1900 but found rather stiff resistance among the ranks of the performers, who banded together in a fraternal organization called the White Rats. A strike, the closing of a few theaters, a few minor concessions from the managers resulted from this protest action, but the triumph, such as it was, was short-lived. In 1906 the managers created the United Booking Office, which flourished on the ten-percent rebate taken from all performers, and never again was the absolute rule of the managers over vaudeville to be questioned. Although a few of the stars had lent their names to the cause of the White Rats, the problems of commissions and rebates were not of vital concern to them.

Of course, the performers had little insight into

the cultural movement of which they were a part. The role of the managers as manipulators of social myths and the role of the stars as social symbols were neither obvious to them nor particularly relevant to their peculiar problems. But it is a mistake to assume that their protest at the turn of the century was purely economic. In a vague way they recognized the mechanical quality of the entire enterprise and resented the insignificant and unsatisfying roles assigned to them. It was a loss of identity as much as economic bondage against which the White Rats launched their brief challenge.

In his book on the White Rats, their leader, George Fuller Golden, tells of the crucial meeting between the delegation of performers and the managers, at the latters' office in the St. James Building. At this confrontation Golden had evidently spoken with some eloquence regarding the equitable treatment to which he believed the performers were entitled. The managers, however, had listened with an infuriating smugness and indifference to this appeal to their better nature. Speaking of himself deprecatingly in the third person, Golden commented that, "One of the many handicaps that our Fool labored under was his ability to see the ridiculous futility of appealing with such sentiments as truth, justice or fair play, in this present age of Iron and Gold." Here, paradoxically, stood the celebrants of the myth of success, chastened by the impersonality of the ideal toward which they had been driving. Golden, no doubt, speaks from the sense of despair and alienation which played no part of the ritual itself, but which in retrospect gives it poignance and emotional depth.[30]

The reasons why these performers remained in vaudeville and prepared the various and lively backdrop against which the stars might shine, are not

THE FOUR COHANS

JOE WEBER AND LEW FIELDS

difficult to find. In spite of the complaints against the U.B.O., the performers were reasonably well paid, and in spite of their relative unimportance, they did receive credit on the programs and in newspaper notices. Then, too, once one was established in the profession, it became a way of life with its own community, its own customs, and its own language. The theatrical trade papers, the *Clipper*, the *Dramatic Mirror*, and, after 1905, *Variety*, told them all that was worth knowing in the world. These folk easily became clannish, developing manners, clothes, and gathering places which were distinctively "show biz."[31] When vaudeville ceased to support them, they still gathered together in such fraternal clubs as the "Cosmopolites" in either New York City or southern California. Even Eva Tanguay, who more than most had brought alive the myth of success, lived out the final years of poverty and physical distress in a lonely bungalow in the Hollywood hills.[32]

The very argot which they spoke connoted their involvement in the myth of success, and in its clipped and comic fashion provided them with a community of value. Many expressions derived from the special demands of the vaudeville show: "headliner," "middle-liner," and "bottom-liner," or "extra-added-attractions" and "held over by popular demand." A woman might be "a great single," especially if she was a "serio-comic" singer like Lottie Gibson who could handle both comedy and dramatic numbers. The song writers were crisply labeled "words and music," the publishers' agents were "song runners," and plants in the audience hired by these agents were "song boosters" and "song pluggers." A recently discovered performer was a "find," and his prospects were good if he could "work right through a piece." Sudden success or failure on the stage were crucial aspects of vaudeville life, and the performers tried to "wow" the audience, to "panic them" or to "knock them off their seats." On the other hand, they lived in dread of "doing a Brodie," or, in other words, to have "flopped," "flivved," or "busted." Failure became obvious when an act "got the bird" or the "raspberry," or was "walked out on," or when the comic instinctively realized that "he was dying on his feet." The respect of the "two-a-day trouper" for the dramatic stage was expressed in the curt word "legit," but his contempt for imported culture was implied by his dubbing classical dancers as "gauze fluffers."[33]

Of course, a certain irony lay behind this sociable clannishness, for in its fellowship and mannerisms lay disillusionment with the mythic values to which vaudeville was committed. Neither the virtues of rugged independence nor aggressive enterprise were particularly honored by the clan, and while material goods were highly prized, they tended to share a spotlight with the satisfactions of perfected technique, applause, and notoriety. Neither the shade of "respectability" nor the demon of pure greed seems to have gained much hold upon these show business folk, and if the ritual they acted encouraged others, less secure in their social roles, to place a premium upon social climbing and the acquisition of capital, that certainly was not their intention. What wealth they accumulated was not so much earned — their performance had its own satisfactions — as bestowed upon them by a grateful public. There is little question that the fantasy of the stage tended to spill over into their lives and to lead to serious problems. Show business clannishness had few answers to the hyperactive imaginations and inflated egos which the ritual encouraged.

Although the Myth of Success said more about the vaudeville managers and the headlined stars than it did about the great body of persons who contributed daily to its propagation across the land, the public nevertheless looked upon the theatrical profession as a whole with a certain envy, mixed with suspicion and curiosity. In the public press interviews with performers and bits of gossip about them tended to identify them with the people, stressing the home town and family background, offering a few hints as to their humble family situations, and suggesting the normal and prosaic aspects of their present lives. The tabloids, however, began early in the century to pick up more provocative material—arrests, divorces, associations with criminals, and other such scandals. The splendidly depraved dream that became "Hollywood" was in the making, and the forces of alienation were at work. The show business community as a whole was becoming an example in the public mind of the way in which the success myth operated, and if it made for selectiveness and pleasure, it also appeared to have its darker and self-destructive side. The people of show business had become unknowingly captives of the myth which they performed.[34]

FOUR

From Sin
to Sociology

WERE THE VAUDEVILLE RITUAL a simple
morality play, like the rags-to-riches versions
of the Horatio Alger story that found their way onto
the popular stage from time to time, problems of
analysis would be all but eliminated. And if the
vaudeville ritual were like primitive ritual, a straight-
forward outgrowth of traditional emotions toward
the cycles of the seasons and of birth, growth, and
death, the problems would be at least simplified.
But vaudeville stood in the midst of a society in
which few values were stable and in which simple
stories of desire, like the dreams of success held by
the masses, became involved in all sorts of compli-
cations. Peripheral symbols of many sorts crowded

their way into the vaudeville performance, and although the Myth of Success provided a core of meaning upon which managers, performers, and the new mass folk seemed to agree, there was no clear consensus as to the precise nature of this success, its relationship to other values, or even the way it was to be achieved. In its very format vaudeville reflected the pluralism and fluidity of social thought during its time and, as a ritual, had to accommodate itself to the most contradictory and ambiguous influences.

In particular, the Myth of Success, as vaudeville revealed it, was directly challenged by two informed clusters of social thought, both of them more consistent and explicit than the Myth of Success, and both propounded by educated and vocal adherents. The first attack was launched by the rural Protestant clergy, who sought to preserve the Protestant ethic in its original purity and who resisted with considerable ferocity the inroads made upon it by urban materialism. The second assault was manned by social scientists and reformers, more cosmopolitan in outlook, but nonetheless deeply disturbed by the emphasis upon fierce competition and the indifference to humane values manifest under the name of Success in the new industrial order. Both of these social doctrines were, of course, key movements in American thought with considerable influence in many directions. The concern of this chapter, however, is limited to their immediate contact with popular entertainment and the way in which the tone of the vaudeville ritual was shaped to accommodate both of these aggressive schools of thought.

Perhaps the central dilemma facing the early stages of mass entertainment was that of presenting to a harshly materialistic social environment a fantastic, dream-like production which had a symbolic relevance. The New Folk were not just dreamers or escapists. If they wished relief from the give-and-take of city life, they also wanted the strength and motivation to face it once again. The dream they cherished was the American Dream of opportunity, prosperity, and happiness—and the entertainment which they patronized had to give expression to the dream.

And yet the ritual was forced also to maintain an aseptic neutrality. Among the New Folk were vast areas of disagreement, not only from group to group but from generation to generation. Folklore for the industrial democracy was still unformed and shifting, and the sensitivities of minority groups had to be continuously protected. The ritual, safe in its fantasy, still had to be rigorously censored and controlled in many of its phases. At few points could individual performers be unleashed to express their own particular visions of life, and above every performance spread the impressive shadow of the vaudeville managers, quick to preserve their enterprise from unprofitable aberrations. Their responsibility for this supervision was never questioned by the paladins of respectability, who regarded show business as a proper form of free enterprise. While groups from the outside were energetic enough in their protests against this or that breach of public manners or morals, never was there a serious attempt to depose the managers or to impose upon them stringent regulations. What the managers well knew was that public good will—the maintenance of a ritual basically offensive to no one sizable group—was the foundation of their commercial enterprise.

B. F. Keith had been among the first to recognize this and in his hard-headed and practical fashion was apt to credit much of his personal success as a showman to what he called the "purity" of his vaudeville entertainment. In 1910, with the advantages of hindsight, he could see how few theatrical performances of the 1880s, excepting the "high class theatre," were suitable for women and children. Reflecting upon the years before vaudeville, he said that "theatrical managers seemed to have quite ignored the wants of the average American family for theatrical amusements." In regard to the policy of his theaters, he said, "I made it a rule at the beginning when I first opened my Washington Street [Boston] museum, that I must know exactly what every performer on my stage would say or do. If there was one coarse, vulgar, or suggestive line or piece of stage business in the act, I cut it out. And this rule is followed in every Keith theatre in the United States today and just as rightly adhered to now as it was originally."[1]

By the twenties the "purity" of vaudeville was still one of its dominant characteristics. A sardonic reporter for H. L. Mencken's *American Mercury* was to acknowledge that: "In all the talk and to-do about censorship of the stage and screen, the one branch of popular entertainment that has been considered by all the authorities, self-constituted and otherwise, to be so pure that it needs no Christian supervision is vaudeville. The heir of Comstock, Mr. John S. Sumner, has not once risen up in wrath against the corrupting influence of the two-a-day, and the Baptist pope, the Rev. John Roach Straton, hasn't even bothered to mention it in his laudable and impassioned discourses."[2] F. F. Proctor advertised that his entertainment was "especially adapted to the tastes of ladies and children" and was "bright in character and wholesome in tone." An English visitor testified that Keith's programs "are as 'pure as the water lily bells,'" and that "is why

69

they draw the very best people who love 'the pure, the good, and the beautiful'. . . .Anyone whose tastes and instincts have the upward trend cannot but be impressed with the Keith methods in America, and desire to have English methods reach the same pitch of perfection."[3] Even an agent for the Watch and Ward Society of Boston could offer nothing but praise for Keith Vaudeville: "I believe it is the highest duty to approve that which is good and condemn that which is bad. Take Keith's theatre as a standard. The performance is elevating and amusing; there is nothing low or suggestive."[4] Proctor is supposed to have been told by a prominent judge: "I've been going to your show every week now with my wife and little girl and little niece, because you've got the kind of show that keeps a family together."

The obsession with "purity" on the part of the big-time managers was not always confined to the elimination of purely scatalogical material. One performer recalled the appearance of a sign backstage in one theater that read: "The use of 'Damn' and 'Hell' is forbidden on the stage of this theatre. If a performer cannot do without using them he need not open here." And the proscription at times also included such vulgarities as "slob," "son-of-a-gun," and "liar."[6] One newspaper cartoon depicted the plight of the performers by showing a manager admonishing one monologuist: "Here, you've got to chop out that swear stuff." To which the artist replies, "Why D--n it sir, that's the hit of my act!"[7]

Even violence could be considered a violation of this "purity" and "refinement." When the Young People's Christian Union launched an organized protest against the showing of motion pictures of the Johnson-Jeffries prize fight, they wrote Keith, who was vacationing at Marblehead. He immediately wired New York: "Can say have issued orders no fight pictures be shown in any house anywhere with which I am concerned—B. F. Keith."[8] This injunction covered twenty-three theaters from Portland to Cleveland; and, although the film concerns threatened legal action, the Independent Managers Booking Office followed Keith's example. John Royal has said that pictures of fires, train wrecks, and the like were also prohibited in deference, it was claimed, to pregnant women who might attend the show.[9]

Mild as these prohibitions seem in retrospect they say much about the development of popular taboos. Both "pure" and "moral" were words that had dropped from the lips of the evangelical circuit-riders as they had spread the doctrines of Protestantism along the frontier and eventually across the continent. The slogan "family entertainment" took on special meaning for a populace attempting to reorient the family unit in the shifting social forces of the late nineteenth century. Even the word "amusement" dulled the hedonistic edge of the gay antics which took place within the vaudeville palaces and provided a euphemism behind which the pleasure principle could do its work.

Vaudeville, in establishing the tone of its ritual, had to come to terms with the dominant Protestant morality and to make clear its position on two important issues. First, there survived the suspicion of the puritanical that any form of pleasure was a form of corruption and that the only legitimate activities for the godly man were the worship of God and the practice of his vocation. The Protestant ethic was concerned with stewardship and the advancement of the kingdom, but it also kept alert to distractions which might occur along the way. Vanity Fair, as it was described from the pulpit, stood

71

ready to lure Christian from his journey to salvation. Second, the Protestant movement had gained its impetus from the rejection of pomp and ritual, and latter-day prophets could, without too much distortion, find in theatrical presentations just such an appeal to carnal, unregenerate man. The ideal of the plain life had found support in the pioneer economy of nineteenth-century America so that the spokesmen for rural virtue were all too ready to condemn the illusory glitter of the stage. Within the ethos of American Protestantism, the myth of vaudeville encountered considerable resistance and could hope to succeed only if it imposed upon itself stringent codes.

What happened, of course, was that vaudeville capitalized upon the uprooting process and offered a compromise to the American as he emigrated to the city. If he would suspend his assumption that the Christian life required a renunciation of pleasure, that a few hours in a palace devoted to mere amusement could destroy his character, then the palace would willingly meet all other objections. It would eliminate the environment of vice typical of some theaters; it would curb obscenity and profanity, and it would in all ways make the performance suitable to the American family as a group. The traditional objections to the wasting of money and the unwholesomeness of nighttime activity could be easily avoided by attending a matinee and sitting in the low-cost balcony or gallery seats. Thus, in abandoning the theological and philosophical basis of the Christian life as it was understood by orthodox nineteenth-century Protestants (in practice many had already found these tenets unnecessary), the American was assured of outward conformity to a code of decency. Vaudeville managers, of course, took advantage of historical circumstances in offering their compromise, for the ground had been seeded decades before. Even the most vigorous salting by the clergy could not subdue inevitable growth. And where the Protestant leaders of society would go, the minority groups could, with safety, follow.

But defining the "moral" tone as a concession that a few showmen made to American religious sensibilities is something of an oversimplification. It does not, for example, explain those allusions to family entertainment and its emphasis upon gentility. Nor does it account for the willingness of hundreds of thousands of church people to take this tentative first step toward damnation. These factors can only be understood in the light of historical developments within Protestantism during the previous hundred years.

With the establishment in the late eighteenth century of a number of permanent theaters in eastern cities, supported by the mercantile and professional classes and tolerated by the Protestant Episcopal Church and the Unitarians, the Calvinist wing of American Protestantism had armed itself for attack. John Witherspoon, a president of Princeton and one of the Founding Fathers, had already published *A Serious Enquiry into the Nature and Effects of the Stage* in 1757, but the issue was to wait for its full development until 1825, when Rev. T. Charlton Henry published his *Inquiry into the Consistency of Popular Amusement with a Profession of Christianity*. His declaration that there was no middle ground, that one was forced to choose between a life of pleasure or a life of Christian godliness, could not have stated the position of nineteenth-century evangelical denominations more clearly. Within the tradition of moral absolutism his logic was impeccable: since the theaters often mocked the clergy, defamed the act of prayer by presenting

73

it upon the stage, and did "everything to stimulate and nothing to restrain the natural workings of depravity," *ergo* the Christian must totally abstain from theater-going.[10]

By midcentury, however, real social problems began to exert their influence upon the clergy. The two bulwarks of primitive piety, the family and the village, showed signs of disintegration under the pressures of industrialism and expansion. The defense of the family became of prime importance, as Horace Bushnell's *Christian Nurture* pointed out,[11] and the clergy found it expedient to encourage "home affections, pursuits, and habits" even up to the point of actual amusement.[12] Although they drew a sharp distinction between domestic entertainment and public entertainment, it is easy to see how subsequent decades could blur the line, and how difficult it would be for the churches who had been preaching family solidarity to object to the "family entertainment" offered by B. F. Keith and his rivals.

The village way was even more directly threatened. Amusements, as one Virginia clergyman viewed them, distracted young people from prayer, impinged upon the Sabbath as a day of worship, and left a record of drunkenness, loitering in the streets, outbreaks of boisterousness, gross insults to passersby, and crime. Even worse than local amusements, however, was the pernicious influence of traveling troupes. This same minister, a Lutheran, warned his congregation that "the readiness of access from the large cities, and the disposition shown by a large part of our population to sustain them, have largely increased the Exhibitions of a demoralizing kind." He specified "concerts of low and corrupting songs," stage dancing, the theater and circus, and he compared the appetite for such indulgences to "the taste of that species of birds which preys upon the dead and the dying."[13]

The protest of the provinces against the corruption of city life has been long current through the western world, but it achieved a particular emotional cast during the late nineteenth century. In the accelerated migration of those years the city folk could easily be one's neighbors and kin. One writer, his book sanctioned by the Methodist Episcopal Church, made a plea to those "Methodists who were once poor and unknown, but have grown rich and prominent in the world," and he reminded them that they "have left the narrow way in which you walked twenty or thirty years ago, have ceased to attend class-meetings, as you once did, and are now indulging in many of the fashionable amusements of the day, such as playing chess, dominoes, billiards, and cards, dancing and attending theatres, or allowing your children to indulge in them."[14] This heartfelt plea is but one example of the personal difficulties which the breakdown of the village life entailed.

Most severely, of course, these problems fell upon the village pastor. His responsibility was to preserve the simple Christian values, to invoke the social pressure inherent in the community church, and to impose his authority as an interpreter of the gospel upon the wavering. Again and again the pastoral arguments repeated themselves and were reechoed in the other protests against the city—the Populist movement, prohibition, and nativism. Sometimes striking blindly without any firsthand knowledge of the evils of the theater which they describe, sometimes conceding that a few exceptions might be granted in the case of Shakespeare, the clergy nevertheless assumed their prophetic role and raised their voices in the name of decency, the home, and the individual. With confidence they followed Henry Ward Beecher in describing the people of show business—those gamblers, circus-riders, actors, and racing jockeys—as "moral assassins," for they were "men whose very hearts are diseased."[15] Do not, they asked, those actors "act a lie" as their nightly business? And what about the mental faculties of spectators dulled by nightly spectacles? The arguments repeat themselves through a vast literature, most of them citing slanted quotations from classic and Christian writers, criticizing the degree of leniency or strictness of other publicists, and (in the sermons) concluding with the inevitable application to the reader, "Will you renounce the vanities of the world?"

As this moralism lost ground it became all the more frenetic. In the period 1900-1915 the editorial pages of the *Dramatic Mirror,* a New York trade publication, followed closely the activities of evangelist preachers and met each slander of the theatrical profession with self-righteous disclaimers.[16] Of course, the sensationalism of the evangelist rhetoric was enough to whet the curiosity of many young folk, and such diatribes as this one by Billy Sunday were fully as effective as publicity for the theater as the provocative items in the gossip columns of the yellow press: "Young women should shun the stage as they would the bubonic plague. The conditions behind the footlights, especially for chorus girls and show girls, is something horrible. Most musical plays employ girls who are at the mercy of men, and half a dozen theatres, were managed by millionaires and their friends, who have the privilege of staying there during rehearsals of the performance and their object is obvious. A girl with a pretty face is soon at their mercy."[17] But while this moralism persevered into the twentiety century as a rabid fundamentalism, its influence declined. Billy Sunday was as much a product of the new ritualism of mass entertainment as he was a critic of it.

Had village righteousness prevailed, the attempt

of vaudeville to acquire the "moral" tone would have been unrealistic if not downright absurd. The Protestant denominations, however, had felt the full force of social and economic developments during the nineteenth century. For reasons too complex to be fully treated here, both the moral philosophy and the social views of the evangelical clergy were to be modified in the crucible of industrialization. While pockets of denunciation and resistance have survived into our own era, their effect upon the urban mass audience after 1900 appears to have been negligible. Even the action of the Methodist Episcopal Convention of 1872[18] in banning an impressive list of amusements fell under rather stringent criticism by prominent Methodist educators and appears to have lost much of its effectiveness by the turn of the century.[19] In the place of negative hostility developed a positive conception of the role of the amusements in urban life.

In this liberalizing process the rise of the Social Gospel was certainly the most obvious, if not the most spectacular, phenomenon, but equally important was the influence of genteel idealism in literature and theology. The harsh logic of the either/or variety was softened by an organic conception of human experience in which the "sensibilities" played a large role. Anxieties over the atmosphere of the theater, which could "grossly deteriorate and debase the affections,"[20] gave way to high-minded attempts to elevate the taste of both audiences and performers. By 1847 the idealism of such Protestant writers as Horace Bushness and Mark Hopkins (Hopkins had drawn the fire of James McCosh of Princeton for his supposed eudæmonism) had inspired a book titled *A Plea for Amusements* (1847) by Frederick William Sawyer.[21]

Rejecting the "old leaven of asceticism," Sawyer

asked that men recognize "the priority of enjoying the bounties of Providence." The cities, for Sawyer, were not centers of vice and inequity, but were the "progressive" and "civilized" centers of the Christian world, where men could insure the "cultivation of *all* their faculties," thus lending "charm to civilized life." Instead of resorting to negative strictures, the church should bend its efforts toward fostering, encouraging, and regulating amusement, and thus develop among the populace "refinement" and "sensibility." Granting that the contemporary theater was "a school of vice," Sawyer saw this fault, as had Mark Hopkins, a direct result of Puritan suppression, not as a reason to despair of reform and elevation.[22]

This emphasis upon "sensibility" went hand in hand with the new social consciousness in American Protestantism. During the eighties the spirit of genteel reform which had motivated Sawyer and others in the previous decades became widespread. Liberal congregations in Detroit and Minneapolis heard sermons calling for an increase in the quality of theatrical performances and for a rise of an "intellectual amusement."[23] When the Protestant Episcopal Church lent its sanction to the activities of the New England Theatre Reform Association, Rev. William Wilberforce Newton rejoiced publicly, "Thank God, our church is coming down to meet the masses and to help solve some of those practical questions which are in the path of the present!"[24] The association's general policy of uplifting the Boston theater was to be shortly taken up also by the Drama Society of Boston and the Drama Committee of the Twentieth Century Club, while a similar movement in Chicago went under the name of the Chicago Drama Committee. A national organization eventually brought together many local groups as the Drama League of America, whose membership strength reached, at one point, 90,000.[25] The mild policy adopted by the league emphasized the "crowding out" of vicious plays by attending and otherwise encouraging approved productions. With the advent of motion pictures in quantity, the focus of "restrictive public opinion" shifted to the National Board of Censorship of Motion Pictures, an organization which, for a time, had the full backing of both the motion picture industry and religious groups; but it bowed, in turn, before the rising Jazz Age and the threat of legislative censorship in many states. It was replaced by the office of Will S. Hays, Presbyterian elder and Indiana Republican, who enforced a comprehensive censorship on all motion pictures.

There was no greater spokesman for the responsibility of Christians to meet the problems of urban growth than Washington Gladden, who had studied under Mark Hopkins at Williams College and was later to acknowledge his intellectual debt to Horace Bushnell.[26] His interest in the YMCA had generated deep concern with the problem of pleasure which he expressed in a book addressed to young people titled *Plain Thoughts on the Art of Living* (1868). In addition to his popularization of Biblical scholarship and his widespread interest in the many problems presented by an industrial society, Gladden remarkably enough contributed a significant essay on amusement. Basically, he advocated that Christians, acting independently of the church but inspired by its teachings, should provide low-cost, mass entertainment for the urban public. His approach was primarily rational and dispassionate, for he sought the means by which human intelligence could control "the force which gathers men into cities," and he advocated that the facts of urban life be examined and acted upon.[27]

79

The facts, as he saw them, were these: first, by 1885 amusement was well established in the cities and the multitudes would prefer to spend "three times as much as a seat in a church would cost on the theatre and variety show"; second, amusement had become a capitalistic enterprise with vast material resources; third, "if the diversions can be kept healthful, a sound national life will be developed," for amusements were "a great factor in the development of the national character"; fourth, commercial entertainment could not help but do more harm than good so long as it was "in the hands of men and women whose moral standards are low, whose habits are vicious, and whose influence upon those with whom they come in contact must be evil."[28]

With these "facts" before them, Christians would find solutions to the problem. One solution was to provide entertainment without commercialism, which would appeal to the higher instincts in man rather than to the lower. Gladden described at length an example of such work already under way, a series of entertainments sponsored by the Cleveland Educational Bureau. The performances were a medley of lecturers, group singing, and concerts, offered at low admission prices and conducted in an auditorium which seated 4,000. The level of decorum and taste was high, Gladden reported, and the series was popular with members of all social classes.[29] Such enterprises were initiated during the eighties and nineties by the YMCA and other civic groups, but they could not begin to fill the demand for daily leisuretime amusement.

In the same year that Gladden's essay appeared in the *Century*, B. F. Keith launched continuous vaudeville and was soon to imitate the highminded tone that characterized the Cleveland bureau's elevating series. Once the clergy and the religious press considered amusement as morally acceptable, the highroad to pleasure was opened to a large, hitherto inhibited group. The influence of Lyman Abbott in the *Christian Union* was strong throughout the urban Protestantism, and in 1879 he had openly criticized the "gospel of work" and narrow attitudes toward the Sabbath, calling for "the play of social life" and a "gospel of rest." The *Union* published special vacation features from time to time and in 1890 the magazine created a department of recreation.[30]

Among the major Protestant denominations the sole remaining bulwark against the inroads of modern life was the Methodist amusement ban. Taking note of the approaching Methodist Convention in 1904, *Everybody's Magazine* conducted an opinion poll among eight prominent leaders in American religious life, including Cardinal Gibbons and the leading spokesman of Progressive Orthodoxy, Newman Smythe.[31] A consensus was established upon two points: first, that many amusements were innocent and harmless, and second, that the churches should avoid making regulations in this area. Cardinal Gibbons took the occasion to warn against so-called "problem plays"; Bishop Kephart of the United Brethren felt that dancing, card-playing, and theater-going never elevated anyone's morals; and Rev. Mr. Smythe cautioned against the cultivation of "selfishness." But even the editors of the "Symposium" seemed surprised by the pervasive liberality of the views expressed. In the quarters where hostility might have been expected, there was articulate moderation. The Baptist representative recognized that there were "coarse and prurient plays" given in "abominable environments," but insisted that "the church can never permanently deny or suppress the dramatic instinct in the human soul." The Methodist reflected upon the arbitrariness of his denomination and criticized its "artificial conscience." The Presbyterian recommended comedies over tragedies for they released the "play-impulse," and added: "We need, then, to play. Play lubricates the stiff, grating machinery of workaday life. It keeps us young." Dr. Remensnyder, the Lutheran, probably expressed the common sentiment when he distinguished between the *abuse* and the *proper use* of a pleasure and cautioned parents to "teach the young to draw the line sharply between that which is meant to excite the sensual tastes and that which illustrates art and enhances nobility of thought and action."[32] Such a view was a drastic modification of the absolute morality that had implemented the attack on pleasure, and it reflected the genteel idealism of the period. Although we should be careful in accepting these statements of prominent clergymen as the unqualified views of American Christianity, they suggest the climate of opinion in which the vaudeville ritual could maintain its moral tone.

The generally permissive attitude toward amusements infecting urban Protestantism gave impetus to mass entertainment. While the emphasis upon sensibility and refinement provided a shield behind which vaudeville and related pieces of showmanship could operate, this rationale was more appropriate to higher forms of culture—the opera, fine arts, poetry, and the classical stage. For the vaudeville audiences themselves, the appeal to purity and uplift was more a snobbish identification with upper-middle class taste than it was a matter of religious conviction. The managers, in adopting the sanctimonious tone, claimed that they were out for the "carriage trade," but the claim itself was addressed to the aspirant members of the new class of white collar workers. For this group, cut off by levels of education and income from the enjoyment of great and

82

expensive art, the appeal to the sensibilities was vaguely desirable, but provided no firm explanation for their leisure activities. What they needed was a justification for fun, a frame of reference which they might not fully comprehend, but which would, at least, provide a basis for distinguishing between vaudeville and grand opera on the one hand, and vaudeville and a revival meeting on the other.

The great wave of ideas which had beached on American shores in the 1870s had not only weakened the hold of orthodox Protestant thought but had strongly affected the directions taken by the Social Gospel. The new biological science which pointed to the evolution of natural forms through a process of natural selection had been applied to social philosophy by Herbert Spencer with devastating results. Evolutionary thought, in offering radical new perspectives upon man and his society, had raised a totally different attitude regarding amusements and recreation. No longer were these diversions either sinful or mere adjuncts to a purposeful life. In the light of scientific observation of animals and man, play was elevated to a functional role in which its potential for release and expression was held to be highly desirable.

Herbert Spencer himself, in his *Principles of Psychology*, had initiated the reevaluation of the play impulse. Working from purely naturalistic premises, he concluded that play among animals and young men resulted from a "surplus of energy" and as such was a natural and commendable activity.[33] In a subsequent address to an American audience he applied this conclusion to American life. Work was a means by which men survived, but was not, as he found Americans prone to think, an end in itself. The evolution of society toward more complex forms of social organization had created, particularly in

America, a "surplus of energies" which demanded release through pleasurable pursuits.[34] Not only did Spencer's widely read speech pose the clear alternatives between the new "science" and the Protestant ethic, but it served to weaken considerably the emphasis of the Protestant reformers upon uplift and purity.

Spencer did not go unanswered by American students of behavior, themselves already committed to evolutionary science.[35] G. Stanley Hall formulated the position most acceptable to academic psychologists when he considered play as a "recapitulation" of former habits of the race and thus not "efficient" in the promoting of happiness or human progress.[36] Neither the professors nor the vaudeville managers were ready, in the first decade of the twentieth century, to declare themselves in favor of pure play. Only with the advent of the twenties, and with the intellectual breakthroughs of Sigmund Freud and Havelock Ellis accomplished, would scholarship and mass entertainment be ready to accept Spencer's point of view regarding the play impulse.

Vaudeville in its formative stages spoke for a generalized conception of the good life rather than for liberated fun-making. Happiness, however, within its ritual was no longer an otherworldly reward for good works, nor was it the endowed privilege of a few saintly members of the community. Happiness was, the ritual implied, already blossoming within the cities and would soon spread beyond the palaces into the daily lives of men. Neither asceticism nor good works, much as they had buttressed the Protestant ethic during its two centuries of supremacy, were relevant to the new rich life in which the godly and ungodly alike were to be flattered, satisfied, and amused. If vaudeville was not, at the turn of the century, ready to lead the New Folk directly into the land of fun, and if practical considerations demanded the imposition of the "tone" of purity and refinement, the direction which mass entertainment would take in the success-oriented, pleasure-seeking, consumer economy of the mid-twentieth century was already being prophesied.

The new biological science, as interpreted and applied to human society by Herbert Spencer, provided a further approach to the problems raised by mass entertainment. American disciples of Spencer, led by William Graham Sumner of Yale University, advocated a doctrine of rugged individualism and strenuous competition in social and economic life, a doctrine congenial to the managerial clique in all phases of show business, and in general to American entrepreneurs and capitalists. The vaudeville ritual itself, insofar as it was a competition among various acts for headline spots on the bill—or for survival— expressed the attitudes of the vaudeville managers like Keith and Proctor. The very Myth of Success, as incorporated in the vaudeville ritual, was to a large extent premised upon the notions of self-assertion, acquisitiveness, and ego-centricity fostered by the Spencerian ethic.

In its more militant aspects, this kind of thought seemed to justify the exploitative and brutal actions of the robber barons, but, as Richard Hofstadter has pointed out in *The Age of Reform*, the main stream of Spencerian thought flowed into channels more in accord with middle class aims. The Social Darwinists, as Hofstadter has called them, resented the affronts to their freedom on the part of monopolists, financiers, and political bosses as much as they resisted socialism. Their activities branched off into many directions. To their mission of preserving the laissez-faire norms of nineteenth-century culture they brought a moral earnestness and crusading fervor which made for grand and ceremonial gestures in trustbusting, conservatism, and cleanup campaigns against corrupt public officials in the big cities.[37] And yet these Social Darwinists had no plan for the future and no program for mass entertainment. Had the Social Darwinists remained alone in the battle for reform, mass entertainment would have mushroomed without any serious efforts at social control.

However, the liberal Protestant clergy, already active in reform, were joined by another wing of post-Darwinians—aptly titled by Eric Goldman the "Reform Darwinists." Influenced not merely by Darwin and Spencer but by such thinkers as Prince Kropotkin, who emphasized the pack instinct inherent in animal life, these Reform Darwinists, like Edward Ross, Francis Giddings, and Richard T. Ely, sought to replace the individual struggle for survival with an ethic of group welfare. Their appeal was to Science rather than to Scripture, but otherwise their aims were not so different from those of the Social Gospel (which was quick to embrace this kind of group evolution), and in the field of mass entertainment they sought a "sociological" approach to the problems which had, by 1910, become ingrained in urban life.[38] Honestly alarmed by the rampant commercialism of amusements—which they regarded as exploitation of the masses—and disdainful of the low level of taste, they sought objective, "scientific" criteria through which their outrage could be expressed. Once they had found these in their sociological "surveys," they translated the results into action by urging public regulation of entertainment centers by police, fire and sanitary inspectors, truant officers, and other officials, and by invoking public opinion in an attempt to raise levels of taste. The so-called "outdoor movement," which sponsored groups for the establishment of parks and playgrounds, was also an outgrowth of this criticism of public entertainment. By 1915 it made little difference to the vaudeville managers whether or not clergymen attended their shows, but they kept a weather eye open for the social worker, with policemen in tow, out to preserve the integrity of the American home.

When the Russell Sage Foundation in New York City found it expedient to establish a department of surveys and exhibits, which it did in 1912, the social science movement in this country had reached its peak of activity and influence. The following year *Survey*, the official organ for the movement, reported "a veritable epidemic of social surveys," dealing with health, education, recreation, charities, crime, and other problems.[39] Academic social science was achieving a prestigious place in the American scene with the work of such men as Lester Ward, E. A. Ross, and Francis Giddings. Their students were in the field, interviewing, counting, and evaluating, and as their data proliferated, more elaborate theories were advanced to account for the puzzling results of their investigations. In the field of recreation alone, full scale surveys were launched in New York City, Providence, Milwaukee, Detroit, Kansas City (Missouri), Springfield (Illinois), and Portland (Oregon). More modest investigations of Philadelphia, Chicago, Scranton, Waltham (Massachusetts), and Indianapolis also found their way into print.[40] On the state level, in 1913 the California legislature commissioned a statewide survey of recreational facilities.[41] Such studies continued to be made even beyond this period, of course, but the significant culmination of them was Jesse F. Steiner's *Americans at Play* (1933), a study national in scope which reflected the direct concern of the welfare state—the New Deal—with public recreation.[42]

These surveys, as their proponents argued, were "a protest against guessing at the solution of community problems," but their supposed scientific objectivity is open to question, and the overtones of middle class opinion are, in retrospect, very obvious. Whether it was the investigator's personal aversion to all sorts of "passive" amusement or whether it was his proclivity to weed out "wholesome" and "demoralizing" segments of a performance, the difficulties of reducing mythic and ritualistic activity to quantitative statistics were insurmountable.[43]

TABLE 2—*CHILDREN SEEN WEEK-DAY AFTERNOONS AND SATURDAY**

What Doing

	Work	Play	Idle	Total
	287	1,088	1,217	2,592
Per cent	11	42	47	100

Where Seen

	Streets	Yards	Lots	Playg'ds	Total
	1,311	855	209	207	2,592
Per cent	51	33	8	8	100

TABLE 3—*WEEKLY ATTENDANCE**

	Below 18	Between 18-25	Below 25
At Moving Picture Shows			
Children under 14 — 2,891			
Boys under 18 — 5,718			
Girls under 18 — 4,838	13,447		
Young people under 25......		21,464	
Total in 10 houses			34,911
At Legitimate Burlesque and Vaudeville Theaters			
Children under 14 — 587			
Boys under 18 — 1,045			
Girls under 18 — 1,173	2,805	5,816	
Young people under 25......			8,621
Totals	16,252	27,280	43,532

*From Francis North, *A Recreation Survey of the City of Waltham, Mass.* (Waltham, 1913).

From the surveys one can gather a fair idea of attendance by class and age group (see accompanying tables), some sense of the relationship between ticket prices and kinds of performance at various theaters, and a vague notion of audience response.[44]

88

(One investigator in New York noted that the audience looked bored.) But otherwise the results were disappointing, as is revealed by the conclusion to the most sophisticated of the local surveys, that supervised and reported by Mark M. Davis in New York City.

Mr. Davis devised scales of value for measuring the moral content of various entertainments, and his results, in respect to vaudeville, based upon the findings of several investigators working independently, were as follows. Occupying a middle position between burlesque (five-sixths *demoralizing* and one-sixth *lowering*) and the motion pictures (half *positive value* and half *not objectionable*), vaudeville was valued as three-fourths *not objectionable*, one-fifth *lowering,* and one-twentieth *positive value.* Davis concluded from his inquiry that vaudeville depended upon "an artificial rather than a natural, human, and developing interest," and was in general characterized by "stupidity." Attempting, with an understandable sense of desperation, to recommend some positive action that reformers might take in regard to vaudeville, Davis suggested the application of "brains," especially in the direction of promoting dramatic art within the format of the vaudeville show. The managers had forestalled this criticism over a decade previously, of course, by introducing farces and sentimental one-acts.[45]

Indeed, under their shibboleths of "purity" and "refinement" the major vaudeville managers had anticipated most of the pressures which the new sociology might bring to bear upon their industry, short of actual government control. The Reform Darwinists, together with the liberal Protestant clergy, might encourage high-mindedness and statistics in order to keep the Myth of Success concealed behind the smokescreen of the moral tone,

89

but the ritual itself operated upon a level which even the most rigorous censorship or suppression in matters of sex, language, or taste would make little difference. Vaudeville as ritual was not primarily concerned with inculcating sexual license or vulgarity—these were merely the symptoms of its underlying materialism. If reform groups objected to these symptoms, vaudeville was ready to make its concessions. What neither reformers nor managers were capable of doing, however, was reversing the tide of mass feeling prompted by the aspirations of the New Folk. As one nineteenth-century clergyman pointed out, in one of the few perspicacious appraisals of the morality of the popular theater in his generation, censorship and suppression were no solution as long as the people desired the kind of entertainment they were getting.[46]

FIVE

The Mechanics of Fantasy

THE SYMBOL-MAKING ASPECTS of vaudeville had also an operational side. Seen from the wings by a detached observer, the performance itself must have seemed rigidly mechanical, for, as with role-players in most highly developed rituals, the vaudeville performers were intent upon the technique and regarded themselves—in their minutes before the curtain—as skilled craftsmen. Those phenomena upon the stage which acquired symbolic meaning in the imaginations of the audience were, as viewed from the wings, the products of a repetitive process based upon rather crude and stereotyped notions of human behavior. Yet this operational quality also encourages a comparison between vaudeville and

91

the primitive ritual. For while each element of primitive ritual becomes minutely prescribed and each has some symbolic meaning, the familiarity and repetition, even apart from symbolic content, bring to the communicant solace, a confirmation of his own sense of reality, and a greater sense of security from the hazards of life.

The Myth of Success from which vaudeville drew had familiar patterns and basic certitudes, but Success, unlike most of the aspirations of primitive myth, depended not upon continuity and stability but upon change and progressive improvement of man's lot. The ritual of the New Folk, then, was required to keep abreast of its age, paradoxically accepting the new even while relying upon the old. An alert, intuitive sense of what Carl Becker has called the "climate of opinion" was the hallmark of every successful performer; to survive along the fiercely competitive bigtime circuits he had to be versatile and flexible enough to change his act from time to time—even, if the occasion required, in the middle of his performance. Anyone present in the wings before curtain time could not help but feel the electric tension charging the atmosphere, for every performer knew that should he fail to sustain rapport with his audience and thus break the feverish pace of the performance, his days as a well paid and admired "artist" were numbered.

To overcome what in older forms of ritual would have been serious gaps—the unmistakable esthetic distance between performers and spectators (a result of both the mass audience and the code of purity) and the impossibility, given the format of the vaudeville show, of any sustained identification with a dramatic character, the vaudeville ritual depended heavily upon a clique of middlemen—managers, stage directors, booking agents and publicity men. These persons, whose native wits had been sharpened by experience in show business or journalism, were, for the performers, part of the great audience to which they played. These middlemen were the ultimate judges of audience reaction, and upon their decisions depended the financial success or failure of the entire industry. The performers lived in awe and terror of such men as B. F. Keith and his representatives, for they were as ruthless as a balance sheet and had an uncanny sense of what acts were doomed to failure.

Within the vaudeville performance the content was constantly changing, in response to popular taste, but the ritual itself retained a basic character through its carefully varied rhythms and its controlled mood.

The rhythm consisted of a series of controlled accelerations toward climaxes of excitement; the mood derived from the comic effect of vivid contrasts. Neither rhythm nor tone could be effectively improvised or left to chance. Each vaudeville bill in the larger theaters was as carefully contrived as a drawing-room comedy by Philip Barry. The audience, largely unaware of managerial strategy, only knew that the peak of the show would be reached with a celebrity performer well along in the bill. The quick transitions from horselaughs to pathos, from girlish charm to baritone gusto, from frantic action to restrained gesture passed too quickly to draw attention to themselves. The fantasy ran on according to the laws of its own being, inviting the spectator to identify but not to participate, leaving him at the close with the sense of waking from some dim, inchoate dream, the order and meaning of which lay buried beneath the threshold of consciousness. The dream might be repeated, but it was not to be dissected or too clearly understood.

A typical performance—a Monday matinee in August of 1912 at B. F. Keith's Boston Theatre—will reveal something of the structure and the pressures of the vaudeville ritual.[1]

Somewhere in the audience of this Monday matinee is Robert Larsen—in performer's lingo, the "Big Noise"—chief booking agent for New England and one of the chief heirs to the authority of the retired Keith. Larsen's reports on the acts today would be forwarded to the United Booking Office in New York and would carry considerable weight in the assignment of subsequent engagements for these performers.

While the audience waits restlessly in the spacious orchestra and balcony, large enough to accommodate 1,500 people, backstage is bustling with show business activity. When the lights out front are dimmed in a few minutes, the audience will be released from their organized and directed lives, but the stagehands, musicians, performers, special effects men, prop men, wardrobe ladies, and press agents—now lounging along the narrow corridors, running over their lines, and making last minute preparations of all kinds—will be plunged into a contest for livelihood that draws upon all of the energy and wit that they can concentrate into a few important moments.

At the "prompt entrance" to the stage (the vaudeville equivalent of "stage right" in the legitimate theater), the stage crew are reviewing the light plot of the one-act comedy drama to be shown today. Neither the man responsible for the large switchboard by the prompt entrance, nor the operator of the "spots" above the stage, is familiar with the play, which was rehearsed in some other city, and only with difficulty are they able to memorize the

94

HARRY LAUDER AS "SANDY McNABB"

FRED NIBLO

involved directions. And lighting, of course, is essential to the fantasy, casting the warm shadows and brilliant glows which convert painted sets and costumed actors into the landscape and characters of a dream world.

As is customary upon the vaudeville stage, the dream takes place in conventional, well-defined locations. The standard sets were a woodland park (a reminder of romantic pastorals, but now stiffly and garishly formalized), a "garden" which combined suburban horticulture with a few plaster hints of Versailles, and a "street scene" with colorful awnings, a freshly painted lamppost, and shop windows. The dream flows from one setting to the next, each symbolizing at one moment a familiar point in everyday life, but the next moment, as the lighting changes or the action intensifies, fading off into a spaceless, unspecified background.

What cannot be recognized from the front of the house, however, is the way in which the settings are determined: not by the appropriateness to the subject matter of the acts but by the order of the performance and the physical demands of the acts. During this typical performance the opening act, "The Dixon Sisters," is set in a "garden in four," a full stage in which the foliage and other pieces are widely spaced across the entire stage, leaving plenty of room for dance routines. Today the Dixon Sisters are followed by Devine and Williams, a comedy team accustomed to a "set in three," which finds them in front of a flat depicting a street scene, on about five-eighths of the stage. But the act to follow this team requires a campfire so that, for this week at least, Devine and Williams must play on a narrow strip between the footlights and the first curtain—a "set in one."

At 2:13 this afternoon the orchestra, which has,

minutes before, squeezed into the pit beneath the stage, strikes up some lively music in march time. Two minutes later, the ornate asbestos curtain rises and the orchestra signals the imminent appearance of the first act by changing to a dance tune. At 2:21, several pulls by a stagehand on a long iron chain raises the second curtain and the Dixon Sisters, three gay soubrettes, skip gaily on stage. They are dressed in frilly blue dresses with abbreviated skirts and wave silver trumpets which they proceed to play in energetic harmony. A blend of saucy sexiness and tomboyish enthusiasm characterizes the initial encounter of the audience. The girls need not say a line—indeed they qualify as an opening "dumb-act" and attention getter—but their whole act suggests personality, youth, vivacity, and material well-being, which forms an appropriate prelude for the entire show. In mid-act the girls scamper off-stage (opposite prompt) and effect a rapid costume change (by pulling their blue outer dresses over their heads) and then dash back before the audience marvelously attired in pink costumes. The finale of their act nearly becomes a cropper as the bridge of a banjo slips out of place, but the girls quickly recover their poise, fake the closing, and reach the wings before the damage becomes evident. The sisters have finished promptly at 2:30 and the comedy "two-act" of Devine and Williams goes on in "one." No sooner are the girls off-stage than their voices, distinguishable by prominent English accents, are heard lamenting the accident, inquiring how their act "went," and asking where Portland and Bangor, their next bookings, might be.

Such acts as the Dixon Sisters represented were characteristic of the vaudeville ritual. While some performers were capable enough as solo acts and could hold the audience through a special talent, many of the acts lacked this substance and depended upon the psychology of the theater—"showmanship"—to carry them through. The song-and-dance acts, which generally included a few fast jokes, were just such a development in which neither particular grace nor interpretative depth was important, but rather timing and personality. The Dixon Sisters could cover their weak instrumental music with a few bars of singing, could distract the audience from their singing with a few dance steps, and could veil their dancing in some eye-catching costume changes. Before the audience was well aware of exactly what was going on, such an act had yielded the stage and was resting up for its next part in the ritual.

Talented or not, the soubrette was an accepted feature of the vaudeville ritual. In the public imagination she occupied a middle ground between Little Nell and the *femme fatale* and kept vaudeville just within the realm of "purity." One trade publication celebrated her in verse:

> Have you met our bright soubrette?
> Roguish eyes as black as jet,
> Golden hair;
> With two dainty little feet
> Just as saucy as she's sweet,
> Young and fair.

Other verses describe how she bewitches men in the audience, keeps them on a string, but—

> Over all the world she'll roam,
> True to one she loves at home,—
> That's her Jack.[2]

Another poet, writing some years later, reveals a greater defensiveness about the soubrette, for we learn that "The soubrette is a much maligned/ And badly treated creature," who in private life, "Like others, is a wife," or has an aging mother to support. The reader is cautioned, "You mustn't judge her harshly, just/ Because she's bleached her hair."[3]

Devine and Williams meanwhile have launched into their routine with a few well-tested jokes. They are practitioners of the "new humor," the crass, unsentimental humor of the city streets, which comes to its punch line quickly and dispenses with the refinements of story-telling technique.

The straight-man asks, "Who was that wall-eyed, pie-faced, old hag I seen you walking up the street with the other day?" "Why that—" says the old-timer, "that was my wife." With these words he hits his partner in the face with a sewing machine, and asks, "Why didn't anyone play poker on the Ark?" Seizing the sewing machine, the partner replies, "I don't know. Why *didn't* anyone play poker on the Ark?" "Because," the old-timer begins as the battered machine poises over his head, "because Noah was sitting on the deck!"—at which point he dodges the blow and pretends to climb up one of the tormentors. This is "typical vaudeville" as the managers and booking agents well know, for Devine and Williams are often inserted into the second place on the bill as pace-setters for the rest of the performance. Their ritual consists of a rapid cross-fire of jokes, puns, riddles, and insults which brings the audience to a pitch of amusement. In a final bid for applause—the index of success for any vaudeville act—they launch into their "sock finish," two choruses of "Remember, Boys, Your Mother Were a Woman."

Abruptly at 2:45 the sign for "The Three Musketeers" goes up and within thirty seconds the stage in "two" is set with a campfire. The curtain now rises upon a trio, arms across each other's shoulders, singing the barbershop chords of the latest song by a home-town (Boston) boy, Newt Newkirk. As the act begins, the manager hastens backstage to the prompt entrance with instructions to push forward the tormentors, perhaps displaced by Devine's antics, and the stagehands quickly respond. The manager returns quickly to the house, but not before he overhears the whispered complaints of Joe Lanigan, the lean monologuist, who is close to panic because of the thinness of one of the Three Musketeers. Supposedly the audience will not appreciate two thin men on the same bill, and here he is to follow one! "I'll get a frost," comes the stage whisper for the manager's benefit, "Wouldn't that make you yell? And Monday afternoon, too. Gawsh."

Functionally, the Musketeers are part of the "build" for the first part of the performance, providing a contrast to the rough antagonism of Devine and Williams in their symbolizing of a sentimental ideal of harmonious brotherhood, and yet preparing the audience for Joe Lanigan's more sophisticated version of city life.

Joe Lanigan is a "name," a comic whom many people have come to watch, and his position as fourth on the bill recognizes this. His anemic face, tight-fitting suit, and oversize monocle—his gloomy entrance and his high-pitched voice—have made him a specialty among the monologuists, and while his routine covers the accepted topics—marriage, politics, streetcars, and the local weather—his delivery has brought him the glory of being a "corker" in the "big time."

After Lanigan completes his monologue, a *corps de ballet* appears as a spectacular close before the intermission and as a concession to genteel "culture." These graceful creatures, under the direction of *prima ballerina* Mlle. Albertina Rasch, are supposedly imported from exotic European capitals, but as the troupe waits nervously in the wings, the shop-girl whine, in the American vernacular, might be heard: "Darn it, Maggie, you didn't hook me up in back. They'll gimme the hook." Mlle. Rasch herself is on edge and scowls last minute advice to the light crew, but, as the curtain once again rises, the entire ballet freezes into a delighted smile. Their performance goes well and the aura of expensive fantasy is captured in their allotted twenty minutes. On stage they point, glide, and kick delicately under the rose and blue lights of some fairyland, and only backstage, where they dash briefly between movements, is their shortness of breath and their heavy perspiration evident. Even the orchestra, none of whose members had seen their score for Mlle. Rasch's ten numbers until three hours before the show, contributes nicely to the lightness and charm of the dance—although Monsieur Modesti, the director, is sure that the cornetist has the wrong music and that the drummer is deliberately falling a half-beat behind the *prima ballerina* in order to ruin the act.

Not every vaudeville performance could support a *corps de ballet*, but this concession to mass notions of education and uplift was typical of the larger houses. On occasion some performances of real quality—a Barrymore, a Caruso, a Nazimova—could be seen in these palaces, and their attempts to mediate between "high" and "low" culture were not entirely misplaced. Yet in the formal structure of the vaudeville show, only the appearance of uplift, not its substance, was required. A scientific lecturer, some slides of news events, a travelogue, or even a soprano giving voice to one of those pieces of heavy Victorian sentimentality which sometimes passed as religious hymns—any of these would strike the balance as against the biting humor and noisy exhibitionism of the other acts. At one time Keith, who would try just about anything, even had a special Sunday program of appropriate music—but this was not, of course, what the public came primarily to see or to hear.

For the benefit of the matinee audience the intermission is a short one, and "The Windsor Trio," which fulfills the booking agent's requirement for the fifth place—"a strong vaudeville specialty with comedy"—takes the stage in "three." It is to be followed by *The Clown*, a playlet requiring a large tent for its setting so that midway through the act a drop falls and the Trio finishes in "one." Backstage the hands scramble to set up the tent, but when the Windsor Trio finishes its act the set is only half erected, and the song and dance men are instructed to return for curtain calls until the stage is ready. They take eight curtain calls before retiring in exhaustion, and still there are seven minutes before *The Clown* is ready. When, at 3:53, the curtain finally rises, the frantic stage crew has forgotten the light plot and during the entire twenty minutes every cue is missed. The cast, in hoarse stage whispers, calls "lights" to the stage crew, and the effect is not only to bewilder the technicians further but to upset the timing and delivery of the actors.

While such fiascos were not typical of vaudeville performances, the very tightness of the schedules made them much more frequent than most managers would admit. The confusion even spills over into the climactic act of the second part of the performance. Bixley and Lerner today play in the spot in which a Harry Lauder or Eva Tanguay would occupy. The particular talent of Bixley and Lerner was for impersonation and burlesque, and the audience is prepared for a series of wacky costumes and extravagant posturings. In their current routine Lerner is supposed to make a quick change off-stage from street clothes to the attire of a Renaissance courtier, including red velvet tights. The accumulated tension is too great, however, and his change is only half effected. His partner Bixley, although he is thrown off stride by the odd appearance of Lerner in trousers and doublet, wisely avoids comment until the curtain, after which he asks, "Where's your tights, you rummy?" Lerner sits shakily on the nearest stool, his face pale beneath the make-up. In spite of this slip, Bixley and Lerner have made their symbolic point. The pretentiousness of the conventional theater has been heavily scored, and the common man is reminded of the "play" — the putting on and off of masks which seems characteristic of the genteel culture that he admires. Bixley and Lerner enact the roles of children in the attic who might amuse themselves with putting on the garb of adults and, for a moment, playing a part through this transformation, but even in the midst of their fantasy are aware of the absurd figures they must seem in the world's eye should they ever take themselves seriously.

Vaudeville was rich in imitators and parodists. To some extent Weber and Fields belonged to this tradition, exploiting the comic values of sporty tweeds or tuxedos on the backs of their illiterate, lower class characters. The blackface comics had effected a comparable humorous contrast by appearing in top hat and tails, while the legions of male performers who, with clumsy gestures and hairy legs, impersonated women and children, is too large for comment. The vaudeville land of make-believe was in part a bitter, self-conscious world, which only humor could resolve. Charlotte Greenwood, probably the best of the impersonators in the early twentieth century, loved and admired for her depiction of ungainly females, had originally aspired to be a soubrette. During one of her early performances in a sister act, the audience had begun an embarrassed laughter at her awkwardness—at which point she discovered her unique talent. Fanny Brice had similarly attempted to play the glamorous sex idol, before finding her proper image as Baby Snooks.

And this same pattern also applies to Jack Benny, vaudeville's high-toned violinist who eventually developed one of the most telling impersonations in American entertainment. Benny's comment on the myth of success took up where Harry Lauder had left it, the parsimonious, would-be capitalist of the lower middle classes. Originally Lauder's Sandy McNabb had been a picturesque, ballad-singing wit but upon arriving in America he had almost at once become the archetypal stingy Scot, straight from the land of hard-core Protestant mercantilism. While Benny's imitation, a generation later, took on the mannerisms of the Jewish dry goods merchant, it offered substantially the same comment on the American businessman, reflecting a consciousness among the New Folk that the dream of success could be debased in the hands of the greedy and the perverse.

As vaudeville became institutionalized, its parodists turned back upon it. Lauder himself was widely imitated, but any outstanding personality was liable to find himself followed along the circuits by an unflattering caricature. The vaudeville travelogues and scientific lectures received a devastating treatment from such performers as Fred Niblo and Doc Rockwell. Comic dancing, burlesqued songs in all styles, and spurious magic acts played side by side with their originals, and the vaudeville audiences appear to have been equally delighted with the real thing and its distortions for humorous effects.

Appropriately, Bixley and Lerner provided the climax for this performance, and the next turn, the acrobats, Kennedy and Melrose, closes the show. Once again the stage is opened up to leave the audience with the sensation of space and depth, and this pair have the "horizon in four"—the last drop with a skyline upon it—in which to perform. Graceful, manly, athletic, they somehow set the seal of masculine competence upon this particular matinee. While the soubrettes and ballet dancers had provided the balance needed by the comprehensive vaudeville ritual, this performance had centered upon the more rugged virtues of masculine play. Devine and Williams, the Musketeers, Joe Lanigan, the Windsor Trio and finally Bixley and Lerner, had tested their adroitness and strength against the background of life in the city. That these concluding acrobats should perform their twists in midair, their cartwheels and their somersaults, before the skyline of the American city was an appropriate piece of closing symbolism.

Each performance would have its own emphasis, of course, and this masculine quality would necessarily recede when an Eva Tanguay or Ethel Barrymore dominated a show. But the sense of the "build" toward key acts—comparable to the sense of climax in plotted drama—and the well-preserved contrasts between successive acts contributed not only to the formalizing of the ritual, but also to the kind of triumphant statement that vaudeville was trying to communicate to its audiences. For instance, there is the subtle weaning of the audience from a world of blaring trumpets and rough-house antics to another world, entirely different, in which people verbalize effortlessly and in which ballet dancers display the beauties of disciplined motion. Or to cite another case, the rapid fluctuations between the sentimental pieties of barbershop quartets and banal melodramas on the one hand, and a harshly realistic humor of a monologuist, on the other, says much about the sentimental-cynical paradox which lay at the heart of the Myth of Success itself. Somewhere between absurdity and anxiety was located a dream of material fulfillment, and if the ritual ran a gamut of responses, it was because the dream itself was made up of ambiguities and inner contradictions. In its multiplicity, in its comprehensiveness, and in its inconsistency the ritual strove to encompass a myth of many facets and many dimensions.

No greater contradiction existed, of course, than between the fantasy-effect and the mechanical-cause of a given performance. While the audience had been momentarily removed from the commonplaces of their lives and their daily routines, the performers were hot in pursuit of the "success" which vaudeville dangled before them. After the show they gathered at the prompt entrance, waiting for the "Big Noise" to appear and tell them how they were faring in the big time.

SIX

The New Humor

TOWARD THE CLOSE of the nineteenth century, Edward Harrigan, the realistic dramatist, was heard to complain: "There's been a great change in the sense of humor in New York. I tell you it's the Irish and Anglo-Germanic people who know how to laugh. The great influx of Latins and Slavs—who always want to laugh not with you but at you—has brought about a different kind of humor. It isn't native, it isn't New York. It's Paris, or Vienna, or someplace."[1] Such testimony that a change had taken place toward a sharper, more critical humor was to become a commonplace after 1900. Wide differences of opinion about the value of this change existed, however, and they ranged from those of the man on the street who attended vaudeville shows weekly to those of the literary critics who solemnly charged that "most fun at the present day, does not grow from a healthy root nor feed a healthy appetite."[2]

Occasionally this "change in the sense of humor" (which was not confined to New York as Harrigan implied) was referred to as the "new humor," and although the term was loosely applied and seldom defined, it generally indicated a humor that was more excited, more aggressive, and less sympathetic than that to which the middle classes of the nineteenth century had been accustomed.[3] Vaudeville made its contributions to this change. While it shared the new humor with other media of popular culture, with newspapers, with humorous magazines like *Judge*, *Life*, and *Puck*, with dime joke books, and with other kinds of entertainment such as burlesque and musical comedy, still vaudeville was both the major market and the leading innovator in this revolution in popular taste.

The contrast between the theories of the new and old humor is well illustrated by two excerpts, dated within six years of each other, from two popular magazines of the period, *Putnam's* and *McClure's*. The first, in verse form, extolls the "kindly" qualities of humor and looks to its basic "seriousness" and "humanity." The second, written by knowledgeable practitioners of stage craft, defines humor as one form of conditioned response, a "reflex action" to unpleasant experiences.

The poem, a contribution to *Putnam's* in 1907 was composed by John Frederick Bangs. Its straight-forward title was simply *Humor,* and directly below the title read the equally flat truism attributed to one Bishop Brewster: "Humor dwells with sanity and common sense and truth."

107

Humor dwells with sanity,
  Truth and common sense.
Humor is humanity,
  Sympathy intense.

Humor always laughs with you
  Never at you; she
Loves the fun that's sweet and true,
  And of malice free;

Paints the picture of the fad,
  Folly of the day,
As it is, the good and bad,
  In a kindly way.

There behind her shaping mien,
  In her twinkling eyes,
Purpose true is ever seen,
  Seriousness lies.

Hers the tender mother's touch
  Easing all distress;
Teaching, e'en though smiling much,
  Moulding with caress.[4]

In striking contrast to this benign tolerance for a morally oriented humor is the blunt opinion of George M. Cohan and George Jean Nathan in an article entitled "The Mechanics of Laughter." Starting from one of the basic assumptions of the vaudeville myth—"It is a mistake to suppose that from the standpoint of the fundamental emotions we are not all alike"—Cohan and Nathan proceed to classify all emotional responses into three groups: "tear-getters," "laugh-getters," and "thrills." Speaking from theatrical experience, they knew that certain stock situations would affect the audience in one of these three ways. Thus, humor is produced on schedule by slapping a man violently on the back, pretending intoxication, using a swear word, interrupting lovers when they are about to kiss, or by stepping on another character's sore foot. Completely avoiding any judgment upon the sadistic elements in most of these situations, and ignoring any possible moral implications in them, the writers can only offer the slightly disillusioned comment that: "Nothing counts in the theatre but the impression of the time being. All the 'mechanics of emotion' are based, from the theatrical craftsman's point of view, on this one solid fact."[5]

The lines of battle could not have been more clearly drawn. The new humor spoke for the New Folk, and was the point of agreement upon which the new mass community might be founded. It drew its material from the main stream of native humor but also reached into the vast reservoirs of ethnic humor, particularly the German and Jewish as they became translated into the American idiom. It sought contact with the elemental experience of the cities, rather than with either "the fad or folly of the day" or abstract moral principles. If the genteel establishment was content to meet the crisis of urbanization with "sanity, truth, and common sense," the masses sought a solution closer to the nerve-ends, more subliminal and more ritualistic. What the practitioners of the new humor on the vaudeville stage might lose in geniality and security, they were to gain in pertinence and explosiveness. They were not really concerned with whether humor might serve as a means of betterment and uplift, but they knew that it was an effective gesture of retaliation against an environment which promised much and yet never yielded quite enough.

The new humor was the antidote for large doses of the Myth of Success. As the performance described in the previous chapter demonstrated, the humor swept in upon the sentimental materialism of the fantasy and brought back into focus the reality of life. Through humor the Myth of Success in its grosser and antisocial aspects was made palatable—its limitations were thrown into graphic relief against its attractions. The dreams and ideals were still ecstatic and pleasurable, but the wise man—the "wise-cracker"—of the new way of life was always there to bring about those sharp moments of recognition in which the audience saw themselves and their lives. The new humor was basic to the ritual, for neither polite wit nor the laconic frontier humor could bring pleasurably before the urban mass man the actuality of his life, or handle effectively his dreams of fulfillment.

Just as the vaudeville show as a whole was expertly fashioned to achieve its effects, the new humor, as the article by Cohan and Nathan indicated, was professional, self-conscious, and deliberate. The task of relieving social tensions had been taken over from the cracker-barrel sages and deadpan Yankee wits, and a whole new generation of comics, for the most part city-bred, competitive hustlers, had sensed the utility of humor in oiling the psychic wheels of an industrial democracy. Monologuists like Andy Rice, Rube Dickinson, Tom Lewis, James J. Morton, George Fuller Golden, James Thornton, Lew Dockstader, Fred Niblo, and Doc Rockwell shaped their fifteen-minute performances as precisely and as skillfully as die-makers, knowing that in their specialty there was no middle ground between success and failure. Spontaneity and improvisation, key characteristics of the American humor described by Constance Rourke, dwindled away under the pressures created by the vaudeville show, while sensitivity to audience reaction was sharpened to an excruciatingly fine point.

Just how much the "comics" had become specialists is indicated by a curious statement by the vaudeville manager, who, above all others, might

MARILYN MILLER

INA CLAIR AS GERALDINE FARRAR

have been expected to understand public taste. Yet even B. F. Keith indirectly admitted to an interviewer that the business of making people laugh was beyond him:

I have sat in the orchestra and seen in the audience some of our most prominent lawyers, judges of the supreme court, ministers, Governors, representative men in all walks of life. A couple of fellows would come on the stage and talk such utter nonsense that I would actually feel ashamed of them—it would seem so absurd—and I would have to get up and go out. And yet the persons I referred to seem to be enjoying themselves immensely. They evidently wanted a little of that sort of entertainment; whether it is so bad that they are amused, I don't know, but the people come week after week to see it, so it must be what they want.[6]

Such reflections, rare among show folk, did not affect the course which vaudeville ran. The "couple of fellows" might stir a sense of shame in Keith, but his awareness that they were, in fact, employees of his doing an excellent job in giving the people "what they want" was overriding.

By 1915 the art of the comic monologue was susceptible to analysis. One writer dissected it into five parts—incongruity, surprise, pure wit, character, and situation—and offered helpful suggestions to aspiring professionals on each part. The very order of the elements, leaving character and situation to the last and placing incongruity and surprise at the head of the list, speaks for the emphases of the new humor in marked contrast to the folksy, narrative cast of the nineteenth-century monologue. In fact, it is doubtful that the generation of Artemus Ward would have recognized the genre that they practiced in the following definition: "The pure vaudeville monologue is a humorous talk spoken by one person, possesses unity of character, is not combined with any other entertainment form, is marked by compression, follows a definite form of construction and usually requires from ten to fifteen minutes for delivery."[7]

There is no clearer statement than this to indicate the drift toward engineered, professional humor. From Artemus Ward to Doc Rockwell, the shift from a leisurely development of character and situation toward an incisive, hard-hitting comedy which would build quickly and efficiently toward excited laughter and applause, was complete. It was suggested that "like ocean waves, monologic laughs should come in threes and nines." The monologue (see subsequent examples for substantiation) should "build" toward several major "points" by means of subordinate giggles and chuckles, and the best material should be used at the close in order to evoke the greatest amount of applause.[8]

One way in which to consider this fast-moving humor, doled out in a string of verbal incongruities, is to say that vaudeville had, in practice, reduced humor to its minimal structural unit, the "joke." That is to say, by 1900 both characters and situations had become stereotyped and standardized to the point where the only novelty lay in the fluid, living language of the cities—in dialect, in boners, in slang, and other surprises of sound and syntax. The exigencies of vaudeville demanded that the audience give tangible, specific proof of their amusement at each bit of verbal gymnastics, and it was not enough to create a ripple of quiet joy—in fact, such situations were deemed embarrassing. Somehow, within the confines of fifteen minutes, the audience had to be pumped into a state of contagious mirth, and the most efficient means to accomplish this was not a drawn-out tale or anecdote, but a series of compressed witticisms which would, by their cumulative force, provoke loud laughter.

That humor should take this course toward compression and frenzy says much about the nature of the audience and their lives. The impulse toward hysteria was rising closer to the surface and given the protective cover of the vaudeville ritual and its sympathetic audience, needed relatively fewer incitements to be released. Vaudeville comics could rely upon the esthetic distance between stage and audience to soften resistance, but the blunt instrument of their attack could only be the joke which could pound away until all barriers were down. Curiously enough, this relationship between the "joke" and the contagious laughter of the mass audience seems to have escaped most modern students of humor, although the producers of television comedy, who rely heavily upon "primed" audiences and taped laughter seem to be well aware of their close connection.

The relative modernity of the "joke" seems also to have been generally overlooked. The word *joke* itself did not enter general circulation until the eighteenth century and did not emerge as a descriptive term in America until the 1860s. The British practice was to apply to verbal humor the word *jest*, since the publication of *Joe Miller's Jest Book* in 1739, and to reserve "joke" for pranks and stunts.[9] Exactly what connections exist between the "practical joke" and the biting, aggressive joke of the "new humor" is not altogether clear, but the assumption seems reasonable that Americans had outgrown the leisurely, literary manner of the traditional Joe Miller and had seized upon a word more violent, more vulgar, and more abrupt, to designate the unit of national humor.

If we look over the titles of American joke books, we see that the first one published in America (1789) contained no reference at all to "jokes" in its long title, but that in 1818 a volume appeared with the

113

title *Joke upon Joke, Being a New Collection of Anecdotes, Bon Mots, Puns, Odities [sic] and most Approved Witty Sayings.* Other popular collections before the Civil War, especially the widely circulated comic almanacs, had brief titles like *The Comic Token, Broad Grins, United States Comics,* or *Chips from Uncle Sam's Jack Knife.* An American edition of Joe Miller omitted the word *jest* from its title and was known simply as *The American Joe Miller.* Not until the sixties did titles like *Old Abe's Jokes, Fresh from Abraham's Bosom* and *Beadle's Dime Pocket Joke Book* begin to appear. Only in the seventies did Henry J. Wehman begin his mass production of the twenty-five cent, paperbacked *Budget of Jokes.* By 1930, there were, according to one authority, sixty titles of this series in print and an estimated distribution of two million copies.[10]

As the name of Henry J. Wehman indicates, the influence of the German Jews was particularly strong in molding the new humor. The concern of Jewish humor with the underdog, its endless cycles of anecdotes dealing with family and street life, its appreciation of the verbal misunderstandings and impasses reached by persons of different ethnic backgrounds — all provided material readily adaptable to the mass urban audience. From the days of Weber and Fields the Jewish communities of the larger cities have produced an endless parade of joke-makers and joke-sayers. The most often persecuted minority group has, paradoxically, come to speak, through its rich tradition of humor, for the plight of mass man.

The transition into the new humor is not difficult to trace. For purposes of contrast, one can take the first three entries from an 1865 edition of the *American Joe Miller* and observe the traces of the leisurely, sometimes pointless, British jests which have been doctored with American subject matter to produce the kind of anecdote familiar to newspaper readers. Even though the point of the jest may be a play upon words, there is enough superfluous detail and characterization to make the situation in itself of some interest.

The editor of the Eglantine says that the girls in Connecticut, who are remarkable for their industry, drink about a pint of yeast before going to bed at night, to make them *rise* early in the morning.

A half-famished fellow in the Southern states tells of a baker (whose loaves had been growing "small by degrees, and beautifully less,") who, when going his rounds to serve his customers, stopped at the door of one and knocked, when the lady within exclaimed, "Who's there?" and was answered, "The baker." "Well you needn't make such a fuss about it; put it through the keyhole."

At a christening, while a minister was making the certificate, he forgot the date and happened to say: "Let me see, this is the 30th." "The thirtieth!" exclaimed the indignant mother, "indeed, but it is only the eleventh."[11]

Now let us examine the "jokes" of the new humor as they appeared in twenty-five cent, paperback books. They are in dialogue form, as were most jokes after 1900 (the he-said, I-said pattern was typical vaudeville) and all excess wordage has been trimmed to the point where the delivery is telegraphic.

"My brother is an oculist in a kitchen."
"What does he do?"
"Takes the eyes out of potatoes."

I asked the hotel clerk how much my bill was.
He said: "What room?"
I told him I slept on the billiard table.
He said: "Fifty cents an hour."

"Is he a hard drinker?"
"Indeed, no! It's the easiest thing he does."[12]

115

Everything about these jokes differs from the others—the material drawn from the vices and weaknesses of the masses, the impersonal relationships sketched out, even the puns which seem to spring more from a contempt for language than the pleasurable discovery of its ambiguities. Notice the forced inappropriateness of this pun:

"She'd wear the trousers if she could."
"What makes you think so?"
"Why, she already has some breaches of promise."[13]

For a brutal indifference to personal relationships, it is difficult to exceed this joke:

"So you went to the ball game yesterday; you told me you wanted to go to your mother-in-law's funeral."
"I did want to, but she isn't dead yet."[14]

And for a bitter revelation of how men, caught up in the complex machinery of the city, cannot even understand what is happening to them, this piece of contrived humor will serve:

A deaf and dumb man was arrested for manslaughter and was to get his hearing the next day. While he was in the cell he was dancing, and singing, so the keeper wrote on a paper, "What makes you so happy?" The deaf man wrote back, "Because I am to get my hearing tomorrow."[15]

In timing, subject matter, and tone, the new humor of the cities had outgrown the familiar pleasantries of the village, the exuberance of the frontier, or the relaxed whimsy of the minstrel show. The terse formula of the joke, easily adaptable to the vaudeville ritual, or the everyday conversation of city life was its major vehicle.

By 1900 there was not only a profession of joke writing in this country, but there were also well-defined procedures, subjects, and markets. From the statements of so-called "jokesmiths," one gathers that the process was not especially creative, most current jokes merely being older materials updated.[16] An editor of *Life* warned against thinking that professional humor could possibly be spontaneous and tells "How I wrote 50,000 Jokes," sometimes at the rate of fifty a day.[17] Editors usually accepted jokes on the basis of the subject rather than originality because they had lost the ability to laugh at jokes, and one editor even ventured to record his list of good topics in a magazine article. This list is worth quoting in full because it shows a heavy preference for the timely and topical, and, like the jokes above, reflects urban culture rather than town or rural life. Notice the number of items which were, because of their suggestion of social and economic status, rather pompous and pretentious to the man on the street. A good deal of the new humor seems to have been the effort of democratic man to reduce those figures of respectability and privilege to his own commonplace station:

old maid, widow, grass widow, bachelor, poet, Irishman, dachshund, woman's bank account, sausages, fiancée, parrot, golf, liquor, incontinence, garter, financier, servant girl, Standard Oil, Hearst, yellow journal, Milwaukee beer, seasickness, amateur actor, Dowie, pie, false teeth, baldness, hair tonic, breakfast food, bad spelling, solecisms, barbarisms, improprieties, mispronunciations, plutocracy, missionary, sleeping car porter, Paderewski, new-rich, Jew, messenger boy, fishing, borrowing, lending, book agent, sea-serpent, goat, Depew, Russell Sage, *Ladies Home Journal*, Bok, Thompson-Seton, Rockefeller, Bishop Potter, Judge Emmons, Ella Wheeler Wilcox, Marie Corelli, Hall Caine, Henry James, Whistler, Bernard Shaw, sky-scrapers, twins, kaiser, lawyer, doctor, automobile, Pierpont Morgan, Carrie Nation, lord, duke, mosquito, Kentucky, Indiana, New Jersey, Chicago,

Boston, Pittsburg, Hoboken, Lynn, St. Louis, Chelsea, Philippines, politician, policeman, anti-anything, tramp, professor, freshman, society, Newport, terminations in "ski" and "vitch," kindergarten, strike, silk hat, land-lady, boarding house, lover, cigarette.[18]

An interesting parallel to this catalogue is a list of subjects humorous to the British public in 1902, compiled by Max Beerbohm. While it compares in many instances with the American list, there seems to be a greater generality and less invention in these topics. Whether this indicates a greater tradition-alism in British humor at the time, or whether it speaks for the conscious search for novelty encour-aged by the vaudeville format, is not certain, but Beerbohm made a special point of the "contempt for the unfamiliar" basic to British humor. His list reads: "Mothers-in-law, henpecked husbands, twins, old maids, Jews, Frenchmen, Germans, Ital-ians, Niggers, (not Russians or other foreigners of any denomination), fatness, thinness, long hair (worn by a man), baldness, sea-sickness, stuttering, 'bloomers,' bad cheese, 'shooting the moon,' (slang expression for leaving a lodging house without paying the bill), red noses."[19]

Like the editors of newspapers and magazines, the vaudeville managers monitored the language of their employees, listening for the four-letter taboo words. Yet the comics kept their psychic antennae active, knowing that audiences that would not respond to bright chatter about missionaries, college professors, and Milwaukee beer were usually highly vulnerable to more primitive kinds of comic material, which they classified on three levels. "Hokum" was a type of broad humor which edged toward actual vulgarity. "Jasbo" was even more explicit, resorting to taboo phrases and allusions for its effect. "Gravy" was a last resource, an abandonment of all inhibitions, a

118

public recital of the latest dirty jokes. Only *in extremis,* when the comic was "dying on his feet," would he resort to "jasbo" and "gravy," knowing that his reputation among the better audiences depended upon the social acceptability of his act.[20]

If the most obvious characteristics of the new humor were the joke and the machined monologue, these are not the only evidences of humor on the vaudeville stage. Humor might appear anywhere in the performance: in the magician's misdirecting banter, in the action of a comic sketch, in the pantomime of a dance group, or in the lyrics of a Gilbert and Sullivan patter song. On the whole, vaudeville humor tended to be verbal, finding its most effective expression in words rather than gestures. To compare vaudeville in this respect to the legitimate stage is to take note of its slapstick and rough-and-tumble aspects, but to compare vaudeville humor to that of the circus or burlesque is to appreciate the degree of language play—admittedly language on rather rudimentary levels, but language all the same —in which the vaudeville artists indulged. The diction was not that of the drawing room or the lecture platform and thus differed markedly with the tradition of graceful, cerebral wit that had descended from the eighteenth-century salons; but it was the American language as Whitman and Mencken have celebrated it: the slang of the cities, the rough coinages of the laboring classes, the pidgin English of European immigrants, backcountry archaisms, and provincial dialects. It is also the language of inarticulated emotions and uncommunicable ideas. In any of the Weber and Fields skits, Joe Weber was likely to blurt out a simple "I luff you, Myer" and catch in a few words the comic pathos of the lonely immigrant who could hardly voice his deepest emotions. Or the monologuist

119

would tell, with a sly wink, of asking the streetcar conductor if the car stops at the Battery. Insufficiently attuned to the language of his own occupation, the conductor misunderstands the word *stop* and replies, "If it doesn't we'll all have to swim."

The pathetic basis for urban humor was symbolized in vaudeville, as it had been in the minstrel show and variety, by the personae assumed by the comics, usually such stylized figures as the black-faced coon, the Jew, the Irishman, the Wop, or the urban dandy. Most of these type characters had been formalized in the decades previous to the rise of vaudeville and had become almost unalterable comic masks by the time they appeared on the vaudeville stage. In fact, there seems to have been a tendency to rely less and less upon costume and props to portray these figures, so clearly were the stereotypes implanted in the popular imagination, and sometimes the dialect itself was enough to carry the act. George Fuller Golden's monologues usually concerned the affairs of Casey, an Irishman, and Golden's imitation of the brogue was in itself, without the aid of costume, enough to make him one of the leading vaudeville comics around 1900.

Harrigan's comment that the public wished to laugh "at you" instead of "with you" must have contained an element of truth, but it seems a mistake to see evidences of racial conflict in this humor. Some members of the audience no doubt felt that the Negro or the immigrant was being justly rebuked for his intrusion into American life, and others may have found the scapegoats they were seeking in these burlesqued figures; but, on the whole, the audience seemed to accept these figures and their strange language as clowns and jesters, as symbolic figures of loneliness and alienation, or perhaps merely as a part of the fantasy world of vaudeville. Many of the comics were themselves of Jewish or Irish stock, and while their comedy was in part a personal rejection of old country mores, the rebellion against their racial identity was only symbolic. The stock figure was a useful projection of the self which even the comics could not take seriously, providing them the advantages of a free personality that could play the fool with immunity.

When the stage Irishman, German or Jew became in the hands of crude performers merely an object of ridicule, the vaudeville ritual was apt to exclude them entirely from the cast. Always solicitous of members of the audience who might leave the theater with bruised sensibilities, B. F. Keith, in the first decade of the twentieth century—after the racial comics of the nineties had run their course—was to censor all material which might be offensive to "the Irishman, the Jew, or the downeast Yank like myself."[21] Keith merely applied the same rule of thumb which led him to ban mother-in-law and streetcar conductor jokes and made certain that the new humor on the vaudeville stage retained its effectiveness as a broadside assault on all phases of city life. When this humor began to single out its scapegoats, and when its appeal became limited to narrow and particular areas of discontent, it was losing its essential character as mass humor. The new humor made its comment upon the disruptions of the melting pot, but it also attended to a wide range of issues in modern city life. To linger too long upon ethnic antagonisms, petty tyranny in the transportation system, or the disruptions in family structure symbolized by the emancipated mother-in-law was to lose sight of the comprehensive task that humor had to perform. Furthermore, if a primary function of this humor was to encourage a sense of community among the diverse groups constituting the American city, then the jokes had to leave off at the point at which members of the audience could no longer laugh at themselves.

The vaudeville comics may have practiced a humor that was new, but they drew upon a strong American tradition in humor in their use of the monologue as a vehicle. Following in the well-established patterns best characterized by Josh Billings, Artemus Ward, Petroleum V. Nasby, and particularly Mark Twain, the monologuists of the new humor had merely to develop the potential which lay within the form. If the earlier generations had tended toward rambling anecdote and narrative, the vaudeville comic merely economized in order to reach his point sooner. If the earlier monologuists had relied upon gestures and nuances of expression, the exponent of the new humor merely broadened the effects and drummed home his point with steady repetition. If the monologuists of the lecture circuits had performed behind the mask of the deadpan expression, an ironic mixture of innocence and wisdom, the vaudeville entertainer assumed the masks of stock comic characters about whose innocence—and ignorance—there was less question. To some extent this adaptation was true of the vaudeville two-act also, but before raising that problem let us examine two passages from vaudeville monologues.

The first is a brief sample of a James Thornton monologue, in fashion about 1900, illustrating again the harsh depersonalization of city life:

While coming to the theatre tonight, I got on a car, the car was full, so was I; every seat was taken, so was my watch, the man alongside of me had a mouth full of sailor's delight. He was endeavoring to expectorate on the ceiling, not having the necessary five hundred for doing it on the floor, the unexpected expectoration of the expectorator, in the opening of the man's map hit the conductor a wallop in the eye. I beg your pardon, says he. My fault says the conductor, I had no right getting in front of a hose.[22]

Thornton spoke for a brash plebeanism, partly defiant and aggressive yet partly overwhelmed by society. Toward this figure the middle class members of the audience might be condescending, but his small-scale rebellion against city life was everyman's. His attack was always specific and concrete, for only those aspects of city life which touched him immediately and personally drew his fire, and yet the corny jokes always implied deeper sources of discontent. The portrait was one of a mass man, inadequate to the demands of a hostile environment yet seeking through verbalization to dispel, if not to subdue, the worst of its threats.

A less obvious persona through which the monologuist might speak was a character like Aaron Hoffman's German Senator. Known in the profession as a "stump act," this monologue begins as a parody upon nineteenth-century oratory, either political or evangelical. The burlesque is generally crude and there is little attempt to develop the character, for once the stump oratory is underway the monologuist lapses into his routine of jokes. In the case of the German Senator, once his image as a bumbling, obsequious politician is established, the voice with which he speaks begins to offer some rather shrewd and cynical comments upon public affairs. Like Mr. Dooley, the Senator strips some of the grandiose phrases and highsounding labels from the realities of high prices, high taxes, marital problems and corruption in government. Like Will Rogers, who was to follow him, the German Senator traveled along the fine line between good-natured humor and social criticism and, like Rogers, found that the more naive and inoffensive one appeared on the surface, the deeper the barbs that might be inflicted. Here is the entire monologue as it has been reproduced in Brett Page's book on vaudeville:

My dear friends and falling citizens:
My heart fills up with vaccination to be disabled to come out here before such an intelligence massage of people and have the chance to undress such a large conglomerated aggravation.

I do not come before you like other political speakers, with false pride in one hand and the Star Strangled Banana in the other.

I come before you as a true, sterilized citizen, a man who is for the public and against the people, and I want to tell you, my 'steemed friends, when I look back on the early hysterics of our country, and think how our forefathers strangled to make this country voss iss it; when you think of the lives that was loosed and the blood that was shredded, we got to feel a feeling of patriotic symptoms—we got to feel a patriotic sump-sumps—you got to feel the patri—you can't help it, you got to feel it.

I tell you, our hearts must fill up with indigestion when we look out to see the Statue of Liberty, the way she stands, all alone, dressed up in nothing, with a light in her hand, showing her freedom.

And what a fine place they picked out for Liberty to stand.

With Coney Island on one side and Blackwell's Island on the other.

And when she stands there now, looking on the country the way it is and what she has to stand for, I tell you tears and tears must drop from her eyes. Well, to prove it—look at the ocean she filled up.

And no wonder she's crying. Read the nuisance papers. See what is going on.

Look at what the country owes.

According to the last report of the Secretary of the Pleasury, the United States owes five billion dollars.

Nobody knows what we owe it for;
And nobody ever sees what we have got for it;
And if you go to Washington, the Capsule of the

United States, and ask them, THEY don't even know THEMSELVES.

Then they say, what keeps the country broke is the Pay-n-more Canal.

It costs the Government nine thousand dollars an hour to dig the canal. THINK OF THAT!

Nine thousand dollars an hour for digging, and the worst of it is, they ain't digging.

Up to date, it has cost a hundred and seventy million dollars to dig a hole—they've been at it for over nine years—and the only hole they've dug is in the United States Treasury.

Look what the cold storage trust have done with the eggs. Sixty cents a dozen—for the good ones. And the good ones are rotten.

Then they say the reason prices are going up is because wages are getting higher.

But why should they raise the price of eggs?

The chickens ain't getting any more wages.

And if meat goes up any higher, it will be worth more than money.

Then there won't be any money.

Instead of carrying money in your pocket, you'll carry meat around.

A sirloin steak will be worth a thousand dollar bill.

When you go down to the bank to make a deposit instead of giving the cashier a thousand dollar bill, you'll slip him a sirloin steak.

If you ask him for change, he'll give you a hunk of bologny.

If they keep on, we won't be able to live at all.

Statistics prove that the average wages of the workingman is one dollar a day.

Out of that, he's got to spend fifty cents a day for food; fifty-five cents for rent; ten cents for car fare.

And at the end of a hard day's work—he owes himself fifteen cents.

Yet the rich people say that the poor people are getting prosperous.

They say look at our streets. You see nothing but automobiles. You don't see half the poor people now that you used to.

Certainly you don't.

Half of them have already been run over and the other half is afraid to come out.

Why, between the automobiles and the trusts the poor man hasn't got a chance to live.

And if only the gas trust gets a little stronger, the price of gas will go up so high a poor man won't even be able to commit suicide.

They'll have him both ways. He can't live and he can't die.

And that's why I am with the socialists.

They say, "Down with the trusts! Do away with money. Make everything equal."

Imagine a fellow going into a jewelry store and saying: "Give me a diamond ring, here's a lemon. . . ."

Then they say that Adam fell for an apple.

It just shows how men have improved.

No man would fall for an apple today.

It would have to be a peach.

And I tell you, it's no wonder that women feel stuck up. They say they can do more than men can do.

That's very true, when you go back to the first woman, Eve.

She was only one little woman, all by herself, and she put the whole human race on the bum.

Could a man do that?

And yet she was only a rib out of Adam's side.

It just goes to show you what a cheap proposition woman was.

Nowadays, when you want to marry a woman, you got to buy a diamond ring, take her to the theatres, buy her taxicheaters, and what's left of your wages you go to spend on candy and tango trots and turkey teas. There's where Adam had it on all of us. . .

I tell you, my dear friends, the way the country stands now, the country stands on the brink of a preci— the country stands on the brink of a precip—and if somebody shoves it, it is going over.

And the cause of all the trouble in the country is the crooked politics.

And that's why the women suffering gents have gotten together and are fighting for their rights.

And you can't blame them.

Now I see where one married woman has hit on a great idea.

She says there's only one protection for the wives.

And that's a wives' union.

Imagine a union for wives.

A couple gets married.

And as soon as they get settled, along comes the walking delegate and orders a strike.

Then imagine thousands and thousands of wives walking up and down the streets on strike, and scabs taking their places.[23]

In importance a close second to the comic monologue among the kinds of humorous presentations in vaudeville was the short dialogue for two persons called the "two-act." At its best it would capture the dramatic talents of Weber and Fields, Smith and Dale, Rogers and Rogers, McIntyre and Heath, or Gallagher and Shean. On the whole, however, it required less individual ability and was more reliant upon situation and action than the monologue was. At least encouraged, if not originated, by the exchanges between the interlocutor and end-man of the minstrel show, this dialogue capitalized upon insult, repartee, and ridicule. Its statement about human relationships may have been a caricature, and its appeal may have been to base aggressive impulses, but in the hands of the masters, the two-act could also make clear the problems of communal living and point out the roads to, and obstacles in the way of, understanding and fellowship.

The "Pool Room Sketch" of Weber and Fields is just such a two-act. Although it uses more props (a ball rack and a pool table) than the run of the two-acts, it is otherwise typical of the genre. It is structured upon an elementary conflict in personalities. Myer (Fields) is a tall, bullying figure, while Mike (Weber) is "a mild, trustful, undersized little innocent, the Mister Common Peepul or Little Jeff of the comic strip." Mike would precipitate the action with his bewildered, "I don't know dis pool business." From there, as Felix Isman has described it, the action flows on inevitably through pain toward a happy conclusion.

MYER. Vatever I don't know, I teach you.

MIKE. Dot seems fair.

MYER. To make der game more interesting, I bet you dot I beat.

MIKE. Oughtn't you to beat? Ain't you biggest?

MYER. Brains in der head, not bigness, vins in pool.

MIKE. Give me otts und I bet you.

MYER. Vat you mean, otts?

MIKE. You should put up more money to my lesterest money.

MYER. I vill not! But I tell you vot I vill do. I vill put up five dollars to your ten dollar.

MIKE. Dot's what I mean.

The squat Weber would guilelessly confide his ten dollars to the lower shelf of the ball rack. Fields would remove it immediately, with his own five dollars, to the top shelf. Weber, watching his maneuver, would return to the rack, raise himself on tiptoe, discover that he could not reach the money, then look questioningly at Fields.

MYER. Remember, now! Der one dot gets der money vins.

MIKE. Let me understandt meinself: der one dot gets der money is der vinner, eh? (MYER, *starting to shoot,* MIKE *seizes his cue.*)

MIKE. Who made idt out you should be firstest starter?

MYER. All right, den ve choose up for it. (*They measure hands on a pool cue in the manner of boys choosing up sides for a baseball game.* MIKE *wins and starts for the money.*)

MIKE. I vin! I vin!

MYER. Dumbskull! You don't vin der money; you chust get shot first.

MIKE. Pardon, please. I oliogepize.

MYER. Hey! Don't get so close to dot table. You got to stand three feets away ven you shoot it.

This was the more ridiculous in that Weber's pillowpadded waistline stopped him a foot short of the pool table. At this warning, he would make a

128

blundering try at a cue's length, then reverse the cue and aim with the large end.

MYER. You can't do dot. Always you must shoot it mit der end dot's got der sponge on.

MIKE. (*examining the tip*) Dot's a sponge? It's very tight for a sponge!

MYER. Remember, you got to break der balls before as you bust dem.

MIKE. (*puzzledly*) I got to bust dem before I break dem? (MIKE *drives the cue ball into the massed numbered balls and the fifteenth ball, by arrangement drops, into a pocket.*)

MIKE. I got him! I got him!

MYER. (*grabbing the ball*) You didn't call it!

MIKE. I did call it! I did call it! I called it to myself!

MYER. Dot's a bad habit, talking to yourselves, und worser in pool. Don't do it some more. Now vot ball you play?

MIKE. Do I got to tell you?

MYER. Sure, you got to tell me.

MIKE. Are you der mayor or somedings? I like to play dis one, only dot one is in de vay.

MYER. All right, I move it for you. (MIKE *also moves a ball, to his further advantage.*)

MYER. Don't do dot! Don't do dot! It ain't allowed you to move balls.

MIKE. You can move dem, und I can't move dem, eh?

MYER. Imbesilly! I moved it as a favor to you. (MIKE *shoots and misses; MYER takes aim.*)

MIKE. Vot ball you play?

MYER. Der round one.

MIKE. Round? All is round!

MYER. Dis one is rounder. (MIKE *picks up a ball to examine it.*)

MYER. Again! Once more, ain't I told you? Drop dot ball! (MYER *manhandles* MIKE *and the game resumes. MYER shoots, misses and drives the white cue ball into a corner pocket. Both jump up and down exultantly.*)

MIKE. Hooray! A scratch!

MYER. Sure! A scratch! Dot gifs me four balls. Only best players can dodge all der other balls und get in der hole. I surprise meinself. (*While* MIKE *ponders this,* MYER *puts the four highest balls remaining on the table in his rack and prepares to shoot again.*)

MIKE. Vot ball you shoot now?

MYER. Der colored one.

MIKE. Vich color? Dey all got colors! (MYER *ignores the question, shoots, misses, and* MIKE *takes his turn.*)

MYER. Vell, vell! Tell it vot you is playing.

MIKE. Pool aind't it?

MYER. Vat ball? Vat ball?

MIKE. Ah! So I got to play a ball?

MYER. How many times got I to tell you you got to name vat ball you shoot?

MIKE. Good! I name one Rudolph. (MYER *menaces* MIKE *with a cue,* MIKE *parrying and thrusting in fencing-master fashion.*)

MYER. Now, vill you tell me?

MIKE. Vich number is the biggest?

MYER. Der fifteen ball.

MIKE. I like to shoot him. Vere is he? (*Both search the table for the fifteen ball.* MYER *finds it in* MIKE's *rack,* MIKE's *only marker.*)

MYER. Here's it.

MIKE. All right, put it down here.

MYER. As a special favor to you, I do it. (MYER *places the fifteen ball back in play.* MIKE *shoots, misses, and scratches the cue ball into a side pocket. He dances jubilantly.*)

MIKE. Hooray! I vin four balls! Dots a scratch like you told me.

MYER. Dot's no scratch. Dot's an itch. Scratches is in the corner pockets, itches in side pockets. Itches is bad. One itch by you gifs me four balls more. (MIKE, *realizing that the game is going against him, jumps on the pool table and leaps from there to the rack, grabbing the fifteen dollars before* MYER *can act. Then* MYER *attempts to take the money from him.*)

MIKE. (*reminding him of his own words*) Der one dot gets der money vins the game. (*Still clutching the money,* MIKE *is dragged offstage by the scruff of his neck.*)[24]

Such a classic act with its heavy overtones of the melting pot brings to life the sensibilities of the public at the turn of the century. The "Dutch" patois is the essence of all attempts of immigrants to learn the American language, for not only does it fail to communicate to one's fellows, but the poor speaker himself barely understands what he is saying. In a society where fellowship is to be gained through wagering and sports, he makes a conscientious effort to conform, but is caught halfway between the acquisitive spirit of the new order and its Anglo-Saxon sense of gamesmanship. That sport was a means toward shared values has dimly entered the consciousness of Mike and Myer, but the disturbing overtones of the confidence game provide the tension necessary for humor. Even the Mutt and Jeff relationship symbolizes the contradictory needs of these new mass men. If on the one hand they desire a dialogue and companionship, on the other they find themselves, by virtue of their urban predicament, in a state of unrelieved competition. In the material order of an industrial society, the very closeness that brings friendship brings also exploitation, antagonism, and ultimately violence.

The role played by the new humor in creating a community of city-dwellers, in establishing norms of taste and behavior, and in releasing the mass man from the strains and pressures of the new order has been fairly well demonstrated by the foregoing samples of monologue and dialogue. What has not been brought out, however, is the degree to which humor became a self-conscious and deliberate means for reaching these objectives, not merely for the professional comic but for the common man. Spurred on by joke books and the examples of vaudeville performers, extroverted citizens in all walks of life took upon themselves the mission of making the office, the kitchen, the shop, the display room, or the construction shack a place of camaraderie and merriment. First testing the communal response, they would then deflate authority images, or set

131

their own mark in the social scale at the expense of those beneath them. About those innovations of a consumer society to which they were not yet accustomed—e.g. the Ford automobile, street cars, elevators—they had an entire battery of extravagant stories to relate. Against those identifiable power cliques such as trusts, labor unions, temperance societies, and women's clubs, they waged a long, raucous war of attrition, not so much to destroy the center of power as to return its members to the common condition of mankind. The backslapping punsters and practical jokers of Sinclair Lewis's novels were the self-appointed priests of twentieth-century society, trying, through the rites of laughter, to simplify and assuage the complex personal and psychological tensions of the era.

Among all the instruments of social coercion, humor has the advantage of being tentative and flexible. Particularly in a society where deep-seated attachments and identities are not always clear on the surface, it becomes the practice for the humorist to deny personal relevance, with a smiling "I was only kidding—where's your sense of humor?" The nineteenth century had known of "the sense of humor," but only as a defense mechanism. James Russell Lowell, for example, had referred to it as a "balance wheel" which enabled men to modulate and restrain their feelings in the face of adversity.[25] Humor itself was, for Lowell's generation, distinct from wit and was a natural and spontaneous expression of universal feelings, "a contagion, or sharing of the sense of excess power, of abundant vitality, of animal magnetism."[26] Thus the faculty which produced this humor could not help but be normal, healthy, and sane. The "sense of humor" had, then, the sanction of what was most wholesome and acceptable in the American tradition.

132

By 1903 a notion of "the sense of humor" had become suitable material for the popular periodicals. One writer claimed it to be "perhaps the most distinctive of all our national traits,"[27] and others intimated that it was the *sine qua non* of all true Americans. In his travels through Europe, "the jocular American abroad" could be considered as a missionary of humor leading the backward nations of the world out of their pessimistic miseries. Readers were warned against making close friends among those unfortunate members of society who lacked the sense of humor and to observe carefully in this light their prospective partners in marriage.[28] Writers in the periodicals tended to agree that the sense of humor was a very serious thing indeed; it was an aspect of individual and social life which should evolve and flourish in America. As one patriot observed, "We have only commenced to be humorous."[29]

Max Eastman perceptively seized upon the phrase for the title of his first book on humor, *The Sense of Humor,* in which he claimed that "the creation of that name is the most original and most profound contribution of modern thought to the problem of the comic."[30] This statement was made, of course, from the standpoint of the psychologist rather than the moralist or philosopher, but Eastman shared with Lowell's generation the belief in the autonomous individual who is capable of independent responses to his experience. His later and more widely read work, *The Enjoyment of Laughter,* developed the didactic strain which was only implicit in *The Sense of Humor* and exhorted the reader to release his native capacity to laugh at life.[31]

Yet the values implied by "the sense of humor" were by no means unanimously agreed upon at the turn of the century. The new humor, in adopting this idea, placed it much closer to the center of social existence than the nineteenth-century moralists had anticipated, and they reacted violently against "the sense of humor" as a form of social criticism. Even Mark Twain, whose position between the new humor and the old was never clearly established, became the object of a devastating critique in 1907 on the grounds that "real humor is unexpected and not professional." The great comic writers, an anonymous critic maintained, have "held up folly to ridicule, not to amuse the groundlings, but to reveal, in a sudden blaze of light, the eternal truths of wisdom and justice." But Twain, the professional humorist, "with a sentimental leer" assures his audience "that his fun is always amiable, as though amiability were sufficient atonement for an imbecile lack of taste." Especially tasteless for this critic were Mark Twain's description of his own funeral and the travesty on chivalry, written with "malignant joy," in *A Connecticut Yankee in King Arthur's Court. Tom Sawyer* and *The Adventures of Huckleberry Finn* were also shameful attempts to capture the spirit of American humor. Far from conveying truth, Twain was "a bull in the chinashop of ideas." And in its concluding statement, this article singled out one of the major difficulties that nineteenth-century humor had brought upon itself. "Humor," it observed, "which should be relief and nothing more, is now an end in itself."[32]

Another writer, in the *Atlantic Monthly*, denounced the current taste in humor on the grounds that it tended toward "mockery and cynicism" and encouraged a lowering of standards and a slackening of principles. He called for "gaiety," not "levity," in the course of life, saying that "we do not know how to amuse ourselves honestly and enjoy ourselves heartily."[33] A further contributor to the *Atlantic*,

134

finding the persistent themes of the tramp and the pie, the Negro and the henroost, husband and wife quarrels, Queen Victoria, and mothers-in-law both lifeless and meaningless, called for the "new joke." For him contemporary humor demonstrated "neither conviction nor steadfast perception, only a momentary sense of the superficial incongruities of life."[34]

While these and similar discussions tended to reflect the ingrained prejudices of the Genteel Tradition, there were, even by 1907, a few attempts to understand the new humor from the analytical viewpoint of modern psychology. One such essay approached directly the problem "Why is a Joke Funny?" Its author, Gilson Gardner, explicitly reversed the position of most nineteenth-century literati and moralists, who held that humor requires sympathy. For Gardner humor was merely "intelligence acting under a particular stimulus" so that it was "quickened and intensified." In an instant of choice the mind decides between the true image and disguise, the true statement and the fanciful play of words, the real course of life and the make-believe. Through laughter the mind "detects" and "repudiates" falsity and error. Gardner incorporated into this theory, which he seems to have adapted from Hazlitt, a subordinate proposition that a common ground is needed for effective humor and that agreement must exist upon what is the real, the true, and the "that-which-should-be." Thus we see why "the average stage comedian builds his jokes upon a theory that a majority of his audience feel that mothers-in-law would be better dead, that marriage is a disappointment, that women type-writers are immoral, that politicians are not respectable, that man's first thought is lascivious, and that heaven and hell are exploded myths.[35] Gardner's insight into the value conflicts implicit in the new humor and its relation to urban subject matter gives his discussion a pertinence that the cries for gaiety lacked.

Another attempt to reconcile theory with trends in popular taste, this time couched in more specifically psychological terms, is an article by Dr. Linus W. Kline, first published in *Popular Science Monthly* and then condensed for *Current Literature.* Dr. Kline rejected the theory that humor is contingent upon a sense of superiority, but otherwise adopted many of the ideas put forward seven years before in Bergson's *Laughter.* Like Bergson, he found laughter to be a product of release and freedom from the restrictive influences of law and habit. All humorous states, he explained, are preceded by a state of tension created by the ordinary functions of the "mechanized mind." "The psychological function of humor is to delicately cut the surface tension of consciousness and disarrange its structure to the end that it may begin again on a new and strengthened base." Humor thus performs a valuable function in guarding between the free mind and the mechanized mind and "saves the individual from the blighting influence of commercial and utilitarian ideals."[36]

In both Gardner's and Kline's theorizing is the recognition that humor itself, and by inference the "sense of humor," was more than a stabilizing influence, to be called upon in situations of temporary imbalance or dislocation. If laughter could be a means by which the mind detected falsity and error, or if it could free the mind from the chains of habit, then the centrality of humor in modern life was obvious. The rise of the joke, the increased respect for the sense of humor, the anguish which Edward Harrigan shared with contributors to the *Atlantic Monthly* that humor was on the side of social revolution instead of bolstering the status quo were all signs that the new humor represented more than a haphazard shift in popular taste. Through humor, the mass man in the midst of urban flux, did his criticizing and judging. In moments of crisis he might fall back upon slogan, aphorism, or creed, but daily life could be endured without dire commitments, in a perpetual suspension of belief, providing that the sense of humor was duly nourished and exercised. To this end the vaudeville comics dedicated themselves. Even B. F. Keith, who admitted fleeing from his theater seat in shame because of particularly absurd vaudeville routines, cultivated his sense of humor, such as it was. Upon being reprimanded by an indignant customer for allowing his performers to appear in silk stockings, he reportedly answered, "I wear 'em myself."[37]

SEVEN

A Modern Totemism and Sorcery

AS OUR PREVIOUS DISCUSSION has pointed out, there is a fundamental distinction between the primitive rituals unearthed by anthropology in many corners of the globe and the ritual of the New Folk. Whereas primitive rituals have nearly always been expressions of a world view in which nature is dominated by unseen occult forces, the ritual of the New Folk celebrates success—the conquest by man, through science and technology, of a purely materialistic natural order. This is not to say that elements of the old magic were not assimilated into the modern ritual; to the contrary, they are applied to the "magic" of science and provide basic themes and gestures from which vaudeville and similar

138

amusements would develop. Within the vaudeville ritual specifically, the totemism with which primitive man had asserted his kinship with other forms of animal life and the sorcery through which he mastered the latent powers of the inanimate world become demonstrations of applied "scientific" technique. The immediate sensation of pleasure effected by these demonstrations upon an audience was symbolic of the entire life of pleasure which technological skill and the application of scientific principles could bring to these folk of the industrialized society.

Popular science of the late nineteenth century is not, of course, a movement which can be easily tied down, for it ranges from the theoretical speculations of Spencerian philosophy to the earthy wisdom of a Thomas Edison. Yet its effective channeling of the Myth of Success into viable social attitudes was unmistakable. At whatever points the new masses sought comfort in a passive acquiescence to their lot, the energizing doctrines of scientific observation and utility quickly interfered. In whatever relics of past magic the New Folk looked for talismans against the machine and its operations, this popular scientism was ready with an agnostic scorn of superstition. Whenever the New Folk tried to humanize its environment, imputing will, heart, or moral sensitivity to the objects of the natural world, the scientific empiricist stood firm in his rationalism, coldly suppressing the vagrant and illogical sentimentality which would place other values above those of ambition, personal well-being, and social competition, but permitting, nevertheless, the rise of paradoxical ideas of nonsupernatural scientific "miracles." Within the vaudeville ritual, especially in its animal acts and stage magic, fundamental attitudes toward science were symbolically communicated even though the audience itself was free to accept this presentation of a serious world-view as mere entertainment.

Of course, the transformation of the animal act and of stage magic was already well underway before the vaudeville ritual reached its institutionalized state. The animal acts were descendants of the equestrian circuses of the late eighteenth and early nineteenth century and of the traveling menageries of the mid-nineteenth century. Stage magic traced its lineage back to eighteenth-century European charlatanry which had been imported into America around 1830 as "mesmerism." Each can claim more remote sources of inspiration, of course, but it is within the century preceding vaudeville that they broke loose from the meshed values of the *volkskunde* and became detached, itinerant entertainments.

Both of these types of entertainment adapted easily to the variegated pattern of the vaudeville performance. In both cases the short, startling effect could be as readily produced as a sustained, dramatic one, and both could rely heavily upon physical action as a medium of expression. The economics of animals and magic acts could be adjusted to circumstances. While the more successful trainers and magicians could transport elaborate properties along the circuits and support a sizable retinue, the more modest acts could be packed in a trunk and performed with the aid of a stage hand. An advantage which animal acts shared with acrobats, dance teams, bicycle riders, and the like was the distinction of being a "dumb act," capable of interesting an audience through those periods of noise and confusion at the beginning and end of a show. Although many performers tended to resent the animals, they seemed to have increased in popularity as vaudeville grew,

and a cursory glance at any collection of vaudeville programs reveals the widespread use of trained
dogs, seals, birds, monkeys, and the occasional
appearance of bears, lions, and elephants.

In similar fashion, stage magic seems to have
flourished through its contact with vaudeville, and
even though the tradition of full-length, evening
performances was still preferred by many magicians,
most of the famous conjurors around the turn of the
century (Kellar, Horace Goldin, Howard Thurston,
Blackstone, Ching Ling Foo, and Harry Houdini)
performed on the vaudeville stage at some time
during their careers. Vaudeville seems to have accelerated the drift which had been taking place in
stage magic following the great days of the eighteenth-century—the breakdown into relatively specialized acts such as hypnotism, mind reading, ven-
triloquism (largely a comic media by 1900), conjuring, and escape art.

The absurdity of the animal acts impressed the
more educated and enlightened vaudeville-goers.
Caroline Caffin lists among "turns" which were
"sometimes incongruous or far-fetched": "bears on
roller skates; ponies who ring out a tune on hand-
bells; and cats, dogs, rabbits, pigeons, presenting
episodes that imitate the doings of the dominant
race—sometimes in a manner far from complimentary . . .[;] monkeys who play billiards, ride bi-
cycles, smoke or drink and behave generally in a
manner so like an extremely ill-bred man that it is
a wonder that some of the audiences do not feel
affronted."[1] From his "Easy Chair" in *Harper's*
William Dean Howells offered a candid assessment
of his personal reaction to one such act:

Perhaps I have seen too much of seals, but I find the
range of their accomplishments limited; and their impa-
tience for fish and lump sugar too frankly greedy before

141

and after each act. Their banjo-playing is of a most casual and irrelevant sort; they ring bells to be sure; in extreme cases they fire small cannon; and their feat of balancing large and little balls on their noses is beyond praise. But it may be that the difficulties overcome are too obvious in their instances; I find myself holding my breath, and helping them along too strenuously for my comfort. I am always glad when the curtain goes down on them; their mere flumping about the stage makes me unhappy; but they are not so bad, after all, as trained dogs.[2]

Neither Caffin nor Howells can be accused of taking a trivial matter too seriously, for both were sympathetic attenders of the popular theater, and both accepted with good humor its concessions to popular taste. Yet their reservations are symptomatic of a widespread apprehension among educated city dwellers that such acts were *not* mere entertainment but rather affronts to basic values. In part incited by the Darwinian controversy to re-evaluate the relationship between man and other members of the animal kingdom, in part merely offended by the utter impracticality and boorishness of highly trained creatures, in part motivated by the high-mindedness of Protestant gentility, these bourgeois reformers created a stir which seems, in retrospect, disproportionate to the number or importance of these acts. While their fathers had accepted with undisturbed aplomb the exhibition of wild beasts, this generation became emotionally transfixed over the plight of an Irish terrier.

In America a fascination with wild animals reached a peak in the decades following the Civil War. At that time the emphasis was largely upon exhibition rather than performance, and the attention of the audience was drawn to size and quantity rather than intrinsic merit or skill. Forepaugh and Barnum were the leading competitors in this area. In fact, Adam

McINTYRE AND HEATH IN 1915

THE ROGERS BROTHERS

HARRY HOUDINI IN 1906

EVA TANGUAY AND LITTLE HIP IN BOSTON, 1907

Forepaugh considered one of the greatest accomplishments of his career to be the accumulation of thirty-nine elephants for one tour, three more of these gluttonous beasts than Barnum ever assembled at one time. Although Forepaugh's reputation has been eclipsed by P. T. Barnum's, his was the keener interest in and knowledge of animals. A man of great physical strength and intense compassion for brute suffering, he usually supervised the care and training of the animals himself, in marked contrast to Barnum, who was inferior in his knowledge of animals and had no personal affection for them. Barnum's biographer says, "So far as we know, he did not keep dogs; he never mentions a cat, and he kept fine horses for his carriage only because they made an excellent impression on the streets."[3]

It was Barnum, however, foremost among the disseminators of popular science, who was sensitive to the change in public taste. His spectacular handling of two notorious elephants gives us an insight into American totemism in the eighties. The first of Barnum's legendary pachyderms was Jumbo, an African elephant that had been captured at an early age by Arabs, sold to a Bavarian collector, purchased by the Jardin des Plantes of Paris, and shortly after traded to the London Zoological Gardens, where he developed into the largest elephant in captivity, eventually attaining eleven feet in height and a weight of seven tons. In 1882 P. T. Barnum purchased Jumbo for breeding purposes for $10,000. The sale achieved international publicity, partially because of the outraged protest by such eminent Victorians as John Ruskin at losing this four-footed natural resource. In spite of his size, which obviously made him a symbol of an expanding nation, Jumbo was a quiet animal and easily endowed with human qualities by the sentimental public,

143

an attitude which Barnum encouraged and exploited. On the occasion of his death in 1885, when he was crushed by a freight train, it was said that he perished while trying to rescue a baby elephant, Tom Thumb, from the oncoming locomotive.[4]

Although the loss of Jumbo was a setback for the aging showman, Barnum was not long in finding another elephant to catch the public eye. With much fanfare, he purchased in India what he claimed was "The Sacred White Elephant, Toung Taloang." The poet, Joaquin Miller, who was later to appear in vaudeville, commemorated the arrival of the White Elephant in New York: "Barnum gold, and Barnum grit" brought the beast from the "storied East," Miller versified, but Americans should remember that it came from "a land of tyranny and tears." The seventh and concluding verse admonished the public not to carry its totemism too far:

> But welcome to the Christian's West,
>   From land of dreams to land of deed.
> You teach us much. Yet it were best
>   You pack this in your trunk to read
> To tyrants on returning East:
> *We worship neither man nor beast.*[5]

In addition to an interest in the size and exoticism of animals, nineteenth-century audiences were fascinated by their savagery. By the time that Frank Bostock, one of the leading lion trainers of the eighties and nineties, was ready to record his impressions in *The Training of Wild Animals* (1903), the performances of the big cats had become a standby of circuses and were occasionally to be seen in vaudeville. The emphasis of Bostock's memoir is upon the heroic aspects of his profession, and through its pages we find a long record of danger and courage. There is a wealth of anecdotes concerning persons—both men and women—injured while handling lions, panthers, leopards, and even tigers for public entertainment. The illustrations in this book show us tall, mustached men, whose expressionless faces and wooden poses give them an air of European dignity while their tight-fitting costumes reveal the slim thighs and full shoulders of men-of-action. Bostock was not only a trainer himself, but he had developed another generation of athletic young men to carry on his tradition, among them Jack Bonavita, who handled twenty lions at once and was praised publicly by Theodore Roosevelt. As a trainer of men as well as cats, Bostock had learned that self-mastery was mastery over beasts. Again and again he reiterated his emphasis upon self-discipline and clean living, insisting that the cats sense weakness in a man even before he recognizes it himself. Such examples of self-reliance as these trainers represented in the cage, with only the chair and whip between them and brute ferocity, were not lost upon the audiences who still admired frontier virtues. The lesson in courage, determination, and heroic calm could hardly have been spelled out more dramatically, unless bull fighting had been successfully introduced into this country.[6]

Bostock's romantic conception of man and beast was, however, modified by his lip-service to what he considered "science." In making a distinction between "trained" and "tamed" cats, for example, he stated, "the trained animal is a product of science; but the tamed animal is a chimera of the optimistic imagination, a forecast of the millennium." He devoted a chapter to "The Principle of Training," in which he referred to the application of scientific observation and reasoning to the problems of compelling the animals to perform; and Bostock was quite serious in disillusioning those who would think that "animals, being controlled by instinct, were quite incapable of comprehending new ideas, and of acquiring and memorizing novel things which they have been taught to do by men."[7] Study, patience, and determination seem to have been the basis of Bostock's technique, and while he claimed the prestige of science, like other trainers he seems to have relied heavily upon an intuitive understanding of beasts and their ways. In a sense, the trainers were pragmatic in their approach— one of them observed that "there are few traditions in our art"[8]—and thus some claim to scientism could be justified. But to the public the danger and horror implicit in snarls and the black whip remained the chief attraction of the "cat acts." While only a few of these acts reached the vaudeville stage, Joe Laurie, Jr., in his book, *Vaudeville*, recites the legends about lions escaping backstage and thus preserves a fragment of the tradition.[9]

The circus was the chief perpetuator of this enactment of frontier myth, but the Ringling Brothers, Barnum and Bailey Circus was forced, in 1925, to retract somewhat. Announcing the discontinuance of all performances by "the fiercer of the jungle animals," the circus management offered four reasons, each reflecting the criticisms of the same middle class reform generation which found the vaudeville animal acts preposterous. First: large numbers of complaints had been received claiming that it was cruel to force animals through stunts toward which they had no inclination. Second: parents no longer wished their children to see men and women in cages of wild beasts. Third: there had long been excessive delay and danger in transferring the animals to the performing cage. And fourth: the public seemed to prefer acts in which animals, such as dogs, seals, and horses took "an interested and playful part."[10]

The notion that some animals actually enjoyed performing would never have occurred to Forepaugh or Barnum, but it was rife in the writings of twentieth-century reformers—many of whom had little personal contact with the animals themselves. On the editorial page of the *Christian Science Monitor* appeared a plea that only animals which responded to kindness be trained for public entertainments. The British House of Commons gave respectful attention to the Superintendent of the London Zoological Gardens when he testified that although older and wilder beasts had no inclination to perform, younger animals and sea lions responded avidly to lures and other kindness. Manuals on dog care and training decried the age-old customs of whipping and beating and called upon owners to exert "patience, kindness, and good temper," secure in the knowledge that animals could learn [*sic*] "naturally."[11]

Throughout the materials that document popular taste during this period and bear upon the way in which the public would respond to the animal acts in vaudeville, the conflict between the conception of animals as savage battlers for survival in a Darwinian state of nature and a view which tended toward a sentimental anthropomorphism is apparent. Yet these conflicting positions, represented by Bostock and the giant circuses on one extreme and the humane societies on the other, shared a common premise. Whatever analogies animal life might have to humanity, in either its frontier or domesticated states, animals were part of the natural environment to be manipulated for human aggrandisement. The point at which the humane societies departed from the Bostockian point of view was in the means by which this control would be effected.

147

The original direction of the humane societies, formed in the seventies and eighties by Henry Bergh and George T. Angell, had been practical and to the point. Beasts of burden and domestic pets were to receive the protection of society equally with higher beings. Only at the beginning of the twentieth century was the issue raised to its symbolic level and the treatment of performing animals made a matter of public debate. Eventually the Jack London Club, whose activities we shall examine in a moment, was established in 1920 for the protection of stage animals.

One particular instance of humane protest reveals the extent of emotional involvement which this reform movement aroused. For example, a Boston matron, Mrs. Huntington Smith, addressing the American humane society in 1905 on the plight of performing animals, asserted that the animal acts of the circus and vaudeville were no better than bullfights. In Spain, at least, the cruelty took place before the eyes of the spectators, but in America "the easily gulled public" was deceived by publicity announcements to the effect that the animals were "Trained with Kindness." On the basis of investigations by the Animal Rescue League in Boston, she charged that, in fact, animals were trained by fear and torture, with "the whip, sharp-pointed goad, hot irons, and starvation." Deeply shocked by the conditions of the large cats she had seen, Mrs. Smith dwelt upon their confinement in narrow cages and their natural repugnance toward discipline. She cited the authority of "a well-known actress in the best vaudeville plays" who could not bear to see animals backstage in the theaters because they were so badly treated. Even dogs and other domestic animals which were easily tamed and receptive to training were compelled to do high jumps, to jump through hoops, and to do other dangerous acts only by means of starvation and the whip. Mrs. Smith further claimed: "I have the word of eye witnesses, who have seen dogs that had been cruelly beaten behind the scenes because they failed to do their tricks, one of them being covered with welts from head to tail, and dogs so overcome with terror when they failed to do a trick the first time that they could hardly crawl to their trainer's feet."[12]

This combination of gory detail and honest outrage permeates the literature of the humane societies but the most powerful expressions were to be found in fiction. Following in the tradition of Anna Sewell's *Black Beauty* (published and popularized in this country by Angell), Jack London wrote a novel, *Michael, Brother of Jerry* (1919), which was to spur the American Humane Education Society to form the Jack London Club. Although this club was without officers or by-laws and seems merely to have been a rallying point for sentiment which had already ameliorated the condition of animals in show business, it did publish a list of procedures for its members to follow. These included the distribution of anti-cruelty printed matter outside of theaters, letter-writing to theater managers and the local press, and the expression of disapproval through hissing at cruel turns in the acts.[13]

The substance and style of London's novel is what readers familiar with *The Call of the Wild* might expect. According to Mrs. London's biography, her husband had been collecting material over a number of years in order to give documentary realism to the story. Some hundred pages of the novel would seem to have been adapted directly from the humane society literature and all examples of cruelty known to have existed throughout the entertainment industry were concentrated within a few months of Michael's experience at the training center and vaudeville houses.[14] In one especially gruesome episode, Michael—an Irish terrier—is carelessly dropped while being shipped in a small, slatted packing case. His toe is crushed in this accident and, upon discovering the injury, his owner whips a jackknife from his pocket and brutally amputates the toe.[15]

Michael is sold, at one point, to a famous animal trainer who, like Frank Bostock, operates a large training center and supplies animals to all parts of the world. In typically melodramatic fashion, the trainer is a respected family man and apparently a gentle person, but "those who from the inside had seen him work were agreed that he had no soul." His philosophy seemed to have been summed up in his observation that: "No dog walks naturally on his hind legs, much less on its forelegs . . . . Dogs ain't built that way. *They have to be made to,* that's all. That's the secret of all animal training. They have to. You've got to make them." While being roughly trained himself, Michael learns about other animals such as Barney Barnato, the mule, who earned the best engagements in vaudeville by his ferocious bucking (prompted by a clown with a spike), and St. Elias, the Alaskan bear, who could never be trained because each time the traditional ring was inserted through the pierced cartilage of his nose he ripped it out, flesh and all. In his tours Michael also learned of the tremendous mortality among the poorly nourished performing animals: one troop of trained poodles required thirty-five replacements over four years.[16]

By 1919 a new situation had been created by the use of animals in motion pictures. While the adaptation of this new medium lies beyond the scope of this study, we might note Jack London's attitude toward the filming of *The Call of the Wild*. He was quite aware that the demands of film were "very different from the vaudeville circuit . . . where the animal is obliged, fair weather or foul, to go through the same act, often of a most unnatural character, from two to four times a day, year in and year out."[17] From the gladiatorial combat of the nineteenth-century circus and menagerie to the twentieth-century use of animals as characters in sentimental dramas, chiefly children's movies and animated cartoons, was a large step and indicates the degree to which animals had become denaturalized into symbolic projections of human desires and anxieties. This sentimental anthropomorphism was reflected upon the vaudeville stage in such performances as "Swain's Cats and Rats," in which natural enemies would exhibit Christian love and charity to one another (under the influence of sedatives, London had alleged), or "The Happy Family," in which the idealized Eden imagined by Elias Hicks would come to life upon the stage. Around a throne occupied by a beautiful woman would gather the lion, the lamb, an owl, some sparrows, a cat, a panther, and whatever other beasts were available to the showman at a particular time.[18]

Science in the guise of behavioral psychology actually turned to performing animals for confirmation of its theories concerning human motivation and habits. Working from Darwin's hypothesis set forth in *Expression of Emotion in Man and Animals,* that an essential continuity of feeling existed through all animal life, this school early developed an elaborate set of experimental techniques, including problem boxes, discrimination boxes, choice boxes, and mazes.[19] Animals for these experiments were usually selected at random, and thus the results of their edu-

151

cation could be considered to be close to norm for their respective species. But when J. B. Watson turned from his laboratory studies to examine professionally trained animals, those who had been selected initially for traits which made them susceptible to training and who had been cultivated by experienced handlers, he found a higher level of intelligence being manifested.

Such an awareness led Watson, in his standard textbook, *Behavior, An Introduction to Comparative Psychology* (1914), to devote a number of pages to the tricks and talents of such performing animals as Clever Hans, a German horse whose tricks included counting into the hundreds by means of tapping his foot, distinguishing between the quantity and kinds of objects set before him, and answering difficult problems in arithmetic. He also discussed at some length the Horses of Eberfield which had been discovered subsequent to Hans' notoriety, two dogs named Jasper and Don—who were supposed to be able to talk—and the chimpanzee, Peter.[20]

Although several other simians were well known in vaudeville, Peter had achieved considerable fame in the hands of Keith's publicity agents. Robert Larsen's scrapbook contains more than a score of clippings covering Peter's activities in Boston in 1909, including long articles headed by such arresting titles as "Peter Visits the State Prison," "Big Monkey Comes to Hub in Pullman; Rides in Taxi and Dines at Touraine," "Noted Monkey Smokes, Dines, Drinks Beer," "Many Famous Guests Meet Famous Simian Host," and "Peter the Great Visits Harvard." Advertisements of his performances announced that "Darwin Was Thinking of Me" and quoted Dr. Dudley A. Sargent of Harvard University as saying that Peter was "The nearest approach to a man I have ever seen." Dr. Sargent, accompanied by Professors Hall and Huntington, was photographed by the press watching Peter light a cigarette.

The conclusions of J. B. Watson regarding Peter are of some interest both for the light they throw upon the reluctance of many behaviorists to abandon traditional distinctions between men and animals in favor of an extreme naturalism and for the serious way in which this scientific discipline viewed what might seem to be an inconsequential amusement. "Peter's vaudeville performance," Watson summarized on the basis of private observation as well as from watching the act on stage, "is most impressive. He skates readily and with accuracy, drinks from a bottle or glass; lights and smokes a cigarette (sometimes after a great deal of 'help' from the trainer); eats with a fork; and can 'ring for the waiter.'" Although Peter's motor development, Watson decided, had brought him nearly to the point where he could compete with man, "his lack of language habits puts him forever below the plane of comparison with man."[21]

Although science and entertainment could thus join hands in a common recognition of the animal kingdom, it may still seem curious that ancient magic and diabolism were also susceptible to a similar up-dating within the vaudeville ritual. Actually, however, the trend had been successfully initiated by a European performer of the mid-nineteenth century. With Robert-Houdin and his followers the trappings of eighteenth-century charlatanry were abandoned and stage magic had become a craft rather than a religion. A handbook of magic published in the United States in 1896 announced that, "With Cagliostro (d. 1795), so-called genuine magic died. Of the great pretenders to occultism he was the last to win any great fame. . . .Science has laughed away sorcery, witchcraft, and necromancy."[22]

The generation which followed Robert-Houdin

153

emphasized the control over nature which man could exert through his knowledge of mechanics, optics, and chemistry rather than through any mystic powers of the spirit. Robert-Houdin, following a predecessor, Wiljalba Frikell, had abandoned the exotic costuming of the charlatans to assume the more professional garb of evening clothes; his stage props were similarly modest, tending to be commonplace pieces of household furniture, dining implements, and the like rather than carved chests, braziers, and oriental vases. His greatest influence, however, was in systematizing stage magic. Not only did he incorporate the *jeux* of fellow *faiseurs* into his own repertoire but he traveled widely, assimilating the local traditions of conjuring in many parts of the world.[23]

The second generation of conjurers, best represented by Buertier De Kolta (1845-1903) and Harry Kellar (1849-1922), continued the refining process of Robert-Houdin and utilized the advancing technology of their day to create new effects. Most notable of these were De Kolta's optical illusions, performed against a background of dark velvet curtains, in unconscious irony, called "Black Magic." During the eighties and nineties, however, the great names in the profession were more and more to be associated with a special kind of performance or even a particular trick. Such specialists in American entertainment were Howard Thurston, who concentrated on card tricks, Thomas Nelson Downs, known for his manipulation of coins, Horace Goldin, who created large effects with rapidity, and, a decade later, Houdini, who received his initial fame in escape art. The two reasons most significant for this specialization were: first, the increased knowledge, on the part of the public, of mechanics, which made necessary an extreme subtlety in the performance of tricks; and,

154

second, the rise of vaudeville as a national institution. Vaudeville, of course, required the brief, spectacular entertainment and permitted the endless repetition of a limited repertoire along the far-reaching circuits. All four of these men were frequently upon the vaudeville stage and owned their professional reputation to it; and it is interesting to note that they were all dead within a decade after the collapse of vaudeville in the late twenties.

But just as Robert-Houdin represented the antiquarian and eclectic view of magic in the nineteenth century, his namesake Houdini (Erich Weiss) stood for the agnostic and efficient twentieth. As Edmund Wilson observed in 1925, Houdini was above all else an "honest craftsman" who was "more interested in understanding how effects are produced than in astonishing people with them." And yet like that other boy's idol of the young century, Tom Swift, his technical proficiency was not limited to a narrow area. During his life he claimed to have mastered every form of magic or deception known to the western world, and he published his findings in numerous books under his name. He was instrumental in the founding of the professional magicians' society and accumulated one of the largest known libraries on all phases of magic and so-called spiritual phenomena. Wilson had considerable basis for crediting this showman with "true scientific curiosity."[24]

Houdini had developed his handcuff and trunk escapes during his early years with museums and traveling shows, where he had also become familiar with the techniques of mind reading, fortunetelling and conjuring. His rise to fame, however, was exclusively the result of his escapes from every type of confinement discoverable: jails, coffins, milk cans, mail bags, packing cases, straitjackets and, of course, handcuffs. He would offer challenges to police chiefs and penitentiary wardens in the cities he visited—first in Europe and then in this country—and would accept conditions which not only increased the difficulty of the escapes but also made them extremely hazardous. Houdini, in fact, seemed to have compensated for the loss of mystery in his acts through an increased emphasis on physical danger.[25]

While some stage magicians of the time loudly claimed that they were conducting "scientific experiments," Houdini merely by his manner and his technique left his audience with the impression that they had witnessed a "demonstration" rather than a "trick." Edmund Wilson was especially impressed by the way in which Houdini talked to the audience, "straightforwardly, with no patter." And Wilson noted that, "The formulas—such as the 'Will wonders never cease?' with which he signalizes the end of a trick—have a quaint conventional sound, as if they were perfunctory concessions to the theatre."[26] The *Scientific American,* which later appointed Houdini to its committee to investigate mediums, ran a series of articles beginning in 1910 on the mechanics of escape art. Those secrets to which they had access were diagramed and described with scrupulous treatment of detail. Regarding the miracle of Houdini's descent into the East River, not only chained but sealed within a packing case, and his ascent a few minutes later, their reporter told his readers: "We do not pretend to give any explanation of Houdini's performances. We can only say that he states that most of the public exposés of this kind are absolutely worthless. . . .Possibly some of our readers have original solutions of these mysteries; if so we should be pleased to hear from them."[27] Thus, Houdini and his generation brought magic to the point where an observer in 1914 could comment: "In these days of materialism no illusionist on the stage makes any pretence to the employment of superhuman agencies. A scientific phenomenon hitherto unknown is the nearest to the insoluble that they will allow themselves."[28]

The irony of Houdini's famous escape art was that it had originally been developed by two well-known spiritualists, the Davenport Brothers, who had used it to demonstrate their mystic powers. Bound first with ropes and then placed in a wooden cabinet, they would cleverly proceed to extricate each other, blow trumpets, bang castanets, and otherwise impress witnesses that, indeed, spirits had joined them in the cabinet. When the cabinet would finally be opened, the mediums would be discovered bound in the same manner as before. Throughout his apprenticeship Houdini had been fascinated by the Davenport Brothers and, after he had already perfected his own techniques, was able to locate the surviving brother and learn the secrets of their performance. According to Ira Davenport's statement to Houdini, the brothers had never claimed supernatural powers; nevertheless, spiritualistic lecturers had always accompanied them on their tours.[29]

Houdini's attitude toward the deceptions necessary to his craft (the packing case in which he entered the East River had a cleverly concealed panel, opening inward) expressed itself in a number of ways. On the stage he would do his tricks without any claims of magical power, and in interviews he would readily acknowledge the trickery involved. Indeed, not believing in any powers beyond the natural himself, his attitude toward those who did was largely compounded of pity. To a reporter for a religious periodical he was supposed to have explained his frequent exposures of mediums by saying: "Tell the people that all I am trying to do is to save them from being tricked in their griefs and their sorrows; and to persuade them to leave spiritualism alone, and to take up some genuine religion."[30] At times he would reflect upon himself and feel that he had been martyred in the cause of truth. Thus: "My professional life has been a constant record of disillusion, and many things that seem wonderful to most men are the every-day commonplaces of my business."[31]

Houdini's reformist crusade against such mediums as the eminently respectable Mrs. Crandon came about after his own authority had been well established and his top billing on the vaudeville circuits was well assured. He had, of course, firm moral reasons for such exposures, and the temper of the scientific age was on his side. But even taking into account the fact that he refused remuneration for serving on the committee appointed by the *Scientific American,* an exposé was good showmanship. Immensely competitive, Houdini did not stop his search for truth with fraudulent mediums. On numerous occasions he turned upon members of his own profession and declared them to be frauds and pretenders. Of the so-called "strong men," he commented that: "Almost all of them have resorted to some sort of artifice or subterfuge in order to appear superhumanly strong. That is to say, they added brain to their brawn, and it is a difficult question whether their efforts deserve to be called trickery or good showmanship."[32] Nor was Houdini's image of himself as a debunker always taken at face value. Sarah Bernhardt is supposed to have asked him in private, as a man who could perform miracles, to restore to her the use of her paralyzed leg; Arthur Conan Doyle persistently pleaded with Houdini, in print and in private, to admit openly that he was psychic.[33]

GEORGE FULLER GOLDEN

LEW DOCKSTADER

Such ambiguity reveals something of the place that stage magic held in the popular imagination. It might emphasize technique and swear by rationalism, but some of its appeal still lay with the primitive obeisance before occult powers which remained at the heart of the modern psyche. Like Barnum, the shrewd magician would associate himself with exotic mysteries. One of Kellar's advertisements read: "Success crowns the season of Kellar, the Great American Magician. His Oriental magic, the result of years of original research in India, enables him to present new illusions that are triumphs of art, and attract enormous houses—dazing, delighting, dumbfounding, and dazzling theatre-goers."[34] Another successful conjurer in vaudeville, Ching Ling Foo, also capitalized upon the mystique of the East, performing in a set of embroidered dragons on curtains of silk, using tiny, almost toy-like, Chinese children to assist him, and presenting his mystifications with "nonchalant wizardry, smiling his inscrutable smile."[35]

Stage magic required a certain cabalistic secrecy in which to flourish, but still most of the sensational tricks were published and widely circulated in cheap handbooks. That it reveal its lore, repudiate its mysteries, seemed to be the only condition upon which a materialistic society would tolerate so primitive and arcane a profession. A paper-covered book of magic selling for thirty cents at the turn of the century, *Herrman's Black Art or the Science of Magic, Witchcraft, Alchemy, Necromancy, Mesmerism, Etc.*, was described in terms calculated to flatter the reader with critical intelligence and yet it said: "The dark night of superstition will never end and no day will ever break to drive away mankind's firm belief in the mysteries this wonderful book unravels. This book opens the sealed doors to all sciences mentioned in its title. . . .With this book in possession all mystery will disappear, and what before seemed to you beyond all human explanation, will become clear as the light of day."[36]

While all of the magic acts shared the ambivalence between the technical and the mysterious, none was on more sensitive ground than the hypnotists. Part of any performance of hypnotic skill, usually announced as a "scientific demonstration," was the participation of members of the audience, and thus the thin veil of fantasy upon which the vaudeville performance depended was momentarily disturbed. Furthermore, hypnotism had outgrown the cultist associations of early mesmerism and had been accepted by many physicians as a therapeutic technique, thus acquiring a kind of prestige not available to conjuring, escape art, and the like. Following the publication of Albert Moll's standard work, *Hypnotism* (1890), there were a number of professional papers delivered to meetings of American physicians and psychologists, but even more significantly a rash of popular, how-to-do-it books appeared under such titles as *Hypnotism: How It Is Done, Practical Lessons in Hypnotism, Plain Instructions in Hypnotism and Mesmerism.*[37] Of these works, the most instructive for our purposes is one called *Stage Hypnotism*, published under the pseudonym of "Professor Leonidas," and subtitled, "A Text-book of Occult Entertainments." True to his profession, the writer does not reveal all, but he tells enough to indicate the amount of hokum and chicanery which went into an interesting and credible performance. Although he retains a serious attitude regarding the "scientific" nature of his craft, the author also admits the use of "plants" in the audience and instructs his readers how to make the simplest of hypnotic effects, such as the loss of sensation in a limb, into a theatrical *tour de force.*[38]

Professor Leonidas distinguished between vaudeville amusements and his independent full-length performance and gave instructions for each. In general, because of the shorter length of time the vaudeville act was more carefully planned and timed, and thus required more deception. However, for a fascinating account of nineteenth-century exploitation of smalltown life by the city slicker, I recommend Professor Leonidas's adventures on the road. There he had full play for his powers of invention and deceit, and his exploits rival those of Mark Twain's Duke and Dauphin. Even with allowance for exaggeration, the awed respect with which the townsfolk regarded him, the display of his hypnotized assistant in the drugstore window—resting within an elaborate coffin—and the careful ferreting out of personal information for the mind reading portion of his act, all ring true. To anyone familiar with the practice of hypnotism, of course, his control over his subjects was obviously superficial and their responses anything but remarkable, but to innocent Americans, confident of their commonsense view of human personality, such performances must have seemed devilish indeed and the hypnotist a being of mystic powers.[39]

Such performers as Professor Leonidas were to lose prestige after 1905 as the result of vigorous protests against their vaudeville performances by the swiftly rising medical profession. The animal acts may have been besieged by humane reformers, but at least laboratory science had placed tentative approval upon demonstrations of animal behavior. Houdini had also been considered as something of a curiosity by physiologists, and his own vendetta against mediums had been in entire accord with the scientific world view. But hypnotism, it appeared, was a natural phenomenon not readily transferable to the vaudeville stage.

Representatives from leading medical schools in

the east, gathered for a symposium on psychotherapeutics, heard the vaudeville performers denounced as "irresponsible mountebanks."[40] *The New York Medical Journal* anathematized hypnotic performances as "a basic fraud upon the public" and explained that "the public induction of hypnotism upon perfect strangers is almost an impossibility, and such complete control as is apparently manifested is a farce." The journal commented upon the use of "plants" in the audience and the familiar staging of the "cataleptic trance" in which the subject, through the aid of a steel frame concealed beneath his clothing, remained absolutely rigid when placed across two chairs and thus could support heavy weights without injury.[41] Two further objections were raised by medical men to the practice of hypnotism outside of their profession. First, that improper hypnotism could seriously damage the will; second, that the extraordinary power claimed by most hypnotists, a vestige of the outdated theories of animal magnetism, was not supported by scientific investigation. As might be expected since these two objections tended to cancel one another, they were not voiced at the same time, but medical authorities seem to have dimmed effectively the lamp of stage hypnotism after 1910. In a similar manner, the appeal of mind readers would be practically extinguished by 1925 through the "exposure" of their methods.[42]

In the vaudeville ritual, the symbolism of the animal act and stage magic held up the mirror to the mass mind. It revealed vestiges of the ancient terrors of the folk in the face of a hostile universe as well as a totemic sense of identification with animals. The awe and reverence of the folk before sorcery and witchcraft had been only partially dispelled by the Enlightenment, and upon its residue of emotionalism the modern entertainer could build his act. But finally, and more subtlely, the very prestige and power of modern science was itself held in superstitious awe by the folk of the new industrial society. Paradoxically, the very champion of the modern age against the ignorance and error of ancient times, was itself deified in the popular mind as a new mysterious and occult activity presided over by a new priesthood of whitecoated scientists and technicians. The control manifested by the animal trainer was equivalent to the control which modern technology had also instituted over a wild and chaotic nature, and the feats of illusion or mental control demonstrated by the practitioners of stage magic were symbolic of man's supremacy, through the application of scientific knowledge, in the worlds which lay beyond the physical—the nether worlds of psyche and animus.

The very changes which took place as these acts evolved, and the kinds of pressure applied by interested groups from society at large, say much about this symbolism. Especially the shift from animals "red in tooth and claw" to those able and apparently eager to work cooperatively under paternal treatment symbolizes the shift from rugged competition as a social ideal toward the more humane social theories of the Reform Darwinists. Even though Darwinism had lowered man's self-esteem by placing him on a closer plane with other animal life, this renewed sense of identification had opened new possibilities for social thinkers and students of behavior. In both the humane movements and in behavioral psychology the symbolizing process, already implicit in the vaudeville ritual, rose to a level of verbal articulation and dispute. As the vaudeville performers and managers appeared to have been aware, the criticisms which these groups leveled against the vaudeville shows were more of a debate over symbolic meanings than an assault upon the ritual itself.

These animal acts and stage magic performances quickly became amusements for children, as do most modern folk rituals, and their meaning underwent even further development in the technological entertainments which superseded vaudeville. But their popularity and pertinence at the turn of the century points up the reevaluation of basic values which took place during this era. An entire world view based upon scientism was in the making, and its new folk expression, necessarily crude and tentative in its symbolism, was being formed. By the gradual conversion of inherited folk attitudes toward animality and spiritism, the New Folk were better enabled to form ritualistically the attitudes and sensitivities appropriate to twentieth-century life.

EIGHT

The Playlets

WHEN "DRAMA" ASSUMED an important place in vaudeville during the 1895-1896 season, mythic elements were added to the ritualistic aspects of vaudeville. So long as the show consisted of a superficially unrelated medley of acts, vaudeville had been under no compulsion to describe or explain or even consciously to organize into some coherent pattern its symbolic content; with the intrusion of what purported to be "imitations of life," however, there was the possibility that vaudeville might have to place its various elements in some kind of overt, related order to accord more closely with the order of life. This was myth—as distinguished from the action of ritual. The inclusion of drama had come

165

about in the first place through the ambition of the vaudeville managers who probably had not thought of the possible consequences of their decision. Earlier, singers, dancers, comics, animal acts, and conjurors had been eminently satisfactory drawing cards, but the star system of Frohman and Belasco had made of the leading actors, and especially actresses, of the popular stage striking symbols of glamour and success, and thereby appropriate candidates for the ritual. These stars, however, needed some sort of vehicle, and by the turn of the century the vaudeville show commonly contained a short play in which the stars of the legitimate stage would take leading roles.

The vehicles for these appearances were a matter of secondary importance at first, but it was not long before a specific genre emerged—the "playlet"— geared to the talents of the performer on the one hand and the values of the New Folk on the other. While Robert Grau, the most active booking agent of the period, claims to have negotiated the first of these appearances upon the vaudeville stage—Charles Dickson and his wife, Lillian Burkhart, to play in a drawing-room one-act called the *Salt Cellar* at Proctor's—he credits a Keith lieutenant, Phillip Nash, with the development of the "playlet" as a dramatic form peculiar to vaudeville.[1] The dramatic press, fairly representative of a genteel middle class position of such matters, suddenly awarded vaudeville formal recognition. The New York *Dramatic Mirror*, which had previously acknowledged vaudeville's existence only in sporadic news items, in October of 1895 initiated a weekly column, "The Vaudeville Stage," which still, however, managed to overlook better than nine-tenths of vaudeville by focusing its coverage upon the "playlet" currently being performed in a half-dozen bigtime vaudeville palaces in New York City.

These playlets, as nearly everyone concerned with them well knew, could never take on the proportions of a serious art form. At best they were carefully tailored vehicles for the established actor or actress, on a level of curtain raisers, fillers, and amusing parlor plays. Characterization was sketchy and typed, plots were compressed and intensified to meet the demands of the vaudeville program, and the effects generally fell within a rather narrow range of humor and pathos. To the extent that contemporary life was acceptable upon the stage, the vaudeville playlets were "realistic," and so long as an accomplished actress like Ethel Barrymore could hold the audience in a drawing-room comedy, the playlets might aspire to sophistication. But the greater proportion of them, whatever the Belasco-inspired realistic elements might be or whatever snatches imitative of Barry dialogue were used, were melodramas or farces directly inherited from the popular theater of the mid-nineteenth century. The broad effect, the direct appeal to the funny-bone or the tear-ducts, the disdain for probability and the heavy reliance upon suspense—these were the dominant traits easily recognizable beneath a few surface changes in the older genres.

But to dismiss these playlets—their total number would appear to exceed 5,000—on purely esthetic grounds is to ignore their staying power and their symbolic importance. Not only did they eventually command a significant mythic place, but they became one of the chief contributions which vaudeville made to radio and television, both of which were to grow fat on short, simplified drama. For good reasons this capsule drama, like its equivalent in printed media, the commercial short story, registered forcefully upon the New Folk. Its very brevity, its recognizable formulae, its uncomplicated characterization, and its tentative and uneasy exploration of new values—all put these playlets closer to the other components of the vaudeville myth than to even the worst productions of the legitimate stage. What the playlets were able to add to the vaudeville ritual, on the other hand, was an amplification of the symbolism already implicit in its many acts. In the playlets the many aspects of the Myth of Success that this study has thus far explored take on positiveness and concreteness. The famous leading man or lady was, of course, the primary symbol—adoration of them made doubly effective by casting them in pathetic roles of nonsuccess—but also the allurements of material prosperity and progress, the means of sloughing off rural, folk attitudes, and the apprehension of the uprooted in the face of the great impersonal city were dramatized over and over again.

For purposes of illustration, let us examine the work of several widely recognized writers of vaudeville playlets, each of whom commanded an important area of specialization. Will S. Cressy was the master of rural types and rural setting; George Ade was known for his good-humored realism in handling urban characters; Willis Steell's best work was in the sentimental vein; Richard Harding Davis wrote suspense plays and melodramas; and although Edgar Allen Woolf ranged widely over the field, his strength lay in custom-tailoring short pieces for popular actors. To all appearances, only Cressy and Woolf were strictly vaudeville writers through a significant portion of their careers and made sizable fortunes from their playlets. The others tended to be writers at large who enjoyed a few successes in vaudeville but who also dabbled in full-length plays, musical comedy, and other types of writing. Both George Ade and Richard Harding Davis, for example, would have been well known in their time without reference to their plays or to their librettos for musical comedies—Ade for his humorous "Fables," Davis for his tales of adventure, and both for their work as newspaper columnists.

First among these playwrights to achieve recognition was Will S. Cressy. During the six years prior to 1897, Cressy with his wife and future vaudeville partner, Blanche Dayne, had played in Denman Thompson's *The Old Homestead*—Cressy as Cy Prime, the eccentric Yankee farmer, and Blanche Dayne as Ricketty Ann, the fey, backcountry soubrette. Cressy's feeling for the drama seems to have been gained largely through his playing in *The Old Homestead*, and there is very little of his own writing which does not contain echoes from that marvelous potpourri of humorous and sentimental clichés. Although *The Old Homestead* was solidly in the tradition of the American rural drama, it wandered for two acts through the big city (as Uncle Josh searches for his lost son), and the play thus included glimpses of ethnic types, Bowery characters, policemen, thieves, bankers, and other characters not usually found in that genre and thus blended the rural and the urban elements. Characteristic of the one-acts derived from *The Old Homestead* are Cressy's first play, *Grasping an Opportunity*, in which a cautious New England farmer is gradually snared and plundered by a wily female book agent, and *The Wyoming Whoop*, in which the Yankee is transplanted to a Western setting as the editor of a small paper and is relieved of his money by a traveling actress.[2]

Cressy's versatility is apparent in the great difference between his rural dramas and such playlets as *Car Two, Stateroom One*, a routine romantic comedy, which cleverly evades the proscriptions of vaudeville's aseptic moralism. In this piece a young man and a

169

young lady on a train discover, to their mutual consternation, that they have tickets to the same overnight compartment. After considerable humorous discussion which ably steers between a rural niceness and an urbane naughtiness, this couple fall in love (they recall they were childhood sweethearts), find a clergyman on the train to marry them, and finally enter the compartment together. In what seems to be a quite different line, dealing with the problems of the immigrant, yet still exploiting the comic pathos of *The Old Homestead*, was a series of playlets concerned with Mag Haggerty, an Irish girl who has become thoroughly American, and her efforts to make her father—who has remained thoroughly Irish—more acceptable to genteel, middle class society. Her attempts to teach the bog-trotting Irishman to dance the quadrille, to read and write, and to dress in a respectable manner were handled in a manner which created sympathy for both characters, even while mildly satirizing the snobbishness of the one and the vulgarity of the other.[3]

Rural drama itself was taking a step away from *The Old Homestead*, and while it was not quite ready to start condemnation proceedings, no longer did it require the wayward sons and daughters to yield to the bonds of family affection and duty and remain at home. Rural drama, within the myth outlined by vaudeville, rapidly became an elegy instead of a paean, and the homey characters, instead of portraying a triumphant combination of shrewdness and virtue, became models by which the older, agrarian generation was shown how to surrender nobly and gracefully. This point is strikingly made in *Brother Dave*, a playlet written in 1909 by Willis Steell for the popular character actor Sam Edwards. Steell, a convert to vaudeville drama after a few minor successes in the purer arts of poetry and poetic drama, chose as his central character a corpulent middle-aged farmer who has supported and provided a home for a distant female relative and her daughter. The girl, Fanny, now eighteen, has thought of the farmer as "Brother Dave," but has understood from her mother that she would marry him.

The dramatic action takes place on the girl's eighteenth birthday and centers upon the clumsy efforts of Brother Dave to discover if Fanny really loves him or is merely marrying him out of obligation. Our sympathy for Brother Dave is aroused by his pathetic account of his previous relations with young ladies, none of whom has bothered to discover the heart of gold beneath his obesity. Fanny is in love, the audience soon discovers, but not with the aging farmer. Her heart goes out to a young farm worker who, like herself, has the upbringing and education which makes him a potential member of the coming industrial order. The focus, however, remains upon the moral issue confronting Brother Dave, and the audience suffers with him as he models his wedding clothes for the ladies; then watches Fanny as she looks at her wedding dress and dissolves into tears. Finally, with a plausibility quite exceptional for this genre, Brother Dave rises to his gesture of renunciation by pretending to Fanny he is really in love with someone else, and asking *her* forgiveness. The pathos receives a further turn of the screw as he masks his suffering and tries to share Fanny's newfound joy. When the curtain drops he, as representative of the older, unacclimated generation, is left alone and suffering upon the stage.[4]

A less moving, but nonetheless skillfully fashioned playlet by Steell was his *Faro Nell*, a story of a California mining camp created for Fannie Hatfield.

Quite obviously modeled upon Bret Harte's tales and probably also in debt to Harte for the sentimental characterizations of the miners, this play had considerable appeal for the urban public as symbolic of the mythic Golden West. Faro Nell, one of a number of emancipated females who appeared in these playlets, is a professional gambler who has become the darling of the rough-and-ready mining camp. So much do the miners adore her that when a worthless character appears and claims as her husband half of her gold strike, the miners refuse to believe him. Nell, overcome by the show of confidence and affection, finally discards her pretense and admits the truth. "You boys was all so good to me—the sheriff—Polly—even Hank—you all thought a woman was somethin' dropped from heaven—an' I'd come here straight from hell." Nell claims sympathy usually reserved for the "fallen women" as she gives in some detail the story of her trials and degradation. Her drunkard father—to whom she was devoted—had persuaded her to marry this gambler, not realizing what a bounder and cad he really was. She had dutifully complied, but both daughter and father were subsequently shocked to learn that the gambler *cheated at cards.* His wickedness was confirmed when he threw Nell out into the street. Nell further relates her father's attempt to find the gambler and kill him, only to return with the news that the gambler was already dead. After her father's death, Nell had sought to make her living in the mining camps, and she had encouraged the attentions of her suitor Dick—a young miner and, of course, a diamond in the rough—only because she believed that her husband no longer existed.

Upon hearing this tale of innocent woe, the outraged Dick slides off seeking personal vengeance. Shots are fired off-stage and Dick returns with the announcement to Nell that he has killed her gambler-husband. In the hectic closing minutes of the play: (1) Nell claims that *she* has shot her husband, (2) the miners cry "She done right; bully for Nell," (3) the sheriff steps forward with the news that, 'There ain't no law for punishing women in Californy this eepock, Nell," but (4) Nell decides to avoid making trouble for the sheriff and so turns the pistol on herself; and (5) Dick knocks the pistol from her hand, and (6) announces that the gambler fired first as evidenced by the pistol in the dead man's hand which is still cocked. Curtain with Dick and Nell holding hands while the miners, massed in front of a bench hiding the dead body, sing "He was seeing Nellie home." While the play depends largely upon the plot and local color for its effectiveness, the essential ingredients of *Brother Dave* are still here, and the nineteenth-century assumption about the essential goodness of man, especially in the primitive and lawless conditions of western life, is the mainstay of the plot.[5]

A third play of Steell's, *The Fifth Commandment*, also illustrates the dynamics of this kind of moral drama as it was presented on the vaudeville stage. The plot here is much more complex than that of *Brother Dave*, and yet it is in some ways a similar story. The problem of family affection is again paramount as we find a young girl living alone with her maternal grandfather, Wingate. He dotes on her, partially because of her deceased mother, his daughter, who married despite of his threat of disowning her, but he allows Alice none of the carefree pleasures of youth. Alice, however, claiming the privileges of her birthday, has admitted to the house two musicians whom she had met in the park and insists that they are to play for her in honor of the occasion. One of the musicians, Carl Winters, sees a picture of the dead daughter (Alice's mother) on the table, recognizes her as his wife, and pretends to the old man that he is a former "friend" of the husband. He tells the story of how the "husband" had left for Europe to make a name for himself as a composer, remaining faithful to his wife, and then had returned only to find that she was dead.

WIN. Better dead than alive, the wife of an adventurer. I taught her to respect the Fifth Commandment—"Honor thy father and thy mother, that thy days may be long" —but she broke the Fifth Commandment; that's why she died so young; and she broke my heart by marrying a man who had no name—no business—no honor.

CARL. Stop! You defame your daughter. She never would have married a man without honor. You killed her faith in him and so she died. Her death was his death.[6]

Carl describes himself as losing his health and ambition—as merely "a wretched outcast waiting for the end"—and the grandfather relents somewhat, but says that since the child believes her father dead, it is best that matters remain so. Whereupon, Carl, discovering for the first time that his wife had left him a child, accuses Wingate of a "hardness" which "killed your daughter and ruined the life of the man she married." At this point Alice appears singing the song she had heard her father playing in the park. It is, of course, the same symbolic song that her mother had loved, and the grandfather— touched at last by sympathy—discloses to the girl that her father has returned. As father and daughter rush into each other's arms, the grandfather intones, "Honor thy father and thy mother — so says the Fifth Commandment."

Here is the theme of family responsibility, recurrent in many of these dramas, but generally reflect-

174

ing a pattern appropriate to the newly urbanized generation. As in the older dramas defending the pastoral simplicity of the American way of life, there is nothing to indicate in these plays that man has any wider responsibilities than family, and it is the duty of the strong within this closed circle to protect the weak from the ravages of the outside world. At times this duty requires the ultimate in self-abnegation and sacrifice. In a kind of grisly competition the sentimental members of these stage families try to outdo one another in forgiveness, humility, and altruism. The spirit of a dead mother, wife, or child would haunt these characters—as it does in *The Fifth Commandment*—as a symbol of guilt, of responsibility withheld when it was needed most. Yet in *The Fifth Commandment*, as in many of these playlets, the message implicit in the plot seems to be a revision of the biblical injunction: "Honor thy children that they will live long. . . ." Behind the nostalgic moralism of family life rears the shadow of progress, the celebration of the success-minded, child-centered family, and a new-found virtue in wandering rather than remaining in the pastoral community.

George Ade—famous for his *Fables in Slang* and other humorous works—has been overlooked as a writer for vaudeville. His dramatic writing seems to have begun sometime in the nineties when his burlesque of local events in Chicago, *The Back Stair Investigation*, was produced in a small theater. In writing it, Ade acknowledged that he had "committed either a misdemeanor or a crime" and considered the real start of his dramatic career to have been *Mrs. Peckham's Carouse,* a one-act comedy written as a result of a conversation at a dinner party with the buxom comedienne, May Irwin.[7] Ade rushed home from the dinner and rapidly wrote the one-act with Miss Irwin in mind for the leading role. She liked the play well enough to purchase it for $200, but circumstances kept her from playing it for a number of years. Not until 1906—eight years later—did she pull it out of her trunk in Boston at a time when her company was searching for a curtain raiser to precede a play titled *Mrs. Black Is Back.* Not only did Ade's one-act prove successful in preparing the audience for the feature comedy, but it soon became well known in its own right. May Irwin took it into vaudeville a few years later, and when she tired of the role after several seasons, her sister Flo Irwin continued to perform it along the vaudeville circuits. The situation was made to order for audiences ready to laugh at reform moralism, for Mrs. Peckham, the central character, is a socially prominent prohibitionist who, in spite of her rigid principles and through her own innocence, becomes intoxicated. Although May Irwin never moved from her chair in playing the part, her "jag" was evidently as convincing a performance as had been seen on the stage, and the comic effect seems to have been devastating to the vaudeville audiences. When she is reviving from her alcoholic haze, her husband assures her that she had only taken two drinks, she replies, "And the strange part of it is that they never had the slightest effect on me!"[8]

During the first decade of the new century Ade was tremendously successful as a writer for the legitimate stage and musical comedy, and his plays, *The Sultan of Sulu* (musical comedy), *The County Chairman* (realistic rural drama), and *The College Widow* (first of the musical comedies to deal with college life) were the basis of his reputation. But, as he acknowledged himself, "I had good luck with the one-act plays after May Irwin . . . started me on a life of shame. 'Marse Covington,' 'The Mayor and the Manicure,' 'Nettie,' and 'Speaking to Father' managed to get by and hang on for the usual span of life."[9]

The reference here to "the life of shame" is not entirely facetious, for there is evidence that George Ade felt, if only intermittently, that vaudeville drama was more than ritual for the new mass man. In an interview for *Theatre Magazine* in 1904, at the height of his success, Ade could offer the following rather humble and commonplace statement of his intentions as a dramatist: "If I have any single ambition in reference to the stage . . . . it is to depict every-day American life in such a manner as to amuse the public and not offend good taste. If, indirectly, I can touch upon some of the weaknesses and foibles of the present moment without slandering my countrymen, or holding our home folk up to ridicule, the plays will have a value which never can attach to an entertainment that is merely farcical."[10] Ade underestimated, in such statements, the quality of the realism which would set him off from such sentimental writers as Cressy and Steell. Instead of the mellow glow of sentimentalism, Ade's plays would radiate an ironic glitter. Where one might expect contrition, forgiveness, and warmth there was inclined to be, in their stead, a cynical self-satisfaction, or bitterness, or indifference. In his own way, however, Ade did stay within the frame of reference created by the tradition of sentimentality and melodrama. The negations which he cultivated for dramatic effect were subtle gestures of criticism rather than outright denials, and if he could face the corruptions and antagonisms of modern life with greater honesty than did his fellow playwrights, often his work betrays an attitude of amazement and surprise which stems from a basic, fundamentally naive, moralism.

If we take, for example, *The Mayor and the Manicure*, we find the ingredients of a sober, sentimental one-act. The Honorable Otis Milford, mayor of Springfield and potential candidate for governor, is accosted in his office by a "loud and showy" female who claims to have a hold upon the mayor's son—or at least letters written by that impetuous undergraduate. The audience is given to understand, however, that not only is Mayor Milford's career at stake, but also the welfare of "the best mother a boy ever had" and the happiness of the sweet, innocent female who doubles as the mayor's secretary and the son's fiancée. Within the situation Ade finds material not for tearful self-sacrifice but for hearty farce. The mayor is a resourceful and experienced politician who turns the tables on Genevieve, "the manicure," through the use of a dummy telephone and through shrewdly guessing that she already possesses a husband. He makes great sport of her sentimental yarn as to how the boy pursued her and played upon her heart. "That pup?" scoffs Milford. And in good-natured sympathy with the woman's attempt at fraud, he finally gives her one thousand dollars, nine thousand less than she had demanded. As the son and his fiancée scamper happily off stage before the curtain, the mayor and the manicurist shake hands in token of their common experience in the ways of the world, and in a piece of realistic dialogue, anomalous in a moral universe, they expose their complacent self-sufficiency.

GENEVIEVE (*Insinuating*). Won't you come out and have lunch with me?
MILFORD. You trot along, Genevieve. You've got yours. I had mine thirty years ago.
GENEVIEVE (*Goes to door, laughing heartily, turns and waves her hand at him*). Good-bye![11]

Similarly in *Nettie*, we find two swindled suitors accepting their lot as fools and retiring in sardonic gaiety from the field, leaving two diamond horseshoes for the adorable schemer, Nettie.

George Ade, like professional writers in many fields, recognized the sentimental and satirical possibilities in the pastoral myth of the Old South. Among all the glorifications of American rural life, the mythic figures of the southern colonel, his decorative women folk, his imposing plantation house, and his loyal Negro servants, were the most blatantly idealized—and most easily deflated for the urban masses. In his playlet, *Marse Covington*, Ade drew upon two of these stereotypes, yet offered a rather subtle and ironic comment upon their fate in the post-Reconstruction decades. The condition upon which these symbols of the old order could be presented to the mass audience, was, of course, that they serve the Myth of Success—a piece of manipulation that presented difficulties on all sides. As a skillful meeting of this problem, Ade's *Marse Covington* offers an informative comparison with another up-dated Southern pastoral drama by Will S. Cressy, in collaboration with Ira Dodge, called *My Old Kentucky Home*.

The plots differ considerably, even though the underlying implications lie close together. In *Marse Covington*, the colonel has lost his wealth and family prior to the action of the play, but retains all of his arrogance and illusions. In the city to which he has wandered, he meets Uncle Dan, "a slavery-days Negro" and latter-day Uncle Tom who has become significantly, a doorkeeper for a gambling establishment. The slight action revolves about the attempt of "Marse Covington" to gain entrance through the steel front door to the casino by working upon the old Negro's sense of loyalty. In *My Old Ken-*

tucky Home, Will Cressy's colonel is faced with the prospect that his only daughter, Jasmine, will run off with a slick-talking, automobile-driving Yankee with the hated name of "Grant."

In both plays the colonels, and with them the proud plantation tradition, go under in radical defeat, and only a shred of their former dignity is left to them. Uncle Dan kindly plays upon the illusions of his former master, describing the gamblers within as "no-good trash," not worth even thrashing, and fabricating a story about some money he had once stolen back on the plantation as a pretext for giving the colonel a ten-dollar bill. The colonel assures Uncle Dan that his prospects are improving and that he will soon want the Negro as a retainer again in "an establishment of my own here in New York." The pathetic close of the play has Uncle Dan conscience-struck by what he realizes as his ultimate betrayal of the Southern myth:

DAN. He got in here mos' befo' I knew it.
[GAMBLER]. Well?
DAN. I threw him *out*.

[GAMBLER]. Good! (*Exits R.*)
DAN. (*Sinking down, sobbing*). Yes, suh, *I threw him out*. I threw him out!¹²

The decline of Cressy's southern colonel is less cleverly arranged, for he discovers in the course of the play that death by heart disease is imminent. When accused by the young suitor of being "a selfish old man," he grimly relinquishes his daughter and retreats into a dream of the past, which he has described during the course of the play: "I was lookin' away off into those years when yo' mammie and I sat hyar under these magnolia trees and watched the little girl playing among the roses and

180

the jasmines we had named her for. And ma old eyes couldn't see the little gal today—standing on the verge of womanhood, looking out across the years into her great big world that her mammie and daddie had never thought or dreamed of. (Smiles sadly)."[13] The original version of the play contained an explicit, wholesale assault upon myth of plantation life, which Grant describes as existence in a "Godforsaken swamp," but the version in which George W. Wilson appeared along the vaudeville circuits in 1907 omitted this harsh comment upon the subject matter of the play, still an object for nostalgia by the community which had superseded it. But as in *Marse Covington* the commitment of playwright and audience to the doctrine of inevitable progress toward an essentially better world is unmistakable. City life may contain hard-boiled gamblers and automobiles whose odors contaminate the pure air of the agrarian countryside (a point referred to several times in Cressy's play) but with the capitalist gamblers and the efficient machine lay the sources of the better life.

For the playlets to turn from the themes of rural drama to those of city life was no easy matter; although the vaudeville ritual encouraged a vague and generalized symbolism, it shied away from too particularized representations of the successful life. That somehow this life would satisfy basic cravings of the mass man—including that of sexual gratification—and that somehow he would enjoy the blessings of wealth, was certainly promised, but exactly how sex and money were to be obtained was largely left to the imagination. But the religious-ethical norms of the middle class were imposed upon the ritual through public pressure, and certainly the enjoyment of sex outside of marriage and the accumulation of wealth outside of the channels of busi-

181

ness or the professions was abhorrent to this middle class. Thus it is that free sex and free wealth (crime) became the highly volatile and sensitive materials with which the skillful molders of the playlet began, around 1905, to concern themselves.

Among the more prominent of these craftsmen were Edgar Allen Woolf, Gordon V. May, Harry L. Newton, Aaron Hoffman, Edwin Muir Royle, and O. E. Young. The transition from rural nostalgia to the themes of city life is sharply indicated in the career of Gordon V. May, for example. May made his original name with such full-length plays as *Bar Haven* and *Red Acre Farms*, but in 1913 he published a collection of theatrical pieces containing, among a wide variety of subjects, a playlet called *After Many Years*, in which a wealthy young widow discovers that a burglar that she surprises is "an old lover," and a playlet named *For the Sake of a Thousand*, in which an artist, attempting to persuade his cronies that he is still a bachelor, dresses his wife in male clothing and passes her off as an effeminate Englishman.[14]

But probably the most accomplished and versatile of these playwrights, one who was considered a "master tailor" in creating roles for legitimate actors, was Edgar Allen Woolf. In the mid-twenties David Belasco was to "discover" Woolf, but by that time Woolf was already credited with two hundred and fourteen plays, playlets, and musical comedies which had been actually performed and some forty others that were never played. Woolf—who had studied under Professors Matthews and Price at Columbia and who made no secret of his familiarity with Aristotle's *Poetics* and Freytag's *Technique of the Drama*—was quite candid about his method of creating a playlet. "When a star comes to me," he explained to an interviewer, "and asks me for a playlet for vaudeville, before I write a line I make a study of the star's former successes in order that I may know just exactly what he represents to the public." In such a fashion he constructed *Lullaby* and *America* for Vera Gordan, *Youth* for Mrs. Gene Hughes, *When Pompadour Was Queen* for Fritzi Sheff, and *Rings of Smoke* for Pat Rooney.

To Woolf, the problems of his art were chiefly technical ones: how to create a dramatic character best suited to the particular performer, how to use costume and setting to exploit the stage personality, how to develop action which would best utilize the dramatic (or musical) talents of the "headliner." These problems were by no means simple ones, and we have Woolf's testimony that the audience in the vaudeville palace was "the most exacting and most difficult audience there is to please." He found that just as much color, action, and dramatic intensity was expected of a twenty-minute skit as would be of a full-length drama. By the twenties, he had given up the hope of ever creating any depth of character or subtlety in structure, and in 1924 he was quoted as saying that since his writing for vaudeville was so "disheartening," he would soon leave the field for other pastures.[15]

Woolf's astute handling of sex in the modern world is typified by *The Lollard,* a playlet described by Brett Page as a "satirical comedy." The comic situation around which the drama develops is the disillusionment of a young wife, who finds that her mate no longer appeals to her. In this state she becomes momentarily involved with a younger, handsomer man in the same apartment, but, through the accidents of the plot and the firm management of her spinster friend, is returned to her husband. Around this basic story-line is built a veil of rollicking humor and irony so that neither the suggestion

183

of marital infidelity, nor even the strong sexual appetites of the characters themselves are more than dimly glimpsed. It is a play which glosses the problem without striking very far at the discontent and frustration which motivate not only the husband and wife, but also the other two apartment dwellers.

The action of *The Lollard* takes place in the apartment of Miss Carey, described as "a hardworking modiste about 45 years of age, rather sharp in manner, very prudish and a hater of men." Into this apartment, uninvited, rushes the ingenue, Angela Maxwell, who announces to the unsympathetic Miss Carey: "Listen, you don't know me, but I've just left my husband." Then, over tea, Angela spills out her troubles. Harry, the husband, it seems, was dashingly handsome at their first meeting at a military ball, but after the wedding he neglected his appearance. Thus, his hair, which had been parted north-to-south and east-to-west in order to conceal the bare patches, was no longer combed "fancy," his shoulders were bereft of their pads, his feet began to look like canal boats, and that very night he had ceased to wear hemstitched pajamas and put on a "cotton flannel night shirt."

After the tea and conversation, both ladies retire —Angela on the couch—but immediately a handsome young man enters the room. Miss Carey explains that he is her "gentleman boarder" and introduces him as Fred Saltus. Miss Carey returns to her bed behind the curtain, while Fred, discovering that Angela has left her husband, begins to make advances. Husband knocks at the door. Fred Saltus retires to his room. Husband (the lollard) enters and a comic arguement ensues. Miss Carey appears, sends Angela to the bedroom, and tells the husband he is a "lollard" and should continue to fool his

184

wife because women want to be fooled. In one of Woolf's delicate aphorisms, Miss Carey scolds: "You can't blame a little woman if she thinks she's getting a man of gold and she finds out she's got a gold brick."

Harry sees his fault and goes off to preen himself. Miss Carey then, upon hearing from Angela that she is in love with Fred Saltus, sets the stage for what Brett Page describes as Angela's "moment of recognition." The spinster cries "Fire" and Fred bursts from his room in his cotton flannel nightshirt, without toupee, *et cetera*. "Where? Where's the fire?" he cries. Miss Carey replies, "Go back to your bed, Mr. Saltus. There was a fire." Harry knocks at the door, Angela opens it, and there he stands in regimentals: "Handsome, young and dapper." Angela purrs, "I'm so tired, Harry—take me home." As he lifts his tired little wife up in his arms, she mutters, "You're not such a bad lollard after all." Significantly, this is not the curtain line, for Miss Carey says, "Now, thank Gawd, I'll get a little sleep."[16]

Somewhere in this little comedy, beneath the frantic entrances and exits, beneath the comic repartee and the virtuoso performance of the kittenish Angela, and beneath the heavy ironies of the plot, lie rather sentimental assumptions, but as in many of the more sophisticated vaudeville comedies, the message of forgiveness and love is diluted with a heady dose of sexiness and wit. Angela is allowed to parade prettily around stage in her pajamas and the appearance of the "gentleman boarder" occasions a number of *double entendres*. Woolf works easily with these caricatures of the demure wife, the handsome suitor, and the spinster, and he manages to shade nicely the blunter edges of the stereotypes. The setting and the situation are convincing enough —an apartment house and a nighttime squabble.

But this is as far as Woolf, or his fellow playwrights, could afford to go within the limits imposed by the current standards of taste and within the time limits imposed by the ritual. Successful sexuality in the playlets, as in the songs and dances of the ritual, was symbolized by physical glamour and all difficulties were easily banished through mutual forgiveness and self-denial, the sentimental ethic of the rural drama transplanted to the city.

In comparable manner, these professional playwrights turned to the problem of wealth and managed to devise a basic formula which was dramatically exciting and which yet contained a symbolic implication of extreme seriousness. This formula, developed in well over 10 percent of the playlets produced on the vaudeville stage, runs something like this. Setting: house of affluent member of the middle class, after dark with only a hall light dimly burning. Curtain: a window slowly opens and a shadowy figure appears, looks around, and then turns on more lights. As this character searches the room, he places valuable possessions into a sack or grip and looks furtively over his shoulder or into the hall from time to time, but he discovers nothing. Nevertheless, he is caught unaware by one of the residents and a situation, potentially violent, develops. No serious harm is done, however, and before the police appear the resident either (a) heroically captures the burglar, or (b) nobly forgives him and sends him on his way, or (c) the impasse is resolved through such familiar theatrical devices as mistaken identity or *deus ex machina*. In any case there is bound to be about twenty minutes of discussion and five or ten minutes of climactic action.

The playlet in which the wealthy widow discovers her former lover in such a situation and shields him from the police has already been touched upon. In comparable fashion, a detective in *Kid Glove Nan* learns that the notorious female burglar of this name has fallen into crime because she was an orphan and, being an orphan himself, he protects her from the law.[17] The storekeeper in *The Alarm* discovers that among the thieves who had emptied his safe was his own son, and since within the canons of sentimental drama familial responsibility precedes civic duty, the father delays the police until his boy is safely aboard his train.[18]

This is not to say that the criminals of these playlets were always long-lost lovers or relatives, and, indeed, there are a number of one-acts which serve to make attractive the cleverness of the professional criminal at the expense of the police. In one play, *A Crooked Man and His Crooked Wife*, we are led to admire the ingenuity with which the wife of a wanted man is able, by clever impersonation, to protect her husband from a particularly dogged detective who has traveled around the world in pursuit of him.[19] And in Edward Harold Crosby's *The Cat's Paw*, we watch a poor, uneducated immigrant caught in the act of burglarizing a house by a resourceful, but sympathetic patrician named Manners.[20] After roundly scolding the poor man and making him surrender his loot, Manners sends him back out the window; and the lordly Manners then finishes his raid of the premises and exits, as he had entered, by the front door. In such plays as Taylor Granville's *The System* and Willard Mack's *Kick-In* (after its success in vaudeville this play was expanded into a full-length drama) the sympathy with the criminal is so far developed that the police are exposed as lacking in both wit and warmth — that is, when they are not absolutely corrupt.[21] Occasionally the police are useful for last-minute rescues, but very seldom does there appear an official with the intelligence, courage, or will to protect the public.

The implications of these playlets are, in retrospect, obvious enough. The search for wealth in its more acquisitive and brutal forms may be undesirable, but it is certainly a drive with which the mass audience must, because of its own commitments to the Myth of Success, sympathize. Better that the resourceful and ambitious be converted and domesticized than handed over to capricious and impersonal authorities. The resentment of the working classes against the squeeze imposed upon them by the industrial revolution comes to a psychological boil in such plays, but also sentimental assumptions about human nature are skillfully manifest in their plots. That the wealth being sought generally belongs to the upper middle class and that this class is in control of the police is implicit in the formula. That the part of the burglar was often played by the featured actor or actress only further points up this symbolism.

One play, however, stands out as a reversal of this basic formula. This one-act, *Miss Civilization*, adapted by Richard Harding Davis from a short story by James Harvey Smith, was created for Ethel Barrymore, who first appeared in the title role in 1906.

Davis had been rapidly proving his competence as a playwright at this time; in the legitimate theater his *The Galloper* and *The Dictator* had both been well received, and the vaudeville one-acts *Blackmail* and *The Littlest Girl* were soon to appear. *Miss Civilization* opened at the Broadway Theatre in New York, but its greatest popularity was to be on the vaudeville stage, where Ethel Barrymore played it off-and-on for nearly a decade.[22]

In the playlet Miss Barrymore is a dignified, self-possessed young lady of the upper classes—the daughter, as she proudly announces, of James K. Gardner, president of the L. I. and W. Railroad. Contemporary journalists saw the "Gibson girl" as an appropriate counterpart to the "Davis man," the square-jawed, athletic adventurer of Davis's novels, and the part of Alice Gardner was perhaps the writer's own approximation of the lofty, cool Gibson-girl type. Alice, upon discovering that three men are breaking into the richly furnished house where she and her ailing mother are spending the night alone (except for the maidservants who are asleep), telephones her father's railroad and arranges to have a carload of trainmen surround the house. She then welcomes the thieves and begins to entertain them with choice food and liquor in order to detain them until the rescue party arrives. She instinctively patronizes these representatives of the lower classes, and their response to her poised charm is, like that of the audience, general bewilderment. When she asks that the flashlight beam be taken out of her eyes, the leader of the three says "Don't you do it. Keep the gun on her." "Oh, I don't mind his pointing the gun at me," Alice states, "so long as he does not point that light at me. It's most embarrassing. (*Sternly*) Turn it down there, please."

Of course, most of Alice's appeal rests in her calculated naiveté. She stands with her hand on the back of a chair as she addresses the leader, Hatch, who has boasted of twenty years experience in crime.

ALICE. Now, I want to ask you some questions. You are an intelligent man. Of course, you must be, or you couldn't have kept out of jail for twenty years. To get on in your business a man must be intelligent, and he must have nerve and courage. Now—with those qualities, why, may I ask—why are you so stupid as to be a burglar?

189

Hatch debates this question with her, not sus-
pecting that she is deliberately delaying him, and
justifies himself by the "fame and big money and a
free life in my business." Alice retorts with a moral
lecture denying the right of these men to success on
their terms.

ALICE. Yes: It's a free life until you go to jail. It's
this way. You're barbarians, and there is no place for
you in a civilized community—except in jail. Everybody is working against you. Every city has its police
force; almost every house nowadays has a private watch-
man. And if we want to raise a hue and cry after you,
there are the newspapers and the telegraph and the
telephone (*nods at telephone*) and the cables all over the—

Hatch interrupts her at the mention of the telephone
and cuts the cord.

Her "Civilization" conquers, of course, with the
arrival of engineers, brakemen, and police who dash
across the lawn and overpower the thieves before
they realize that they have been deceived. That
Alice has fulfilled an obligation to organized society
is implicit in the police chief's line: "My congratulations, Miss Gardner. They're the worse lot in the
country. You're a brave young lady. You ought—"
But Alice breaks in, "speaking with an effort and
slightly swaying," and lets us know in her curtain
line that she is still feminine and still aware of her
filial duties also. "Hush, please," she says to the
police, "Don't—don't alarm my mother. My mother's not as strong as—as I am." The stage direction
indicates that she closes her eyes and "faints across
the arm of the Chief of Police."[23]
It took the combined authority of Davis and
Barrymore, of course, to make a vaudeville playlet
an occasion to lecture the masses, and their depar-
ture from the formula was not openly criticized. But
very seldom in these plays do figures of the social
or economic status of Alice Gardner come off as well

DOC ROCKWELL

CONSUL THE GREAT

as she did in this play, and only the callous and brutish character of Hatch and his fellows justifies her strong defense of the commercial establishment of which she is a symbolic representative. That her father's wealth is retained by force is made apparent, and similarly her sexual detachment from these rough men is based upon strongly entrenched social habits. Her possessive insularity, based upon chastity and wealth, may have been feared by the mass audience, but it also served to symbolize an enviable success.

The gambit by the vaudeville managers—the offering of well calculated snippets of drama based upon contemporary life—appears to have been successful, partially because of a plentiful supply of actors and actresses from the legitimate stage but also because of the rapid development of a guild of writer-craftsmen who understood the demands of vaudeville as a media. By 1914, not only had Brett Page's thoroughly professional book, *Writing for Vaudeville*, appeared, but also a number of magazine articles under such titles as "Vaudeville Appeal and the Heart Wallop," and "Advice to Vaudeville Playwrights."[24] While Belasco and Frohman were pushing show business toward the heavily costumed feature with full stages and long performances, the vaudeville playwrights were learning the lessons of compression, immediacy, and the exploitation of talent—virtues upon which radio and television were subsequently to place a great premium. Among all of the entertainment forms of the first two decades of this century, vaudeville seemed to move most surely toward the efficient and effective use of resources appropriate to an advanced technology. Ironically enough, of course, the microphone and motion picture camera were to displace the vaudeville stage by virtue of their even greater efficiency and effectiveness.

Some idea of the hard-headed calculation that went into the vaudeville playlets can be gathered from Page's handbook. There were, for example, ready-made sets in all of the larger vaudeville houses, and the writer who could tailor his drama to one of these had reduced the cost of production considerably. A standard box-set could usually be adapted for four basic scenes: center-door fancy, the parlor set, the kitchen set, and the office set. And the timing of a playlet also imposed definite limitations upon the writer. Exits and entrances, costume changes, interpolated songs, or dances—even the heavily emotional scenes were timed with stopwatch precision. A time plot for a one-act musical comedy reveals nine separate pieces of business, each allotted a unit of time of from two to seven minutes. A sample from this rather extensive list reads: "Opening ensemble . . . 2 minutes; Dialogue introducing plot . . . 4 minutes; Solo . . . 3 minutes." The climax, "a big love scene," takes a full seven minutes, leading into a "duet . . . 4 minutes"; and finally, in two remaining minutes, come the "dialogue: plot solution—the final arrangement of characters." Add to these problems those of the wardrobe, stage lighting, and the particular demands of a leading man or lady—to say nothing of the problems of staying in "good taste," while introducing novel and striking dramatic elements— and one can appreciate the competence, if not the originality, of the best vaudeville writers.[25]

This emphasis upon technique, together with the kinds of symbolism and thematic material employed in the vaudeville playlet, paved the way toward the two-reelers, soap operas, and television detective dramas and westerns of subsequent decades. Fifteen to thirty minute drama was to become staple fare in American entertainment.

NINE

The Palaces

THE TWENTY-FOURTH OF March, 1894, two days before the opening performance at B. F. Keith's New Theatre in Boston, two thousand invited guests, including "leading dignitaries of the State and city" as well as "representatives of the wealth and culture of New England," inspected this luxurious building and admired, if one is to believe the publicity releases, its beauty, its comfort, and its safety.[1] Mrs. Ella Butler Evans reported in the Augusta (Georgia) *Herald*: "The age of luxury seems to have reached its ultima thule. The truth of this has never been impressed upon one so forcibly as in a visit to Keith's dream palace of a theatre. . . .It is almost incredible that all this elegance should be placed at the disposal of the public, the poor as well as the rich."[2]

Such journalistic hyperbole was needed to do justice to this amazing edifice, and to others like it around the country. Not even American state houses captured quite so much glare and opulent color as did these adaptations of southern European architecture. To the mass man Keith had brought a literal elegance and scale which had been the exclusive property of the privileged classes, but the rococo filigree and the polished marble were symbolic also and reinforced the rituals played out upon the stage. They were testimony to the success of vaudeville, to the success of the showman who had brought them into being, but, even more, to the ideals of material comfort, pleasure, and well-being which were the property of all who might enter. For the American audience such palaces represented a denial of both smalltown architecture and of the sooty dullness of commercial buildings. The magnificence of such public buildings as the Boston Public Library, which the firm of McKim, Mead, and White had designed a few years before in a more austere version of a "Renaissance style," could only approximate the aura of gaiety and release evoked by these buoyant symbols of the new city.

To some extent the assimilation into vaudeville theaters of materials and motifs characteristic of public buildings and private palaces from Vienna to Lisbon was a reflection of the shifts in American taste brought about by the altered pattern of immigration during the last decades of the nineteenth century. Whereas the architects of the Genteel Tradition had seen in the architecture of Italy and had translated into terms of the United States the qualities of fluidity and proportion, the peasants and artisans of southern Europe had perceived in their architecture its grosser qualities, its color, profligacy, and grandeur. The palaces, which the European masses had regarded from afar but which in the New World they were permitted to enter, and the cathedrals had testified alike to further dimensions in life than those of field and marketplace. To the immigrant the spiritual promise of his religion had been manifest in the hues, lines, and lights of the cathedrals, and when he came to the secular society of the United States, he could not help seeing the symbolic promise—not for the life hereafter but for the present life—in the vaudeville palaces. By its proportions and decor the vaudeville palace made easier the immigrant's translation from the rites of a ceremonial religion to the ritual of secular amusement.

Keith's New Theatre was not, of course, the first of the elaborate show palaces to rise upon the American urban scene: Madison Square Garden, noted for its capacity of 40,000 persons and the chaste dignity of its Italian Renaissance decor, had preceded Keith by a few years, and both the Metropolitan Opera House in New York and the Chicago Auditorium had been completed before 1894.[3] But Keith's theater did have two claims to distinction. It was the first of the palatial vaudeville houses, for many years unrivaled in size or magnificence except by the over-ambitious Proctor's Pleasure Palace. And, it was the first of the new, grand theaters in New England, anticipating by six months the opening of the Castle Square, a legitimate theater on Tremont Street, smaller than Keith's, but even more lavishly appointed. All of these theaters—in and out of vaudeville—were symbols of material progress, of course, and the lesson of enterprise was not, in any case, lost upon the public. The Boston *Herald* took special note of B. F. Keith's New Theatre and was quick to point out its significance in the context of American capitalism. Its editorial congratulations were extended not only to Keith but to the city itself, as it boasted that "Keith has given to Boston the proud distinction of possessing the handsomest and most costly theatre in America, and the finest place of amusement in the world owned and controlled by one individual."

That European playhouses and opera houses had to some extent anticipated this generous luxuriousness appears to be true, but the American theaters, like Keith's New Theatre, were faced by quite different problems from those posed by European cities. Whereas the European playhouses generally stood isolated on sizable plots of ground, the vaudeville palaces had to be squeezed into the valuable real estate left between large department stores and commercial offices in downtown areas. Such a problem was met by the New Theatre in Boston, and the bold solution of it pointed out the way to rather unique architectural conceptions.

In essence, Keith's architects met the problem of crowding a theater onto a narrow lot by a concentrated variety of ornamental detail on the front of the theater and by a system of foyers and lobbies which whetted the expectations of the audience as it approached the house proper. The narrow frontage upon Washington Street was covered with a plentitude of decorative detail — ornamental iron work, stained glass, pediments, cornices, and incandescent lighting — proclaiming loudly the presence of Amusement among the stolid, work-weary faces of hotels, department stores, and office buildings. Here the brownstone hostility of the crowding structures on either side was relieved by a bold opening on the street level, framed by an arch on marble pillars, bearing a transom of opalescent glass with the inscription "B. F. Keith's New Theatre" prominently in the center. A dozen large electric lamps were placed along the arch and also high among the pilasters and gargoyles of the second and third story facade. On either side of the grand entrance, just within the loggia, were two circular ticket offices constructed of "Sienna marble" and plate glass, and surmounted by domes fancifully worked in stereorelief and embellished with touches of gold and ivory. From the street one could glimpse, through this wide penetration, the inlaid mosaic in the floor of the loggia, and the wainscoting of "Sienna marble" relieved by large, brightly polished mirrors.[4] All this brilliance, the passing shopper or salesman knew, was only a taste of what lay inside—for only about twenty-five cents admission.

The narrow lot which made necessary the sequence of lobbies and corridors leading from the street to the orchestra and balconies was utilized to its full advantage, both as display space and for the circulation of large numbers of people. In making one's way toward a seat in the house one first passed through a lobby foyer in Nile green containing an ornamental fireplace with a marble mantle and a large plate mirror. Then one entered the main foyer with its walls in "rich old rose," mirrors again, and large panel paintings "by the eminent artist Tojetti," marble wainscoting, a floor of white marble tile, "elegant vases and jardinaires," "a magnificent hall clock," "sofas and tete-a-tetes [sic] in frameworks of burnished brass, and upholstered in leather"—all lit by three hundred incandescent lamps in fixtures of brass burnished to a gold finish. From this foyer one might climb up or down on large marble staircases to rooms for gentlemen and ladies, or pass through swinging doors, upholstered with leather and decorated with silver plates, to the orchestra

197

reception-room. Through three gigantic archways one gained the auditorium, an equally gorgeous place with walls treated in green and rose "in a brocaded silk effect," cherry wainscoting to the rear of the orchestra, and convenient railings upholstered in soft, green plush. Looking upward from the front of the house one could see the balconies carefully worked in white and gold similar to that which appeared on the twelve private boxes, six on either side of the auditorium. Even the ceiling had been carefully designed with hand paintings and stereo-relief so that nowhere was one conscious of the sheer mass and great weight such a structure represented, but only aware of its spaciousness, its lightness, and its exotic grandeur. Above the heavily gilded proscenium arch were three more panels by Tojetti, from which draped ladies of heroic proportions, emblematic of Dancing, Comedy and Music, beckoned the viewer to join them and their cupids in a chaste carouse.[5]

Keith's New Theatre was not entirely a creation of the fancy, nor was it dedicated to a literal duplication of the baroque. Exits and entrances were planned to provide egress from the building in case of fire, and all floors were furnished with wide iron fire escapes. Public statements asserted that "Almost every appliance for extinguishing fire known to science is at hand at all times, and the stage, besides being provided with a fire-proof curtain, could in ten seconds be drenched with a perfect torrent of water." Technology had also contributed to heating and ventilation, for like other large theaters constructed during the nineties, Keith's contained a large fan in the basement which sent warm air from the furnace (or cool air in the summer) up through the interstices in the iron framework of the seats. Ventilators under the balconies and in the dome released the rising air. An electric light plant in a sub-basement generated sufficient power to light 6,000 units of sixteen candlepower apiece; the cost of electrical installations in the theater supposedly reached $60,000. Stage lighting as advanced as any then in existence was controlled from a switchboard measuring six by seven feet, containing thirty-four 50 ampere double pole switches and twenty-seven regulators. These could be manipulated separately or through connecting rheostatic switches operated in series to produce various intensities of light in both the stage and house.[6]

As some of these details of construction indicate, the planners of American theaters were not solely concerned with the sensual man and his response. Audiences were made up of prudent, practical persons who were well informed by the press of the dangers in mass gatherings, particularly the threat of fire. All knew of the great city fires of Chicago and San Francisco, and particularly the theater fires—the worst of which was the Iroquois Theatre fire in Chicago in 1906 in which hundreds of lives were lost. What made the Iroquois Theatre tragedy so impressive was that the building itself was less than a decade old at the time and had been constructed according to the most approved methods of the time. The gains in space which the use of structural steel brought about had decreased the danger of direct burns from the flames themselves but had introduced two more lethal dangers: the generation of hot air in a confined space such as the flyloft with a capability of asphyxiating an entire balcony full of persons before they could leave their seats, and the hysteria of the audience as it becomes a blind mob seeking egress and crushing those who fall before it. In the Iroquois Theatre fire the crowds had funneled into a blind alley with terrific loss of

199

life. Although that theater had been designed to be emptied in five minutes, firemen had reported a steady stream of people leaving the building for fifteen minutes after the initial outbreak of the fire.

Keith's New Theatre and Proctor's Pleasure Palaces had already by 1906 taken many of the necessary precautions. A longitudinal section of Proctor's reveals two large vents over the hanging loft for the release of smoke; Keith's stage could be drenched "with a perfect torrent of water" within ten seconds of an alarm.[7] Some fifty exits throughout the entire Palace were available to the patrons of Proctor's, and there were separate staircases for the gallery, dressing rooms, and box seats. On the Fifty-eighth Street side of the building was a large outside balcony, which was supposed to be of use to the audience attempting to leave, and also to firemen. On the ground floor were five emergency exits from the auditorium proper: two of six feet in width at the rear of the foyer, two more to the left, and a twelve-foot exit leading directly from the right side of the auditorium to Fifty-eighth Street. At Keith's model theater there were three large exits to the rear of the parquet, three on the right side, a public exit to Mason Street from the opposite side and four exits from the stage—all in addition to the main exit on Washington Street. The upper tiers opened onto iron fire escapes as well as onto their regular wide staircases.[8] We must assume, of course, that local ordinances forced many of these precautions upon the proprietors, but there is reason to feel that such managers as Keith and Proctor were anxious to preserve their reputations and those of their circuits, to say nothing of their huge investments in combustible property.

Structural steel had brought other problems than those of safety. From the initial trials of German

200

and English engineers in the seventies and eighties, builders had learned to produce theaters in which the stage was comfortably visible from nearly every portion of the house and in which the acoustics were remarkably improved. American architects seem to have gone a step further than their British or German fellows in the projection of the upper tiers into the auditorium, conveniently close to the stage. According to published figures, the balcony in Proctor's Pleasure Palace was only thirty-three feet from the curtain, the gallery front thirty-six feet; the balcony in Keith's New Theatre was about forty-four feet distant from the stage and the gallery only a few feet more. Compare these figures with the fifty-two foot reach of the Lessing Theatre in Berlin (ca. 1888), with the sixty-two feet of empty air in the Royal Alhambra of London (1883), or the fifty-seven foot gap from curtain to balcony of the Paragon Variety Theatre of London.[9]

Perhaps the Americans were fortunate in not having the traditional "pit" to influence their designs; perhaps they built larger balconies because of the increased number of medium-priced seats they would provide; but whatever the reason, the gain in terms of immediacy and clarity would appear to have been considerable. Unfortunately the size of the balconies seems to have precluded the bold use of cantilever girders to support the upper tiers, and thus iron posts dotted the auditoriums and obstructed sight from a few seats in even the best of the palaces. Further efficiency was promoted, however, by the narrowness of many American theaters, excepting of course those which had been converted from the old-time opera houses, for one finds most of the vaudeville theaters with proscenium widths of less than forty feet.[10] The reduced opening naturally served to channel sound from the stage and direct it forward into the house, and the elimination of excess beams and supports inside the dome tended to give sound an easier passage to the audience. Another advantage of the general narrowness of the vaudeville houses was that it encouraged experimentation with seating arrangements. In the parquet, especially, the judicious combinations of straight, parallel rows in front and semi-circular rows toward the rear, and the gentle incline of the floor in order to give the maximum of vision, show that McElfatrick and Sons, at least, were sensitive to the problems of hearing and seeing.[11]

Such efficiency in architecture, and in other phases of management as well, explains a great deal about the rise of vaudeville. From the first, the managers, unfettered by traditional notions of what "good theater" might be, were responsive to public demands and were willing to test new techniques for attracting larger audiences. No better example of their inspired opportunism exists than that of the first "continuous performance." Keith's letters retell the story of its origin on July 6, 1885: "The continuous performance idea came to me as a sort of half-dream between waking and sleeping, about two years before I tried it. I had forgotten about it entirely, until the summer of 1885, when I was at my wit's end what to do in order to have the appearance of success, or in other words, to have an audience. I found that when the curtain was lowered everyone left the place, and it was hard to get others in for the next performance." Keith adds parenthetically, "I have never since been at a loss to know what to do as regards policy." The first act on the bill that day was S. K. Hodgdon who lectured on "The Arctic Moon," a small, handmade newspaper composed by the members of a U. S. expedition who had suffered and died through the long arctic night of 1883-1884. (Keith subsequently kept the small newspaper on the wall of his office, protected by glass, perhaps to remind his associates how much can be done with very little.) When Keith had informed Hodgdon that he was to go on immediately after the concluding act, he is supposed to have replied, "Really, Mr. Keith, it's no use to go out there; they are all the same people and have been here for two hours now, but of course I will go if you say so." "Well, Sam," Keith said, "I'd rather you would."[12]

Once started, the "continuous performance" was largely responsible for changing Keith from a proprietor of a small museum to the owner of a circuit of theaters. Hodgdon, who was later to become president of the United Booking Office, had not recognized what Keith had dimly perceived. Amusement for the city-dweller had ceased to be merely the evening pastime of the leisure class and had long outgrown the older traditions of the holiday gathering for circus or carnival. No single time schedule could accommodate the many different routines of city folk and only round-the-clock amusement, available for whatever duration of leisure one might have, could hope to draw the mass audience. For the members of the audience which Sam faced for the second time that day, in 1885, the repetition of his lecture was far more satisfying than being emptied back on the street with another hour or two of leisure to while away. Two decades later some of Keith's larger theaters had been converted back to the "two-a-day," but the policy of meeting public demand had been established. For the early risers and for the farmers who had brought in an early morning load of produce to the market there was a "milkman's matinee," and for the benefit of those who wished to catch the late evening train back to the suburbs, the last performance ended at 10:30.[13] Proctor had a similar experience in New York. During his partnership with Charles Frohman in 1889 he had noted that their theater on Twenty-third Street commanded a valuable location for attracting women who would come in from the suburbs for the day to the nearby shops and department stores. When he separated from Frohman, he had begun a two-a-day policy with full vaudeville, but then, evidently learning of Keith's tremendous success in Boston, converted to the "continuous" in 1893, running his shows from 11 a.m. to 11 p.m.[14] His advertising slogan for a time was: "After Breakfast go to Proctor's / After Proctor's go to bed."[15] Keith followed with more "continuous" at the Union Square Theatre and during the nineties the trick caught on rapidly with other managers. Some cities did not accept it, Providence for example,[16] but elsewhere it met the problem of amusement for complex city lives. Some harried mothers are supposed to have sent their children off in the morning with a box lunch and then collected them toward evening, often locating their offspring through an announcement from the stage.[17]

Keith's antenna in matters of gentility was E. F. Albee, who was responsible for the palaces' motto of "Cleanliness, Comfort, and Courtesy." The larger Keith theaters maintained large crews of service personnel to provide all three for the benefit of the mass audience, but even the smaller theaters retained costumed ushers and an adequate maintenance staff. Marble walls, mirrors, brass, and carpeting required, of course, constant attention, and the thousands of electrical fixtures which did away with the traditional dinginess of low-cost theaters were maintained by a corps of electricians.[18] Lest the public sit on the plain, wooden benches typical of the variety

204

houses, the vaudeville management provided folding seats, opera chairs, or at the best theaters, "automatic assembly chairs."[19] To protect him from the customary open urinals and dirty, zinc wash basins, Keith offered "a gentleman's smoking and reading room, and the finest toilet and retiring rooms in the country." More delicately, the Keith programs suggested that for the mass woman—henceforth a "lady"—there were "suites of rooms for exclusive use of lady patrons, furnished with dressing cases and every toilet requisite—all free." The delicate sensibilities of the urban folk were further seduced—and their egos gratified—by the distribution through the theaters of "fragrant floral displays," "the purest artesian well water," and "writing materials furnished free—gold pens, sterling silver handles, monogrammed paper and envelopes."[20] Much of this must have been sheer hokum, but Keith knew his audience and its aspirations, and if his theater was not in actuality a private club for millionaires, at least there was no harm—and much profit—in pretending that it was.

Under the byword of "comfort," the palaces became temples to conspicuous consumption. But not only was the patron moved to enjoy a few hours of creature comfort, the attractive hand-out program was bursting with suggestions as to how he could consume more goods and services. The appeal of the advertisements was to glamour through cosmetics and corsets, to the gay life in restaurants and cabarets, or to the victory over the common discomforts of city folk by means of corn plasters and laxatives. By 1915 the full page color advertisements of cigarettes—of all consumer items the most quickly and irradicably consumed—had begun to appear. And for those persons whose hunger for pleasures had outstripped their incomes, there were the invitations of the loan offices to borrow now and pay later.

Such materialism, however, could not fill the pockets of loneliness, and the bigtime palaces tried to recapture some of the lost sense of human contact through a policy of "courtesy." Keith's New Theatre program announced that toilet and retiring rooms on each floor were "in charge of attendants who will extend every courtesy to patrons,"[21] while his chief competition announced that "Politeness is exacted from all who wear the Proctor regalia." Proctor's publicity folder of 1902 stated that "uniformed superintendants, ushers, and attaches [*sic*] pay careful attention to the wants of patrons at all Proctor's theatres."[22] Even William Dean Howells is supposed to have been delighted at the courtesy shown by employees when he visited Keith's.[23]

This notion of service appears to have reached, at times, extravagant extremes. In some theaters printed cards on silver trays were tendered to cigar smokers, requesting them to cease smoking for the convenience of other patrons.[24] The matter of the ladies' hats, those large, opaque displays fashionable in the nineties, proved to be the ultimate extension of Keith's principle of courtesy. So many complaints about them had been received that Keith and Albee in conference decided to meet the problem by prohibiting the hats entirely. After repeated public announcements, this policy was put into effect — courteously, of course. "Some lady would seat herself," Keith recalled, "and either through forgetfulness or ignorance of the regualtion, would not remove her hat. The usher would approach her carefully and state the case, and the hat would immediately come off. Then there would be a round of applause, showing that the audience appreciated it as much as we did." On those few occasions when the lady stood by her right to wear the hat, "Our rule was to have

WILL CRESSY

B. F. KEITH

the party approached by the usher first, second by the assistant head usher, then by the head usher, and lastly by the management, who would request the party to leave if the hat could not be removed." Keith added, "I am happy to say that very few went out."[25]

Courtesy along the vaudeville circuits was carried even into the audience itself, and the gallery gods were generally instructed by means of ushers—and if need be by the police—in the attitudes of well-mannered, polite society. At the inception of his circuit, Keith had taken upon himself the process of uplift and education, as his own account of the opening of his Providence house well illustrates:

I succeeded in securing the largest house in the state, then known as Lowe's Opera House, which had previously played only the highest class of attractions, but its gallery, like many others of this character, was filled with an element, not bad, but inclined to be demonstrative, which had been entirely in conflict with the rules of my one-room establishment with neither gallery or balcony. So during the first performance in this new large house, the gallery commenced its usual demonstrations, most complimentary, but in a very noisy way, so I stepped out onto the stage and explained to this portion of the audience that it would not be allowed to continue these demonstrations any longer. I said, "You can't do that here. You know you did not do it in my other house, and while I know that you mean no harm by it, and only do it from the goodness of your hearts, but others in the audience don't like it, and it does not tend to improve the character of the entertainment, and I know you will agree with me that it is better to omit it hereafter." As I walked off, I received a round of applause from the whole house including the gallery. And that was the last of the noise from the gallery gods.[26]

As Keith later noted, apropos of the gentility and refinement of his theaters, "The public needed to be educated in these matters."[27] What he understood, of course, was that the process of initiation into the new society was a gradual process and that certain elements in the audience were likely to lag behind. The symbolism, however, was clear. Adaptation and survival in the crowded streets, shops, offices, and places of amusement in the city depended upon a recognized code of behavior. That the palaces should be primary symbols of this improvised gentility and expedient courtesy was quite in accord with the basic intention of the vaudeville managers and with the spirit of the ritual as a whole. Success in urban life was a conquest of environment, both social and physical, and while the ritual through word and gesture could communicate the immediate and visceral realization of this conquest, the palaces were its permanent symbols. The vaudeville palaces were not tributes to either humanity or beauty, any more than was the ritual, but were solid and substantial monuments to wealth, power, and prestige. In the shadow of the palaces, as well as in the dim light of the orchestra, the city was no longer a thing of stone and steel and was, in this brief space, filled with human warmth and passion.

In some dim way B. F. Keith worked his way into the heart of this problem and emerged with a further piece of symbolism. It was no freakish coincidence that within a year of the moment when Henry Adams stood rapt in meditation, strongly moved by the exhibition of the giant dynamo at the Columbia Exposition of 1893, Keith was to lavish funds upon the electrical equipment for his new theater and to invite the first patrons to inspect it. And it was no mere whim which made him encourage this visiting of the subterranean reaches of the theater, first installing a $69 red velvet rug in the furnace room to attest to the cleanliness of the equipment, and eventually maintaining an antiseptic gloss in the entire power plant. Not only were pipes, flues, walls, and carpet kept spotlessly clean, but soon the area was decorated with marble-topped tables, potted plants, and a case of mahogany lined with plush for the repair equipment. In the boiler room the coal came down a chute of polished brass, to be shoveled into the furnaces by firemen in white uniforms, who would, on request, use a shovel of "solid silver." From the far parts of New England entire families traveled to observe this symbolic conquest, not only of power, but of the dirt and grime which had been power's invariable companion ever since the development of the steam engine.[28]

Everything about this exhibit connoted the values which adhered to the Myth of Success. Even the approach to the shrine from the entrance of the theater was along marble staircases and marble corridors. Thirty-two feet below street level, the marble surfaces broadened into a "reception room," where electroliers cast a subdued light of green and pink. Across one wall of this room spread a switchboard in white marble, on which sixty-six pilot lights had been artistically arranged to form a double scroll. Nearly six dozen switches in various hues of copper, bronze, and nickel plate completed this display. From the reception room visitors passed to a gallery, from where could be observed, beyond a glistening railing, the massive, humming generators, painted in light brown with only a few touches of nickel plate and tended by technicians in white trousers. Along the gallery, in unconscious irony, were vases of freshly cut flowers; in one corner was the stolid rolltop desk of the chief electrician.[29]

Here, with all the prodigality and satisfaction of a pharaoh building his tomb, B. F. Keith constructed his inner shrine to genteelized power. Dynamo and audiences alike within these palaces were to be domesticated through daily pampering, and if there was too little that was truly human and too much that was merely garish about this showman's tribute to the idols of a materialistic society, the same might be said about the ritual entertainment that the New Folk demanded and he supplied.

TEN

The Patterns of Ritual Meaning

WHILE VAUDEVILLE AS RITUAL enacted for the New Folk the myth with which to meet the challenge of the Industrial Age, its lessons were not lost upon the entertainment forms which displaced it. As a symbol of the modern American's search for commonality of vision, as an expression of the mechanical containment of vast energy and frantic rhythms, and as an invitation to the dazzling wonderland of comfort and convenience brought about by technology and capitalism, vaudeville took a permanent place in the popular imagination. Movies, radio, night clubs, musical comedies, and television would appropriate its values and purvey them more widely and profitably. Advertising, public relations, the Hollywood ethos, the slick magazines, and other taste-makers of our time would be less hesitant and ambivalent about the messages derived from vaudeville. But the ritual in its totality, its spectatorial awe before splendor and diversity, its sublimation of deep-rooted conflicts in mores and belief, its humor, pathos, banality, purity, and innocence, was not really transmittible.

That vaudeville, absorbed by the new media, was out of business by 1930 can hardly be questioned. In April of that year even the Palace, last stand of the big time, had been wired for sound.[1] Since 1926 the multimillion dollar circuits had been wobbling, ducking the economic punches of the radio and record companies and the knockout blows of motion pictures. Less than a hundred theaters throughout the country were booking any vaudeville acts at all, and only a dozen of these could be considered "big time."[2] During 1927-1928 the major circuits sold out to the financial syndicates already in control of much radio and record production. The mammoth RKO (Radio-Keith-Orpheum) made gestures toward placing vaudeville once more on its feet, but only the well-established name acts were able to survive the stringent economic measures necessary to present attractive "live" entertainment. *Variety* reported that "Vaudeville in 1930 stood motionless on a treadmill that moved backward."[3] In that year alone 1,500 acts left vaudeville for good, and the Palace continued to lose $4,000 a week. In 1931 only 675 vaudeville acts were to find a full week of work.[4] The scattered and well-meaning attempts to revive vaudeville over the ensuing decades could not reverse the inexorable process. Mechanization had brought the stars, the skits, and the music of the times into every neighborhood and into the majority of homes.

But doomed though it was by the technical progress it had glorified, to vaudeville as an institution belongs the credit for recognizing the new audience —the folk of the industrial cities. Mechanized media, lacking the stimulus and rapport of a living audience, could never have responded so well to the mythic needs of this folk population. But with the audience made ready by vaudeville, with the canons of taste laid out and the points of symbolic reference clearly understood by performers and public, it was possible for the silent pictures and then the "talkies" to move into the old vaudeville palaces, while radio took over the function of providing a "continuous performance." Furthermore, vaudeville answered the needs of the heterogeneous American audience, and expressed the particular Myth of Success in terms not readily duplicated in other parts of the globe. Britain and Australia, with whose music halls vaudeville maintained a close relationship by borrowing ideas and exchanging performers, were really not the same, never so explicit in their projection of a Myth of Success as was the peculiarly American institution.

Of course, through vaudeville the New Folk were being weaned from their varied cultural heritages— both rural Protestant Anglo-Saxon and eastern European. The vision projected by vaudeville of a community of men in pursuit of leisure and material well-being was closer to the visions of revolutionaries, both bourgeois and worker, in other parts of the world than it was to the older visions, moral and pastoral, of the eighteenth and early nineteenth-century Americans. Through ritual the New Folk were able to dull the bitter edge of transition into the mechanized and over-populated environment of the twentieth century, and, to a degree, they were able to use the ritual both as an emo-

tional safety valve and as a means of self-rec-
ognition.

That vaudeville was also a means by which the
newer arrivals became "Americanized" would certainly appear to be true, and the indoctrination into
accepted standards of dress, manners, speech habits, and social goals became an integral part of the
Myth of Success as the vaudeville audience recognized it. That the ritual was also a process by
which the people of show business became "Americanized" was also true, but the irony of the managers and stars is that, in achieving the dream of
success, they overshot their mark. By virtue of their
achievements they were placed outside of the community into which they had sought acceptance, and
instead of being priests of the new order, they became all too often its sacrificial victims. Closer to
the New Folk was the common run of performer
who yearned for the astronomical contract figures
that spelled success but settled for bread and butter
along the circuits. He could bask in the synthetic
glow of ritualized success—wear the costumes,
speak its lingo, and frequent its restaurants, but he
could also descend into the mass once more, hum-
bly accepting a less exotic, but still specialized
economic role and enjoying the styles, slang, and
haunts of the common man.

As an instrument of Americanization, vaudeville
made its concessions to the waning establishment
of genteel Protestant professional and mercantile
groups, particularly in the area of sexual taboos, but
it more readily responded to the ethos of the generation of wardheelers, managers, technicians, and
reformers who would largely supplant the traditional American establishment. This rising stratum of
American society understood and lived by the success and progress and encouraged the humor, the

popular science, the antiagrarian drama, and the conspicuous consumption of vaudeville. In contrast to the authoritarian social control of the Genteel Tradition, the reform generation tended to be permissive, allowing the ritual to run its course except when their own prejudices, humanitarian or scientific, were violated. Lacking a coherent plan for an industrial utopia, however, the programs of this new class tended to be fragmentary, short-lived, and even ceremonial. Thus while they gave lipservice to the traditional moralism of the Anglo-Saxon middle class, they freely allowed the New Folk to devise and perpetuate their ritual celebration of science, consumption, and success. While the bankers and schoolmarms would have fashioned the emigrants to the American city into millions of young Ben Franklins (somewhat genteelized), the employers, department store managers, and political bosses were quite glad to have ranks of tamed clerks and efficient typists, whose dream lives might include glamour and wealth — so long as these fantasies were contained within a mechanized and conventional dream world.

Obviously the vaudeville ritual denied the validity of certain basic Christian principles. Where Christianity sanctified poverty and turned men's eyes toward heavenly rewards, vaudeville extolled the gospel of wealth and sought happiness in immediate existence. Where Christianity marked man's place in history through a framework of revelations, the vaudeville myth knew no past nor future, only the sensuous and climactic rhythm of its man-made, man-centered ritual. Christian, of Bunyan's allegory, had resisted the temptations of Vanity Fair, knowing how earthly pleasures defeat the aspirations of the soul toward the Heavenly City. Vaudeville symbolized Vanity Fair, the city of men's new dreams. Salvation was no longer an arduous hike along a cruel path but a willingness to open the senses to the brilliant wares that Vanity Fair had to offer.

The problems which the new industrial order had posed for the Christian churches were, of course, staggering. Liberals sought for a Social Gospel with which to come to terms with the world; fundamentalists fell back upon the simplified religion molded on the American frontier; the Roman Catholic Church, largely made up of national groups in metropolitan areas, struggled to maintain its otherworldly dogma through the confessional and the discipline of the Mass. Their prestige assailed from the outside by the agnosticism of Darwinian naturalism and their authority vitiated from within by sentimental or fundamentalist evasions of historical realities, the churches were pressed to define a workable ethic for modern man. While they attacked specific vices and back-slidings, they left crucial issues of materialism, business ethics, and personal morality largely unresolved.

In practice, however, only the most violently fundamentalist sectarians pictured the vaudeville version of Vanity Fair as a latter-day Sodom and Gomorrah. The back-country prophets found a limited response in the urban centers, for most of the city dwellers had already declared a truce, even if they had not made their peace, with the demons of technological materialism. Vaudeville had risen out of, and was the expression of, complex social forces that they had already encountered in the shop, in the street, and even in their homes. The Myth of Success had not originated in the minds of shrewd showmen or vain performers; they only ministered to it. If the myth ran counter to Christian values, if the lessons of the Saturday matinee and the Sunday

216

morning sermon ran off in two different directions, so also were the lives of many Christians involved in serious contradictions. Vaudeville purity and vaudeville refinement were, of course, artificial attempts to resolve the basic conflict, and thus the myth itself acknowledged its own uneasy tenure within a nominally Christian society.

In a far more significant respect, however, vaudeville took over a function of the historical church: through its inculcation of the people with some sense of common humanity, a feeling for community which transcended the boundaries created by ethnic origins, specialization, and the impersonalism of urban life. In its own naive fashion, and upon its shallow foundation, vaudeville and later show business were able to point the way toward a neoprimitive ecumenicalism. While its ritual was not traditionally religious in its intent or symbolism, yet it shared with primitive religious rites a fascination with gesture, language, and the rhythms of everyday life.

The contention between the ritual of vaudeville and Christian thought, however, has not been in practice so vigorous as the contrast between it and the heirs to the humanistic tradition in literature, philosophy, and the arts, probably because the Protestant ethic in America had always supported various forms of the Myth of Success, while the literary community, in the tradition of Emerson, had never felt quite at home with it. For the adherents of reflective thinking and refined sensibility, however, vaudeville stands at the fountainhead of the torrent of vulgarity, commercialism, and "puerilism" which has inundated American culture. Even the rise of museums, libraries, mass education, symphony orchestras, and the publishing boom has tended to further rather than to restrain the slogan

217

thinking, sentimentality, and simplistic moralizing of the mass man—so runs the alarmist train of thought. The humanist plea for independent thought and awakened sensitivity is even now heard along the channels of communication which have done most to retain parts of vaudeville. But the challenge to these media to produce a steady output of first-rate drama, music, or intelligent discussion has, of course, been met by only a few scattered educational television and high-frequency radio stations. It may be unrealistic to hope that the barriers between the New Folk, on the one hand, and the artist and scholar, on the other, will ever be successfully razed.

For the literary mind particularly, the myth and rituals of materialism seem like unhealthy and destructive monsters; for the working anthropologist, they are lacking in the very character of myths and rituals. Lost are the traditional—and acceptable—concerns with man's origins, his destiny, and his struggle with cosmic forces. Lost also is traditional dignity given by ancient custom in a stable community. Narrative seems to be a bygone art and the picturesque rituals of the folk have disappeared in a panorama of minstrels, buffoons, and acrobats. The popular myths and rituals express themselves in a transparent symbolism which offers only a tangential commentary upon the abiding, universal concerns of mankind.

Yet the literary mind has already had to make its terms with American literature and is well aware of the unceasing quest for new forms and symbols within the other American arts as well. Whether his ordering principles have been those of rational theology and its direct descendant, natural philosophy, or whether he has sought coherence in the forces of the imagination, the unconscious, or in the drama

of experience itself, the American artist's plight—
and his task—has consisted of being dissatisfied
with even the most radical of his experiments. The
history of the novel with its violent fluctuations between realism and romance, the frantic retreats of
lyric poetry away from and then back to formalism,
the hectic development of the short story—part allegory, part case-history—all attest to the rapid movement of the literary intelligence across the realms of
form in the quest for, if not truth, then at least, a
true voice. Although one cardinal declaration of the
Romantic movement was for artistic freedom, critical realism also put forward its claim to attention
by asserting its contemporaneity in the face of stale
metaphors, rhetorical clichés, and well-worn plots.
Imagism, expressionism, symbolism, and impres-
sionism have, in their very rivalry, kept alive the
tendency to improvise, to experiment, and if need
be, to abandon totally whatever elements of the
artistic vision that do not square with present
circumstances.

If such has been the experience of literate and
aware persons in American culture, it is hardly surprising that the semieducated have not been rigidly
traditional in their expression, that those in the
front lines of American venture have not adhered to
primitive forms expressive of folk or feudal societies.
Although popular culture, by nature of its collective
quality, does not lend itself to the startling originality or to the rational discipline of personal art, it
too has met the problems of innovation on its own
terms. The day appears to have passed for occult
forces, a spiritualized nature, for the gods and demons of a bygone folklore, but man's psychological
impulse to objectify his dreams and to create the
symbols through which he can handle them still remains. The lesser gods were dead by 1900; the de-

mons were political; the cosmic forces were harnessed in the service of man—as was evident in the incandescent lamp and the trolley car. Although the problems of life and death, and of the other world, had not lost a significant place in human existence, the pressing problem of identity—as such modern writers as Arthur Miller, Ralph Ellison, and J. D. Salinger have so poignantly demonstrated—has become even more important in modern life than the mystery of death. Even modern drama, the ritual of the educated elite, up against a dead-end of realism, has itself, in the "epic theater" and the "theater of the absurd," moved more toward a ritualistic and symbolic art which at times is forcefully reminiscent of old vaudeville. The step from the vaudeville playlets of Edgar Allen Woolf to Edward Albee's *The American Dream,* is not so long as Off-Broadway would like to think.

As for the thinness and banality of much vaudeville ritualism, it should suffice to point out its tremendous rapport with its audience. Instead of doubting the communal values in mass entertainment, the literary mind should examine its own symbolism and ask which of its outpourings are anything more than the private and obscure projections of the alienated soul. The language of the masses is that of gesture, movement, and the emotionally charged phrase—a simple, stereotyped set of images easily grasped by those with no learning and little capacity for discursive thought. Though the vaudeville playlet, for example, was deliberately and admittedly devoid of artistic quality, it was thus all the more accessible to the masses and all the more effectual in communicating its mythic truths. Even the novelists at the turn of the century, much as they assumed a critical posture toward the vacuousness of city life, responded to the powerful influence which popular entertainment had upon their working class characters. Frank Norris' brute protagonist, McTeague, goes to a cheap variety show and is "dazzled" and "stupified with admiration."[5] Crane's Maggie is swept up in the fantasy of a Bowery theater and identifies readily with its Cinderella heroines. Dreiser's touching portrait of show business glamour and self-deception in "My Brother Paul," and his companion portrait of Sister Carrie during her years of lonely success upon the stage, both testify to the mythic values implicit in mass entertainment.

Certainly these myths and rituals were temporary ones, and one should not be surprised when revivals of the old formulas fail to work their magic. Like the realism and naturalism of the vintage years—that preached by Howells and taken seriously by Norris, Crane, Dreiser and others—the ritual resurrected today is more nostalgic than it is pertinent. As Alfred Kazin and Howard Mumford Jones have made unequivocally clear, realism and naturalism in the nineties were temporary redirections of psychic energy. The platitudinous idealism of the Genteel Tradition had failed to work for the rising generation of artists and intellectuals, and they turned for sustenance toward a vitalizing empiricism. Though this took the forms of a photographic esthetic, a critical irony and humor, psychological analysis, or a concern with applied economics, this realism and naturalism was a confrontation of the life of the times. It shared with vaudeville an imaginative involvement with the life of the cities and with the problems of the mass man, a recognition of the importance of fantasies and daydreams for the silent masses, and a disdain for traditional myths. Yet neither this literary empiricism nor the entertainment ritual, except perhaps in certain inspired

221

works or gestures, could produce anything more than period pieces. In defying tradition, in seeking a personal engagement with history, in refusing to probe deeply into the mythic universe created by science and success, both the literary genre and the folk ritual doomed themselves. Their magic powers waned with the passage of history, and even as relics their value and meaning is uncertain and ambiguous.

What vaudeville had to tell the New Folk about the Myth of Success during the years from 1885 to 1930 cannot be fully encompassed in one person's study. Each inevitably emphasizes those aspects of the myth which move him most profoundly and must find those angelic or demonic images which suit his view of modern life. The materials of this myth may be endlessly true, but they are also endlessly mutable and open to interpretation. That vaudeville was a significant part of its times, that its ritual lingers in modern mass entertainment, that it had a symbolic function in its era seems incontrovertible. But to be wholly precise about what the Myth of Success means to individuals and to American society as a whole—to explore fully the value conflicts which it occasions and to define comprehensively all of the functions of its ritual—is ultimately impossible. To assert, nevertheless, as this study has, that the meaning of vaudeville lies in the nature of man; that because he affirms his existence through a power to symbolize, man can shape his destiny; that vaudeville was a ritualistic expression of inchoate emotions and half-understood ideas in America at the turn of the century—is hopefully a meaningful statement about the human condition.

Notes

ONE
  [1] Contemporary thought regarding myth has not yet reached a clear consensus, and the relation between myth and ritual is a matter of considerable debate. Although the present study has had to delve further into the theoretical implications of myth than other comparable works in American studies, such as Smith's *Virgin Land* and Hofstadter's *Age of Reform,* clarity still demands firm and workable definitions of terms. *Myth,* as it is used in these pages, is a constellation of images and symbols, either objectively real or imaginary, which brings focus and a degree of order to the psychic (largely unconscious) processes of a group or society and in so doing endows a magical potency upon the circumstances or persons involved. *Ritual* is a repetitious and public presentation of the materials proper to mythical thought, which shares with myth its concern with psychic life, but which, because of its dramatic medium, operates more fluidly and more instantaneously. The word *rite,* often used interchangeably with *ritual,*

has been excluded from this discussion because of its more explicit connotations of religious worship. These definitions are, on the whole, a compendium and distillation of the definitions to be found in the following sources: Henry A. Murray (ed.), *Myth and Myth Making* (New York, 1960), pp. 318-49; Susanne K. Langer, *Philosophy in a New Key* (Cambridge, Mass., 1960), pp. 36-50, 152-60; and Ernst Cassirer, *The Philosophy of Symbolic Forms*, II (New Haven, 1955), pp. 38-41.

[2] Cp. Mark Schorer, "The Necessity of Myth," in Murray, *Myth and Myth Making*, p. 355: "Myths are the instruments by which we continually struggle to make our experience intelligible to ourselves. A myth is a large controlling image that gives philosophical meaning to the facts of ordinary life; that is which has organizing value for experience."

[3] The pioneer work in this field was Arthur M. Schlesinger, *The Rise of the City, 1878-1898* (New York, 1933), but other significant contributions have been Henry Nash Smith, *Virgin Land* (Cambridge, Mass., 1950); Richard Hofstadter, *The Age of Reform* (New York, 1955); Henry F. May, *Protestant Churches and Industrial America* (New York, 1949); Eric F. Goldman, *Rendezvous with Destiny* (New York, 1952); and Samuel P. Hays, *The Response to Industrialism: 1885-1915* (Chicago, 1957).

[4] Cp. Susanne K. Langer, *Philosophy in a New Key*, p. 49: "Ritual is a symbolic transformation of experiences that no other medium can adequately express. Because it springs from a primary human need, it is a spontaneous activity—that is to say without intention, without adaptation to a conscious purpose; its growth is undesigned, its pattern purely natural, however intricate it may be."

[5] Cassirer has particularly stressed the manner in which myth and ritual operate below the level of conscious thought. Thus the myth-making process becomes one of immediacy and of what he calls an "interpenetration" of idea and object: "Rites cannot be explained as a mere representation of beliefs; on the contrary, the part of myth which belongs to the world of theoretical representation, which is a mere record or accredited narrative, must be understood as a mediate interpretation of the part which resides immediately in the activity of man and in his feelings and will. Seen in this light, rites are not originally 'allegorical'; they do not merely copy or represent but are absolutely *real*; they are so woven into the reality of action as to form an indispensable part of it." *Philosophy of Symbolic Forms*, II, p. 39. See also Stanley E. Hyman, "The Ritual View of Myth and the Mythic," in *Myth a Symposium*, ed. Thomas A. Sebeok (Bloomington, 1958), pp. 84-94.

[6] This point was originally suggested to me by Richard Chase, *The Quest for Myth* (Baton Rouge, 1949), pp. 7-30, 69. Other passages in this book bear directly on this problem of myth-making in modern civilization.

224

[7] Charles and Mary Beard, *The Rise of American Civilization*, II (New York, 1937), p. 397.

[8] Kenneth S. Lynn, *The Dream of Success* (Boston, 1955). The discussion of the Alger tales in the first chapter of this book is particularly good.

[9] Cp. Howard Mumford Jones, *The Pursuit of Happiness* (Cambridge, Mass., 1953), especially his discussion of the modern "technique of happiness," pp. 131 ff.

[10] Jones quotes Dorothy Thompson's article from the *Ladies Home Journal*, LVIII (April 1941), 6, to the effect that "In this democracy it has become a public duty to be as happy as one can be."

[11] R. G. Collingwood, *The Principles of Art* (New York, 1958), pp. 57-104. Johan Huizinga, *Homo Ludens: The Study of the Play Element in Culture* (Boston, 1955), p. 205.

[12] The divergencies among folklorists are well known, but the principal positions are well represented in John Ball (ed.), "A Theory for American Folklore: A Symposium," *Journal of American Folklore*, LXXII (1959), 197-242.

[13] Caroline Caffin, *Vaudeville* (New York, 1914), pp. 9-23.

[14] Gilbert Seldes, *The Seven Lively Arts* (New York, 1957), pp. 300-301.

[15] Cp. Susanne Langer, *Philosophy in a New Key*, p. 158: "But the driving force in human minds is fear, which begets an imperious demand for security in the world's confusion: a demand for a world-picture that fills all experience and gives each individual a definite *orientation* amid the terrifying forces of nature and society."

TWO

[1] Michael Bennett Leavitt, *Fifty Years in Theatrical Management* (New York, 1912), p. 189.

[2] Bernard Sobel, *A Pictorial History of American Vaudeville* (New York, 1961), p. 24.

[3] See *A Dictionary of American English*, IV (Chicago, 1949), pp. 2407-408. C. P. Sawyer, "Mirrors of Variety," Boston *Transcript*, Oct. 2, 1926, cites other references. In the Harvard Library is a dramatic piece with musical interludes, *Le Secretaire de Madame* by Mm. E. Labiche and Marc Michel (Paris, 1857), which has the subtitle, "Comedie-Vaudeville." *Dramatic Records of the Lion Theatre*, Harvard Theatre Collection (this collection is hereafter referred to as HTC), contains a program of the Vaudeville Saloon (corner of Boylston and Washington Streets, Boston, Mass.) ca. 1840.

[4] Leavitt, p. 186.

[5] Page, *Writing for Vaudeville*, (Springfield, Mass. 1915), pp. 1-2, gives the complete story; his facts are corroborated by Funk and Wagnall's *New Standard Dictionary* and to some extent by *The Oxford Universal Dictionary*.

[6] E. G. Chancellor, *The Pleasure Haunts of London* (London, 1925), p. 137, says this theater in the Strand was first opened in 1870. See also Phyllis Hartnoll, *The Oxford Companion to the Theatre* (New York, 1951), pp. 823-24.

[7] Albert F. McLean, Jr., "The Genesis of Vaudeville: Two Letters from B. F. Keith," *Theatre Survey*, I (1960), 90. (This source is subsequently referred to as "Keith Letters.")

[8] Boston *Herald*, Jan. 13, 1895.

[9] Robert Grau, "The Amazing Prosperity of the Vaudeville Entertainer," *Overland*, LVII (June 1911), 608.

[10] New York *Clipper*, Jan. 2, 1892.

[11] George C. Odell, *Annals of the New York Stage*, XV (New York, 1949), p. 352.

[12] Carl Wittke, *Tambo and Bones: A History of the American Minstrel Show* (Durham, N.C., 1930), pp. 147-48.

[13] Constance Rourke, *American Humor* (New York, 1931), pp. 89-90.

[14] John R. Betts, "P. T. Barnum and the Popularization of Natural History," *Journal of the History of Ideas*, XX (1959), 353-68.

[15] Wittke, p. 91; Dailey Paskman and Sigmund Spaeth, *Gentlemen Be Seated* (New York, 1928), pp. 175-76; Frederick W. Bond, *The Negro and the Theatre* (Washington, D.C., 1940), pp. 47-49.

[16] Edward Marks, *They All Sang* (New York, 1934), pp. 60-70.

[17] Bond, pp. 39-41; Oscar Handlin, *Race and Nationality in American Life* (New York, 1957), pp. 120-28.

[18] Paskman and Spaeth, pp. 91-93.

[19] Leavitt, p. 183.

[20] Felix Isman, *Weber and Fields* (New York, 1924), pp. 22-23.

[21] David Warfield, "My Own Story," HTC.

[22] John Corbin, "How the Other Half Laughs," *Harper's Weekly*, XCVIII (Dec. 1898), 30-48.

[23] New York *Dramatic Mirror*, Dec. 25, 1897.

[24] Odell, XV, 350-51.

[25] Glenn Hughes, *A History of the American Theatre, 1700-1950* (New York, 1951), pp. 292-93; James L. Ford, "Our National Stage," *McClure's*, XXXII (March 1909), 497-98.

[26] F. Anstey, "London Music Hall," *Harper's Monthly*, LXXXII (Jan. 1891), 190-202. See also Archibald Haddon, *The Story of the Music Halls* (London, 1935), and C. D. Stuart and A. J. Park, *The Variety Stage* (London, 1895).

[27] New York *Dramatic Mirror*, Nov. 20, 1897; Haddon, p. 86.

[28] H. L. Mencken, *The American Language* (New York, 1936), pp. 237, 347. For Mencken "vaudeville" was the equivalent in American speech of the English "variety," for he noted that its Americanization had extended to the pronunciation *vawdvil*. A survey of the dictionaries show considerable divergence on pronunciation and suggests that Mencken's contrast may have been too hastily arrived at. Although *The*

226

New Century Dictionary (1927) recognized the corruption *văd' vil, Webster's New International,* for example, does not, but accepts *vod' vil, vo de vil,* or the British *vō' de vil* and tries to avoid the extreme Americanization represented by the deletion of the second syllable. The almost total rejection of the long "o" of *vōd* in common speech, in spite of the preference of many dictionaries, has prevailed, and thus the American thirst for cosmopolitan dignity has been compromised with the flat homely quality of the American vernacular. *The NBC Handbook of Pronunciation,* comp. James F. Bender (New York, 1957) recommends VOHD vil, however.

[29] Charles B. Davis, "The Vaudeville Club," *Harper's Weekly,* XXXVI (Dec. 1892), 1243, and XXXVII (Feb. 1893), 116.

[30] Douglas Gilbert, *American Vaudeville* (New York, 1940), p. 244.

THREE

[1] This account of American urbanization and the formation of the New Folk draws upon a wide range of reading and course work, but I would cite as the two chief contributions to my understanding of these problems: Oscar Handlin, *The Uprooted* (Boston, 1951) and Richard Hofstadter, *The Age of Reform* (New York, 1955).

[2] Maldwyn A. Jones, *American Immigration* (Chicago, 1960), pp. 178-79.

[3] Hofstadter, pp. 218-19.

[4] C. Wright Mills, *White Collar* (New York, 1951), 161-88.

[5] Mills comments extensively upon this need of the new middle class to feel important, pp. xvi-xix, 251-58.

[6] According to Michael M. Davis, *The Exploitation of Pleasure* (New York, 1911), p. 27.

[7] Figures are from various editions of *Julius Cahn's Official Theatre Guide* (New York, 1896-1910).

[8] New York *Herald Tribune,* Sept. 5, 1929.

[9] Keith's New Theatre Program, 1914, HTC.

[10] William M. Marston and John H. Fuller, *F. F. Proctor, Vaudeville Pioneer* (New York, 1943), p. 155.

[11] *Cahn,* II, pp. 37-58, 84-88, 95-101, 137-47. *Cahn,* XV, pp. 47, 74-82, 111-19, 125-41, 208. E. M. Herlihy (ed.), *Fifty Years of Boston* (Boston, 1934), pp. 400-401.

[12] Davis, p. 28 (Table VII).

[13] Davis, p. 25 (pertinent figures from Table V).

[14] Constance Rourke, *American Humor,* (New York, 1953), p. 74.

[15] Constance Rourke, *The Roots of American Culture,* ed. Van Wyck Brooks (New York, 1942), pp. 262-74.

[16] W. J. Cash, *The Mind of the South* (New York, 1956), pp. 94-95.

[17] Mark Twain, *The Adventures of Huckleberry Finn* (New York, 1948), p. 147.

[18] R. G. Collingwood, *The Principles of Art* (New York, 1958), pp. 64-65.

[19] Robert Grau, "The Growth of Vaudeville," *Overland*, LXIV (Oct. 1914), 392-93.

[20] Grau, pp. 393-96.

[21] Grau, pp. 393-96.

[22] Felix Isman, *Weber and Fields* (New York, 1924).

[23] Ward Morehouse, *George M. Cohan* (New York, 1943), pp. 41-43; Edward Marks, *They All Had Glamour* (New York, 1944), p. 287.

[24] Donald Day (ed.), *Autobiography of Will Rogers* (Boston, 1949), pp. 30-32.

[25] Obituary in New York *Times*, Nov. 6, 1933.

[26] Abel Green and Joe Laurie, Jr., *Show Biz* (Garden City, N. Y., 1953), pp. 91, 131.

[27] [Bert Levy], "Benjamin Franklin Keith, Discoverer of 'Polite Vaudeville,'" New York *Herald*, July 7, 1912.

[28] Boston *Sunday Herald*, Feb. 2, 1896. Equivalent tributes were paid to F. F. Proctor in the posthumous biography sponsored by his widow and written by William M. Marston and John H. Fuller.

[29] Boston *Globe*, Jan. 4, 1908; New York *Telegram*, Dec. 22, 1909; Boston *Journal*, Jan. 31, 1908. Clippings in Scrapbook of R. G. Larsen, in the author's possession.

[30] Robert Grau, "Fortunes Made on Actor's Salaries," *Overland*, LXV (Feb. 1915), 131-32.

[31] George Fuller Golden, *My Lady Vaudeville and Her White Rats* (New York, 1909), p. 138.

[32] S. Morace Mortimer, "The Old Vaudeville Troupers," New York *Times*, Dec. 23, 1934.

[33] Obituary in New York *Times*, Jan. 12,1947.

[34] Walter J. Kingsley, "Vaudeville and Revue," New York *Times*, July 8, 1923. "The Argot of Vaudeville," New York *Times*, Aug. 11, 1918. See also the glossary in Green and Laurie, pp. 527-31.

[35] See Howard S. Becker, "The Professional Dance Musician and His Audience," *American Journal of Sociology*, LVII (1951), 136-44, for a revealing study of the alienation of the modern entertainer.

FOUR

[1] "Profits in Clean Vaudeville," *Literary Digest*, XLIII (Oct. 1911), 603-605.

[2] Marian Spitzer, "Morals in the Two-a-day," *American Mercury*, III (Sept. 1924), 35.

[3] "The Model Playhouse of the Century," publicity flier, ca. 1894, HTC.

[4] Program for Keith's New Theatre, 1910, HTC.

[5] William T. Foster, *Vaudeville and Motion Picture Shows* (Portland, Ore., 1914).

[6] Brett Page, *Writing for Vaudeville* (Springfield, Mass., 1915), p. 105.

[7] Boston *Sunday Post*, Aug. 18, 1912.

[8] Telegram in Larsen Scrapbook.

[9] In Alva Johnson, "Profiles, Vaudeville to Television, III," *New Yorker*, XXII (Oct. 5, 1946), 36.

[10] T. Charlton Henry, *Inquiry into the Consistency of Popular Amusement with a Profession of Christianity* (Charleston, S. C., 1825), p. 42. See also: C. W. Andrews and others, *The Incompatibility of Theatre-going and Dancing with Membership in the Christian Church* (Philadelphia, 1872); O[rville] D[ewey], "Fashionable Amusements," rev. of *Tract 73*, *Christian Examiner*, VIII (1830), 201-20. Reference is made to *Tract 130* in Martha Clark, *Victims of Amusements* (Philadelphia, 1849), p. 16.

[11] Horace Bushnell, *Christian Nurture* (New York, 1860), passim.

[12] J[ohn] H[opkins] Morison, *Amusements* (Boston, 1859), pp. 7-8, 11.

[13] Charles P. Krauth, *Popular Amusements* (Winchester, Va., 1851), pp. 26-27.

[14] Hiram Mattison, *Popular Amusements, An Appeal to Methodists* (New York, 1867), p. 3.

[15] Mattison, p. 30.

[16] Representative editorials in the *Dramatic Mirror* went under such titles as "Ignorant Vilifiers," Oct. 12, 1901; "Self Evident Debate on 'The Theatre is an Evil Not to Be Eradicated,'" Oct. 20, 1906; "And yet Another Survey of Clerical Opinions on the Stage," March 16, 1907.

[17] William Ashley Sunday, "Amusements," (ca. 1917). I am indebted to Dr. William McLaughlin for bringing this sermon to my attention and sending me a transcript.

[18] Mattison, pp. 56-58; *Doctrines and Discipline of the Methodist Episcopal Church, 1912* (New York, 1912).

[19] "Christianity and Amusements, A Symposium," *Everybody's Magazine*, X (May 1904), 697; "The Methodist Amusement Ban," *Literary Digest*, XLIV (June 1912), 1260.

[20] W. DeLoss Love, "The Relation of Amusements to the Education of the Sensibilities," *Congregational Review*, X (May 1870), 237-39.

[21] On Hopkins see Mark Hopkins, *The Law of Love and Love as Law* (New York, 1881), pp. 39, 330-31, 342. Also see his treatise *The Connection Between Taste and Morals* (Boston, 1852).

[22] Frederick W. Sawyer, *A Plea for Amusements* (New York, 1847), pp. 96-103, 237, 242-43.

[23] S. W. Sample, *Theatre and Church—A Sermon* (Minneapolis, n.d.); T. B. Forbush, *The Theatre* (Detroit, 1881), p. 8.

[24] William Wilberforce Newton, *Christianity and Popular Amusements* (New York, 1877), p. 12.

[25] Richard H. Edwards, *Popular Amusements* (New York, 1915), p. 135.

[26] Washington Gladden, *Recollections* (Boston, 1909), pp. 118-19.

[27] Gladden, pp. 90-91.

[28] Washington Gladden, "Christianity and Popular Amusements," *The Century Illustrated Magazine*, XXIX (Jan. 1885), 388.

[29] Gladden, *Century Magazine*, XXIX, 390-92.

[30] Ira V. Brown, *Lyman Abbott: Christian Evolutionist* (Cambridge, Mass., 1953), p. 75.

[31] *Everybody's Magazine*, X, 696-701.

[32] *Everybody's Magazine*, X, 700-701.

[33] Quoted in J. L. Gillin, "The Sociology of Recreation," *American Journal of Sociology*, XIX (May 1914), 826.

[34] Herbert Spencer, "The Gospel of Recreation," *Popular Science Monthly*, XXII (Jan. 1883), 358.

[35] Gillin, 827. See also Edward S. Robinson, "Play," *Encyclopaedia of the Social Sciences*, XII, 160.

[36] G. Stanley Hall, *Adolescence*, II (New York, 1905), passim.

[37] Richard Hofstadter, *The Age of Reform* (New York, 1955), pp. 148 ff.

[38] Eric F. Goldman, *Rendezvous with Destiny* (New York, 1952), pp. 93-117.

[39] Shelby M. Harrison, "Surveys and Exhibits," *Survey*, XXXI (Dec. 1913), 359.

[40] For New York: Michael M. Davis, *The Exploitation of Pleasure* (New York, 1911). For Providence: Francis R. North, *A Recreation Study of the City of Providence, R. I.*, (Providence, 1912). For Milwaukee: Rowland Haynes, *Recreation Survey, Milwaukee* (Milwaukee, 1911). For Detroit: Rowland Haynes, *Detroit Recreation Survey* (Detroit, 1913). For Kansas City: Rowland Haynes and F. F. McClure, *Recreation Surveys of Kansas City, Mo.* (Kansas City, 1912). For Springfield: Lee F. Hammer, *Recreation in Springfield, Ill.* (New York, 1915). For Portland: Foster, *Vaudeville and Motion Picture Shows*. For Philadelphia: "The Movies in Philadelphia," *Survey*, XXXII (May 1914), 176. For Chicago: Louise de Koven Bowen, *Five and Ten Cent Theatres* (Chicago, 1911). For Scranton: Lavera Berlew, *Recreation Survey of Scranton*, (Scranton, 1913). For Waltham: Francis North, *A Recreation Survey of the City of Waltham, Mass.* (Waltham, 1913).

[41] *Report of the State Recreational Committee* (California, 1914).

[42] Raymond Moley, *Commercial Recreation* (Cleveland, 1920). Charles B. Raitt, *A Survey of Recreational Facilities in Rochester, N. Y.* (Rochester, 1929). Jessee F. Steiner, *Americans at Play* (New York, 1933).

[43] North, *Waltham*, p. 20.

[44] North, *Providence*, p. 60.

[45] Davis, pp. 4-5, 21-33, 44-45.

[46] J. F. W. Ware, *May I Go to the Theatre?* (Baltimore, 1871), pp. 13-14.

FIVE

[1] The description of a typical performance draws freely from a feature article in the Boston *Sunday Post* of August 18, 1912, but I have also incorporated details and observations from my general reading in vaudeville materials.

[2] *Dramatic Mirror*, Dec. 25, 1885. See also Leon Mead, "A Little Soubrette," *Dramatic Mirror*, Dec. 25, 1891, and Norman Hapgood, "The Life of the Vaudeville Artiste," *Cosmopolitan*, XXX (Feb. 1900), 399.

[3] *Dramatic Mirror*, Oct. 26, 1895.

SIX

[1] Quoted in Douglas Gilbert, *American Vaudeville* (New York, 1940), p. 111, from an interview with Frank C. Drake of the New York *World*.

[2] "A Plea for Seriousness," *Atlantic Monthly*, LXIX (May 1892), 628.

[3] Burgess Johnson, "The New Humor," *Critic*, XXXX (April-June 1902), 331-38, 526-32. Also for Great Britain, cp. J. L. Toole, "The New Humor and Non-humorists," *National Review*, XXI (June 1892), 449.

[4] John Kendrick Bangs, *Putnam's*, III (Oct. 1907), 54.

[5] George M. Cohan and George Jean Nathan, "The Mechanics of Laughter," *McClure's*, XLII (Nov. 1913), 69-71. Nathan's independent judgment was expressed in "The Ten Commandments of Vaudeville," *Bohemia Magazine* (July 1909; clipping in the HTC files).

[6] Boston *Herald*, ca. 1905 (clipping in HTC files).

[7] Brett Page, *Writing for Vaudeville* (Springfield, Mass., 1915), p. 70.

[8] Page, pp. 87-88.

[9] In 1741 Henry Fielding wrote of "tossing men out of their chairs, tumbling them into water, or any of these handicraft jokes." "An Essay on Conversation," *Works*, XI (London, 1903), 274.

[10] Harry B. Weiss, *A Brief History of American Joke Books* (New York, 1943), pp. 8-15.

[11] Robert Kempt (comp.), *The American Joe Miller* (1865), p. 1.

[12] *Wehman Bros. Combination Prize Joker* (New York, 1896), p. 4.

[13] *Wehman Joker*, p. 5.

[14] *Wehman Joker*, p. 9.

[15] *All Star Joke Book and Minstrel Guide* (Boston, 1918), p. 37.

[16] John Albert Macy, "The Career of the Joke," *Atlantic Monthly,* XCVI (Oct. 1905), 498-510. See also Thomas Masson, *Our American Humorists* (New York, 1922), "Foreword," and Arthur Sullivant Hoffman, "Who Writes the Jokes," *Bookman,* XXVI (Oct. 1907), 171-81.

[17] Masson, pp. 432-43.

[18] Macy, pp. 502-503.

[19] Max Beerbohm, "The Laughter of the Public," *Living Age,* CCXXXIII (Aug. 1902), 52-57.

[20] "The Argot of Vaudeville," Part II, New York *Times,* ca. August, 1918, clipping HTC.

[21] "Keith Letters," p. 88.

[22] *New Book of Monologues,* No. 1 of Wehman Bros.' Handy Series (New York, 1908), p. 37.

[23] Aaron Hoffman, "The German Senator," in Page, pp. 435-43.

[24] Felix Isman, *Weber and Fields* (New York, 1924), pp. 166-70.

[25] James Russell Lowell, "Democracy," *Democracy and Other Addresses* (Boston, 1887), p. 3.

[26] Charles Johnson, "The Essence of American Humor," *Atlantic Monthly,* LXXXVII (Feb. 1901), 195-202. On the matter of distinguishing between humor and wit, see Oliver Goldsmith, *Works,* I (New York, 1850), 452; William Hazlitt, "On Wit and Humor," *Works,* VIII (London, 1903), 15; Mark Twain, "How to Tell a Story," *The Man That Corrupted Hadleyburg* (New York, 1900), pp. 225-34. See also Melville D. Landon, *Wit and Humor of the Age* (Chicago, 1883), pp. 9-13, and "Wit and Humor," *Atlantic Monthly,* C (Sept. 1907), 427-28.

[27] "The Dominant Joke," *Atlantic Monthly,* XCI (March, 1903), 431-32.

[28] Elisabeth Woodbridge, "The Humor-Fetish," *Outlook,* XC (Nov. 1908), 540-42.

[29] Gerald Stanley Lee, "A Rule for Humor," *Critic,* XXXIII (Oct. 1898), 291-94.

[30] Max Eastman, *The Sense of Humor* (New York, 1921), p. 168.

[31] Max Eastman, *The Enjoyment of Laughter* (New York, 1936).

[32] "The Limitations of Humor," *Living Age,* CCLIV (Aug. 1907), 560-64. (Condensed from "Musings Without Method," *Blackwood's,* CLXXXII [Aug. 1907], 276-86.).

[33] *Atlantic Monthly,* LXIX (May 1892), 625-30.

[34] "The Need of the New Joke," *Atlantic Monthly,* LXXXV (March 1900), 717-18. For further statements supporting traditional views of humor see: Ella MacMahon, "Is Humor Declining?" *Living Age,* CCXLIII (Oct. 1904), 310-16; Arthur B.

Maurice, "The Humor of Nations," *Outlook*, LXXXV (March 1907), 609-13; Robert Haver Schauffler, "The New German Humor," *Outlook*, XC (Nov. 1908), 542-46.

[35] Gilson Gardner, "Why Is a Joke Funny?" *Putnam's*, III (Oct. 1907), 55-61. For an earlier attempt to blend moral idealism and psychology see S. H. Butcher, "The Evolution of Humor," *Harper's New Monthly Magazine*, LXXX (May 1890), 898-908.

[36] Linus W. Kline, "The Nature, Origin, and Function of Humor," *Popular Science Monthly*, LXXIII (Aug. 1908), 144-56. See also his technical presentation, "The Psychology of Humor," *American Journal of Psychology*, XVIII (Oct. 1907), 421-41.

[37] Statement of William E. Collins, in personal interview with author, Nov. 1951.

SEVEN

[1] Caroline Caffin, *Vaudeville* (New York, 1914), p. 217.

[2] [William Dean Howells], "Editor's Easy Chair," *Harper's New Monthly Magazine*, CVI (April 1903), 814. For further views on animals see [Howells], "Easy Chair," *Harper's Monthly*, CXII (April 1906), 796-99.

[3] HTC files. M. R. Werner, *Barnum* (New York, 1923), p. 332. John R. Betts, "P. T. Barnum and the Popularization of Natural History," *Journal of the History of Ideas*, XX (1959), 368.

[4] Betts, pp. 333-46.

[5] Betts, pp. 350-51.

[6] Frank Charles Bostock, *The Training of Wild Animals* (New York, 1903), esp. pp. 202-18. Magazine articles also expressed the heroic attitude toward jungle animals, e.g., Samuel Hopkins Adams, "The Training of Lions, Tigers, and Other Great Cats," *McClure's*, XV (Sept. 1900), 386-98; Harvey Sutherland, "Training Wild Animals," *Current Literature*, XXXII (June 1902), 709-10; Cleveland Moffat, "The Wild Beast Tamer," *Current Literature*, XXXII (Jan. 1902), 88-89; Hjalmar Hjorth Boyesen, 2nd, "Training Wild Animals," *Cosmopolitan*, XXXIV (Dec. 1902), 123-32; "Training an Elephant," *Current Literature*, XXXV (July 1903), 75; Samuel Hopkins Adams, ed., "Notes From a Trainer's Book," *McClure's*, XXIV (Dec. 1904), 188-97. See also Carl Hagenbeck, *Beasts and Men* (New York, 1909).

[7] Bostock, pp. 182-85.

[8] Hermann Boger, "Training Wild Beasts," *Independent*, LV (Oct. 1903), 2555.

[9] Joe Laurie, Jr., *Vaudeville* (New York, 1953), pp. 155-57.

[10] "Abandoning Wild Animal Acts," *Literary Digest*, LXXXV (April 1925), 33.

[11] "The Ethics of Wild Animal Training," *Review of Re-*

views, LXVI (Aug. 1922), 212; S. T. Hammond, *Practical Dog Training* (New York, 1882), p. 1; B. Waters, *Fetch and Carry* (New York, 1895); Oliver Hartley, *Hunting Dogs* (Columbus, Ohio, 1909).

[12] Mrs. Huntington Smith, "Cruelties Connected with Training and Exhibition of Animals" (a pamphlet published by the Animal Rescue League, Boston, ca. 1905).

[13] William J. Schultz, *The Humane Movement in the United States 1910-1922* (New York, 1925), p. 133. Full information on the humane movement can be found in this book and its predecessor, Roswell C. McCrea, *The Humane Movement* (New York, 1910). Other sources are George T. Angell, *Autobiographical Sketches* (Boston, 1924), and Clare Morris, "Riddle of the Nineteenth Century: Mr. Henry Bergh," *McClure's*, XVIII (March 1902), 414-22.

[14] Charmain London, *The Book of Jack London*, II (New York, 1921), 305.

[15] Jack London, *Michael, Brother of Jerry* (New York, 1919), pp. 204-205.

[16] J. London, pp. 207, 234-40, 307-309.

[17] C. London, p. 306. See also "Cruelty Charged in Training Trick Animals for Stage and Movie," *Literary Digest*, LXVI (Sept. 1920), 102-11.

[18] Laurie, pp. 165-68.

[19] See M. E. Haggerty, "Animal Intelligence," *Atlantic Monthly*, CVII (May 1911), 599-607.

[20] John B. Watson, *Behavior, An Introduction to Comparative Psychology* (New York, 1914), chapter IX. See also: Lightner Witmer, "A Monkey with a Mind," *Psychological Clinic*, II (1909), 179; L. K. Hirshberg, "Don, The Talking Dog," *Scientific American*, CVIII (May 1913), 502-503.

[21] Watson, pp. 311-14.

[22] Albert A. Hopkins, *Magic: Stage Illusions and Scientific Discoveries* (New York, 1897), p. 6.

[23] J[ohn] M[ulholland], "Conjuring," *Encyclopaedia Britannica*, VI (1956), 262.

[24] Edmund Wilson, "Houdini," *The Shores of Light* (New York, 1952), pp. 174, 176.

[25] Harold Kellock, *Houdini* (New York, 1928), pp. 132-38, 148-71, 201-202.

[26] Wilson, p. 176.

[27] "Handcuff Releases Under Difficulties," *Scientific American*, CVII (July 1912), 58. Typical of *Scientific American* articles were: Hereward Carrington, "Handcuffs and Escapes Therefrom," CIII (Dec. 1910), 460, 469; and "Sacks, Bags, Boxes, Trunks, Mail Cases, Packing Cases and Escapes Therefrom," CIII (Dec. 1910), 482, 489-90.

[28] Caffin, p. 187.

[29] Harry Houdini, *A Magician Among the Spirits* (New York, 1924), p. 100.

234

[30] "A Warning Against Spiritualism," *Literary Digest*, LXXXVI (July 1925), 32.

[31] Harry Houdini, *Miracle Mongers* (New York, 1920), p. v.

[32] Houdini, *Miracle Mongers*, p. 192.

[33] Kellock, pp. 14-15. Bernard M. L. Ernst, *Houdini and Conan Doyle* (New York, 1932), describes this strange friendship.

[34] Hopkins, p. 26.

[35] Caffin, p. 190.

[36] Advertisement on inside front cover of *Wehman Bros. Combination Prize Joker* (New York, 1906).

[37] Prof. Leonidas [pseud.], *Stage Hypnotism* (Chicago, 1901).

[38] Leonidas, p. 9, (Leonidas refers to the plants as "trained subjects").

[39] Leonidas, pp. 23-42.

[40] Ernest Jones and others, *Psychotherapeutics, A Symposium* (Boston, 1910), p. 67.

[41] "A Medical Denunciation of 'Vaudeville Hypnotism,'" *Current Literature*, XLVII (Aug. 1909), 215.

[42] Laurie, pp. 110-11.

EIGHT

[1] Robert Grau, "The Growth of Vaudeville," *Overland*, LXIV (Oct. 1914), 393; Robert Grau, *The Businessman in the Amusement World* (New York, 1910), p. 144.

[2] Denman Thompson, "The Old Homestead," typescript, HTC, n.d. *Grasping an Opportunity*, rev., *Dramatic Mirror*, Nov. 24, 1906. *The Wyoming Whoop*, rev., *Dramatic Mirror*, March 30, 1907.

[3] *Car Two, Stateroom One*, rev., *Dramatic Mirror*, March 3, 1906. *Mag Haggerty's Reception*, rev., *Dramatic Mirror*, May 3, 1906.

[4] Willis Steell, *Brother Dave* (Boston, 1909). Steell's earlier works were *The Death of the Discoverer* (Philadelphia, 1892); *A Juliet of the People* (produced Jan. 1901); *The Morning After the Play* (Boston, 1907).

[5] Willis Steell, *Faro Nell* (Boston, 1912) in *Plays with a Punch* (Boston, 1916). See also: Steell, *A Bride from Home* (Boston, 1912).

[6] Willis Steell, *The Fifth Commandment* (Boston, 1907). See *Dramatic Mirror*, May 18, 1907, for a report on a court case in which Steell lost his rights to the play to the leading actor, Julius Steger.

[7] Fred C. Kelly, *George Ade, Warmhearted Satirist* (New York, 1947), pp. 160-61.

[8] Kelly, p. 162. New York *Herald Tribune*, May 24, 1936. See Norman Hapgood, *The Stage in America* (New York, 1901), pp. 98-100, for a description of May Irwin's technique in acting a "jag."

[9] Kelly, p. 202.

[10] "George Ade Talks of His Stage Ideals," *Theatre*, Nov. 1904 (clipping in HTC).

[11] George Ade, *The Mayor and the Manicure* (New York, 1923); rev., *Dramatic Mirror*, Nov. 23, 1907. See also *Nettie* (New York, 1923).

[12] George Ade, *Marse Covington* (New York, 1923); rev., *Dramatic Mirror*, Jan. 26, 1907.

[13] Will Cressy and Ira Dodge, "My Old Kentucky Home" typescript, HTC, ca. 1907. See also the burlesque by James Madison, *My Old Kentucky Home*, in Brett Page, *Writing for Vaudeville* (Springfield, Mass., 1915), pp. 594-624.

[14] Gordon V. May, *Half Hours of Vaudeville* (Boston, 1913).

[15] New York *Herald Tribune*, Dec. 14, 1924.

[16] Edgar Allen Woolf, *The Lollard* (ca. 1914), in Page, pp. 493-512.

[17] Edward Elsner, *Kid Glove Nan*; rev., *Dramatic Mirror*, May 18, 1907.

[18] Marion Roger Fawcett, *The Alarm* (ca. 1912), in *Plays with a Punch*.

[19] Kenneth L. Andrews, *A Crooked Man and His Crooked Wife*, in *Plays with a Punch*.

[20] Edward Harold Crosby, *The Cat's Paw*, typescript, HTC, ca. 1906.

[21] Taylor Granville, *The System* (ca. 1912), in Page, pp. 537-74. Willard Mack, *Kick-In*, typescript, HTC, n.d. See Mack, "Vaudeville Playlet," New York *Dramatic Mirror*, March 3, 1915, concerning the expansion of this play.

[22] Richard Harding Davis, *Blackmail* (ca. 1910), in Page, pp. 513-36. For information on Davis's career see: Fairfax Downey, *Richard Harding Davis: His Day* (New York, 1933).

[23] Richard Harding Davis, *Miss Civilization*, in *Farces* (New York, 1906), pp. 314, 321, 325, 329, 332.

[24] Representative articles are: Tom Barry, "Vaudeville Appeal and the Heart Wallop," *Dramatic Mirror*, Dec. 16, 1914; C. Hamilton, "The One-Act Play in America," *Bookman*, XXXVII (April 1913), 184-90; W. C. Lengel, "Advice to Vaudeville Playwrights," *Green Book*, IX (April 1913), 726-31; E. F. Reilly, "Writing Drama for Vaudeville," *Editor*, XXXVII (May 1913), 279-83.

[25] Page, pp. 44-57.

NINE

[1] "B. F. Keith's New Theatre in Boston, Mass.," publicity booklet, HTC, ca. 1894.

[2] "The Model Playhouse of the Country," publicity flier, HTC, ca. 1894.

[3] William H. Birkmire, *The Planning and Construction of American Theatres* (New York, 1896), pp. 2-7.

236

[4] "Keith's New Theatre." The description of the theater and illustrations have been reprinted, for the most part, in Birkmire, pp. 48-56.

[5] "Keith's New Theatre."

[6] "Keith's New Theatre."

[7] Birkmire, p. 34; "Keith's New Theatre." See also John R. Freeman, *On the Safeguarding of Life in Theatres* (Transactions of the Society of Mechanical Engineers, 1906), pp. 34-35, regarding the operation of the automatic sprinkler system in Keith's Philadelphia Theatre.

[8] Birkmire, pp. 50-51. William Paul Gerhard, *Theatres: Safety from Fire and Panic* (Boston, 1900), p. 15.

[9] Gerhard, pp. 38, 52-53 (Floor plan); "Lessing Theatre, Berlin," *American Architect*, XLIV (May 1894), 58; "Royal Alhambra," *American Architect*, XLV (Aug. 1894), 71-72; "Manchester Palace of Varieties," *American Architect*, XLIX (July 1895), 36-38.

[10] *Cahn's Official Guide* gives stage measurements.

[11] Birkmire, pp. 52-53, 82-93.

[12] "Keith Letters," p. 80. Information on Hodgdon from HTC.

[13] HTC.

[14] William M. Marston and John H. Fuller, *F. F. Proctor, Vaudeville Pioneer* (New York, 1943), p. 49.

[15] Marston and Fuller, p. 50.

[16] "Keith Letters," pp. 94-95.

[17] Marston and Fuller, p.50.

[18] "Keith's New Theatre."

[19] Birkmire, pp. 52-53.

[20] "Model Playhouse."

[21] "Model Playhouse."

[22] Marston and Fuller, p. 79.

[23] Hartley Davis, "In Vaudeville," *Everybody's Magazine*, XI (Aug. 1905), 234.

[24] Edwin M. Royle, "The Vaudeville Theatre," *Scribner's*, XXVI (Oct. 1899), 485-95.

[25] "Keith Letters," p. 93.

[26] "Keith Letters," pp. 93-94.

[27] "Keith Letters," p. 93.

[28] "In the Center of Things," publicity booklet, HTC, ca. 1891.

[29] Birkmire, pp. 53-56.

TEN

[1] Abel Green and Joe Laurie, Jr., *Show Biz* (Garden City, N.Y., 1953), p. 354. The specific information here is from

Show Biz, but the story also unfolded in the trade papers and the New York *Times.*

[2] Green and Laurie, p. 264.
[3] Green and Laurie, p. 353.
[4] Green and Laurie, pp. 353-55.
[5] Frank Norris, *McTeague* (New York, 1952), p. 72.

A Note on the Sources

WHILE THE SOURCES for this study have been amply designated in the notes, a few comments upon the major ones may be useful for both the vaudeville buff and the scholar.

The three books on vaudeville which deserve closest attention are: Carolyn Caffin, *Vaudeville* (New York, 1914), a series of sensitive critical essays on vaudeville as seen by a member of the audience; Joe Laurie, Jr., *Vaudeville* (New York, 1953), the recollections and insights of a vaudeville performer; and Bernard Sobel, *A Pictorial History of Vaudeville* (New York, 1961), a book directed at the popular audience but, in spite of its style and format, a reasonably accurate and informative account of

239

vaudeville history. For detailed information, less cogently presented, there are Abel Green and Joe Laurie, Jr., *Show Biz* (New York, 1951) and Douglas Gilbert, *American Vaudeville* (New York, 1940). The inside view of vaudeville can be found in Brett Page's handbook, *Writing for Vaudeville* (Springfield, Mass., 1915), and in two books by an actor's agent, Robert Grau, *Forty Years Observation of Music and the Drama* (New York, 1909), and *The Stage in the Twentieth Century* (New York, 1912).

Naturally vaudeville provided a fascinating subject for journalists and feature writers. Among the many articles appearing in periodicals of the era, I would cite four: Hartley Davis, "In Vaudeville," *Everybody's*, XI (Aug. 1905), 231-34; Robert Grau, "The Growth of Vaudeville," *Overland*, LXIV (Oct. 1914), 392-96; Edwin Muir Royle, "The Vaudeville Theatre," *Scribner's*, XXVI (Oct. 1899), 485-95; and Charles R. Sherlock, "Where Vaudeville Holds the Boards," *Cosmopolitan*, XXXII (Feb. 1902), 411-20. Most of the metropolitan dailies published reviews, articles, and features on vaudeville personalities and performances, while the files of theatrical publications, *Variety*, the New York *Clipper*, and the New York *Dramatic Mirror* are, obviously, rich in material.

The intellectual and emotional climate in which vaudeville flourished has been treated in scores of works, but I would single out for special mention: Oscar Handlin, *The Uprooted* (Boston, 1951); Arthur Meier Schlesinger, *The Rise of the City, 1878-1898* (New York, 1933); Richard Hofstadter, *The Age of Reform* (New York, 1955); Henry Farnum May, *Protestant Churches and Industrial America* (New York, 1949); Samuel P. Hays, *The Response to Industrialism: 1885-1915* (Chicago, 1957); and C. Wright Mills, *White Collar* (New York, 1951). Two important works dealing with the history of the popular American sensibility are Carl Bode, *The Anatomy of American*

Popular Culture (Berkeley, Cal., 1959) and Howard Mumford Jones, *The Pursuit of Happiness* (Cambridge, Mass., 1953). Among the writings around the turn of the century, those which most adequately assess the function and value of mass entertainment are Michael M. Davis, *The Exploitation of Pleasure* (New York, 1911); Washington Gladden, "Christianity and Popular Amusements," *Century,* XXIX (Jan. 1885) and "Christianity and Amusements, A Symposium," *Everybody's,* X (May 1904), 696-701. Quite different, but equally provocative later interpretations of popular entertainment may be found in Gilbert V. Seldes, *The Seven Lively Arts* (New York, 1957) and Reuel Denney, *The Astonished Muse* (Chicago, 1957).

Much information about vaudeville can be discovered indirectly in books about related theatrical entertainments. Specific data on people, places, and events is best located in the fifteen volumes of George C. Odell's *Annals of the New York Stage* (New York, 1945) and in the annual editions of *Julius Cahn's Official Theatre Guide* (New York). A useful perspective upon the development of legitimate drama is gained from Glenn Hughes, *A History of the American Theatre, 1700-1950* (New York, 1951), while a comprehensive view of American entertainments is contained in Foster Rhea Dulles, *America Learns to Play* (New York, 1940). Two complementary accounts of popular music of the period are Edward Marks, *They All Sang* (New York, 1934), the remembrances of a music publisher, and Neil Leonard, *Jazz and the White Americans* (Chicago, 1962), a thorough historical analysis of the important shift in popular music brought about by the rise of jazz. The particular entertainment forms to which vaudeville was most closely related are described most effectively in: George L. Chindahl, *A History of the Circus in America* (Caldwell, Idaho, 1959);

Cecil Smith, *Musical Comedy in America* (New York, 1950); Bernard Sobel, *Burleycue* (New York, 1931); and Carl Wittke, *Tambo and Bones: A History of the American Minstrel Show* (Durham, N. C., 1930).

The material upon individual personalities in show business is voluminous and can be found in newspaper clippings, scrapbooks, magazine articles, reference works, and books. Three revealing autobiographies bear mentioning, however. George Fuller Golden, *My Lady Vaudeville and Her White Rats* (New York, 1909) centers about Golden's effort to create a union of vaudeville performers. Bert Levy, *For the Good of the Race and Other Stories* (New York, 1921) is a somewhat fictionalized account of a performer's life along the vaudeville circuits. "Genesis of Vaudeville: Two Letters from B. F. Keith," *Theatre Survey,* I (1960), 82-95, is Keith's own story, edited and introduced by me, of his early life and his role in the development of vaudeville. Four biographies were particularly valuable in preparing this book: Felix Isman, *Weber and Fields* (New York, 1924); Alva Johnson, "Profiles, [John F. Royal] Vaudeville to Television," *New Yorker,* XXII (Sept. 28, 1946), 32-41, (Oct. 5), 34-44, (Oct. 12), 36-45; William M. Marston and John H. Fuller, *F. F. Proctor, Vaudeville Pioneer* (New York, 1943); and Ward Morehouse, *George M. Cohan* (Philadelphia, 1943).

Index

243

245

247

248

249

ALBERT F. McLEAN, JR., a native of Boston, is a graduate of Williams College and holds the Ph.D. degree in American Civilization from Harvard University. He has taught at Tufts University and is presently professor of English at Transylvania College. He is the author also of a recently published book on William Cullen Bryant.